Global Markets and Financial Crises in Asia

Global Markets and Financial Crises in Asia

Towards a Theory for the 21st Century

Haider A. Khan
University of Denver
USA

First published 2004 by
PALGRAVE MACMILLAN
Houndmills, Basingstoke, Hampshire RG21 6XS and
175 Fifth Avenue, New York, N.Y. 10010
Companies and representatives throughout the world

PALGRAVE MACMILLAN is the global academic imprint of the Palgrave
Macmillan division of St. Martin's Press, LLC and of Palgrave Macmillan Ltd.
Macmillan® is a registered trademark in the United States, United Kingdom
and other countries. Palgrave is a registered trademark in the European
Union and other countries.

ISBN 0–333–76076–X

This book is printed on paper suitable for recycling and made from fully
managed and sustained forest sources.

A catalogue record for this book is available from the British Library.

Library of Congress Cataloging-in-Publication Data
Khan, Haider.
    Global markets and financial crises in Asia: towards a theory for the
    21st century / Haider A. Khan.
        p.   cm.
    Includes bibliographical references and index.
    ISBN 0–333–76076–X (cloth)
    1. Financial crises—Asia.   2. Capital market—Asia.   3. Monetary
    policy—Asia.   4. International finance.   5. Globalization—Economic
    aspects—Asia.   6. Asia—Economic conditions—1945–   I. Title.

    HB3808.K53 2004
    332'.042'095—dc22

                                                            2003058077

10   9   8   7   6   5   4   3
13 12 11 10 09 08 07 06 05

Printed and bound in Great Britain by
Antony Rowe Ltd, Chippenham and Eastbourne

For
Katsuhito Iwai

Izumi Otomo

Masanori Tanabe

and

all my teachers

the path
for teachers of
the Good Law
led me to
an unexpected mountain.

(adapted from *The Tale of Genji*, 'The floating bridge
of dreams')

Contents

List of Figures

List of Tables

Acknowledgements

My sincere thanks to Helene Wieting, Shuemm-Yow hiao and Rey-Ching Lu at GSIS, University of Denver, Prof. Iwai, Prof. Miwa and the staff at the CIRJE at the University of Tokyo, Prof. Kamoike at Tohoku University, and Dr Eisuke Sakakibara at Keio University for their generous assistance.

I am grateful to Amartya Sen for several discussions on economics and ethics. Erik Thorbecke, as good a friend and guide as always, has been among the pioneers in integrating financial aspects in the economy-wide modeling of developing economies. I have learned much from him. Several talks by Joseph Stiglitz in Manila and Tokyo and a conversation with him at the Aoyama Gakuin University were also most helpful. Conversations with Henry Wan were, as usual, illuminating.

I am also grateful for stimulating comments from participants in seminars I gave at Tohoku University, Tokyo University and the Bank of Japan on bounded rationality and neuro-fuzzy modeling of bank behavior. Special thanks are due to Prof. Kamoike, Prof. Iwai and Dr Shiratsuka for inviting me to make these presentations.

I have also benefited from many discussions with many other friends and colleagues, including Shigeru Ishikawa, Jesus Estanislao, Michael Sheeran, Laurence Harris, S.-W. Nam, Choong Yong Ahn, D. Huang, T. Chung, T. Rowe, M. Majumdar, J. Foster, K. Basu, R. Kanbur, Peter Ho, Tracy Mott, J. Svejnar, Victor Lippit, A.R. Khan, P. Pattanaik, A. Bhaduri, James Chung, J. Dean, J. Koo, J. Woo, K. Chang, T. Sekine, Q. Khoda, A. Kumssa, K. Sonko, G. Groshek, A. Basuseno, C.-S. Lin, Alan Gilbert, K.S. Jomo, Ha-Joon Chang, Hasan Ferdous, Joao Carlos Ferraz, Yujiro Hayami, K. Otsuka, Peter McCawley, M.G. Quibria, Pradumna Rana, Ramesh Adhikari, Barbara Stallings, Akira Suehiro, T. Karigane, H. Nishida, Masahiro Kawai, Chris Rodrigo, Chris Walker, Mohammad Irfan, S.-Y. Liao, R.-C. Lu, H.H. Khondker, Anwar Hossain, Peter Warr, John Weiss, Toru Yanagihara, M. Yoshitomi, Juzhong Zhuang, Izumi Otomo, Cindy Houser, S. Bhandari, Monzurul Huq, Sudipto Mundle, Don Parker, Debraj Ray, Myo Thant, F. Harrigan, Ghon Rhee, Peter Van Ness, Joseph Szyliowicz, T. Tatara, David Goldfischer, Rana Hasan, Micheline Ishay, Tom Farer, Ilene Grabel, B. Hughes, N. Suleiman, N. Umari, K. Kulkarni, David Levine, J. Nakagawa, M. Hakogi, Iwan Azis, Doug Brooks, Jesus Felipe, M. Fujimura, Ira Gang, K. Sakai, John McCamant,

H. Montgomery, Ken Ohno, E. Sakakibara, Tetsuji Okazaki, Yukiko Fukagawa, F. Kimura, Hitomi Tomii, Atsuya Tsukasa, M. Tanabe, E. Pernia, J.S. Lee, R. Nag, Y. Iwasaki, S.N. Oh, K. Jalal, Moto Noguchi, Joseph Fan, Sudipto Dasgupta, Ronnie Dasgupta, Michael Herrmann, Phillip Phan, Karin Hillen, James Jacobs, Michelle Fulcher and Jim Cole. My apologies to anyone whose name was omitted inadvertently. I alone am responsible for the views expressed in this book.

Nick Brock's careful editing of the manuscript saved me from a number of errors. I am most grateful to him. All remaining errors are mine.

1
Introduction: The Mangled Miracle and the Alchemy of Finance

> GRONTE: It seems to me you are locating them wrongly: the heart is on the left and the liver is on the right.
> SGANARELLE: Yes, in the old days that was so, but we have changed all that, and we now practice medicine by a completely new method.
>
> Molière, *Le Médecin malgré lui*

It was the best of times, getting even better – if that can happen – when things came crashing down in Asia. Nothing as dramatic as what happened in Asian financial markets in 1997 has occurred since the great crash of the 1930s. This is not mere hyperbole, but the sad truth about the Great Asian Crash of 1997. When economic historians look back they will mark not only Asia's progress and unparalleled growth, but also its rapid descent into chaos within a few short months. But Asia was by no means an exception. In 1994, another crash had taken place in Mexico, and in 1998 Brazil and Russia also faced financial crises. Finally, in early 2002 Argentina descended into an economic and policy chaos that was not foreseen by the media pundits or many mainstream financial forecasters. At about the same time, starting with the Enron scandal, the serious misgovernance of several large US corporations came to light. Thus, as far as international finance and corporate governance are concerned, the twentieth century ended not with a bang, but with a whimper. While the twentieth-century crises may have been merely unfortunate, the twenty-first-century ones seem like stubborn recklessness. Is there a way of theorizing that will help us to explain these crises opening the way for better policy formulation in the future?

In order to arrive at an adequate theory of these crises we need to ask: do these crises share something in common, or are they merely idiosyncratic events – each one a unique tragedy, but with no connections to the others, or any deeper common causal mechanisms? If the 'uniqueness' hypothesis is true, then the logical implication is that no single underlying causal structure can be expected to have operated in all cases. On the other hand, how plausible is the uniqueness claim? This is the first question which any serious student of these crises must consider.

At the same time, if all of these cases, including the Asian case, turn out to have been unique, the sequence of crises still poses many difficult and embarrassing questions. In this book, I will focus mainly on the situation in Asia. Clearly, in this instance we need to ask: How did it happen to Asia? How did a devaluation of the Thai baht in July 1997 precipitate a cascading wave of currency crisis spreading all the way to Korea in less than six months? How did Asia develop the symptoms of a debt crisis that was not supposed to happen there?

Not only did Asia suddenly develop a debt crisis; it also seemed to have been plunged into a full development crisis. Output plummeted precipitously in the affected countries. Living standards followed suit. Unemployment rose. Millions of poor people added to their anguished lives even more misery. Millions more became poor even by the modest official standards used to measure poverty. It is no exaggeration to say that Indonesia, Thailand and South Korea were pushed into depressions comparable to the historic crisis that engulfed Europe and North America in the 1930s. Although recovery did occur in Korea, it is questionable if the former growth rates can be restored on a sustainable basis for long. Recovery in Thailand has continued to be fragile. Finally, Indonesia still could not emerge from the multiple crises as of spring 2002.

We need to think long and hard about the causes of these crises. According to the euphoric descriptions during the heydays of Asian growth – and Russian, Brazilian and Argentinean economic prospects heralded by Wall Street and the believers in the so-called 'Washington consensus' – these economic disasters were not supposed to happen. Yet they very palpably did happen.

In the case of Asia, in particular, when the dizzying growth was replaced with a sobering shakedown, there was immediately a cacophony of condemnations of the 'Asian way' of doing things. Wise heads were shaking in Washington in triumph as fingers were being pointed at Asian heads of state and government officials. Some wise Western economists would even write articles with titles such as 'I told you so'.

Yet in sober moments most reflective people – professional and non-professionals alike – had to admit that the Asian crisis, in particular, was baffling in several respects. For one thing the so-called macroeconomic fundamentals seemed sound in Asia going into crisis. For another, in contrast to the situation in Mexico or other Latin American countries in the 1980s most of the debt was not sovereign. It was a private sector debt crisis. So once again, the question arises, how did this come to be?

This book is really an attempt to answer this deceptively simple question by appealing to the historical facts, and economic theory. It will turn out that a fully satisfactory analysis and the crises that followed, must include a consideration of both international and national political economies. It is also hoped that, through a greater understanding of this unusual crisis, the global forces that dominate our economic lives can be better controlled through necessary institutional innovations. But before we proceed any further, it will be instructive to examine briefly some attempts to explain the crisis away, as it were, initially. The insights gained from this exercise will help us appreciate the genuine intellectual challenges posed by the Asian crisis.

A few months into the crisis in 1997 the dominant view of the crisis from the United States was a round condemnation of the Asian version of capitalism. Robert Wade (1998a) termed the events, somewhat dramatically, 'the death throes of Asian state capitalism'. According to Wade, 'the chairman of the US Federal Reserve, Alan Greenspan [became] the most prominent if not the most eloquent, exponent of the idea'. Indeed Greenspan in early December 1997 had said:

> The current crisis is likely to accelerate the dismantling in many Asian countries of the remnants of a system with large elements of government-directed investment, in which finance played a key role in carrying out the state's objectives. Such a system inevitably has led to the investment excesses and errors to which all similar endeavors seem prone...

> Government-directed production, financed with directed bank loans, cannot readily adjust to the continuously changing patterns of market demand for domestically consumed goods or exports. Gluts and shortages are inevitable...

Greenspan further linked this position with what he identified as a global move towards 'the Western form of free market capitalism'. The note of triumphalism was barely concealed. 'What we have here is a very dramatic event towards a consensus of the type of market system we have in this country', he said in his testimony before the US Senate Foreign Relations Committee in February 1998.

Speaking on Korean national television George Soros advised the Korean government to invite foreigners buy up Korean companies and to let the rest go to the wall. Stanley Fischer of the IMF blamed domestic causes such as the failure to dampen overheating, the maintenance of pegged exchange rate in the face of credibility problems, and the lack of prudential regulations and political will.

On the face of it Fischer's list of problems is not incorrect. But the problem is that such analysis lacked depth, which was revealed in 1998 when IMF was forced to change its stance. In retrospect the flaws in this analysis have become much clearer. We will offer a detailed critique of the then dominant US Federal Reserve-Treasury and IMF views in Chapter 5.

For the moment let us turn to an alternative explanation offered by 'structuralists' such as Wade, and, more surprisingly, by 'dissident' neo-classicals such as Jeffrey Sachs. In this view the problem was a crisis of confidence in an otherwise sound but underregulated system. Sudden investor pull outs then caused a severe debt-deflation. As Wade (1998) describes this view:

> These, then, are the pre-conditions of the Asian crisis: (1) Very high rates of domestic savings, intermediated from households to firms via banks, creating a deep structure of *domestic* debt. (2) Fixed-exchange-rate regimes, with currencies pegged to the US dollar (apart from Japan, and partially, Korea), that created the perception of little risk in moving funds from one market to another. (3) Liberalization of capital markets in the early to mid 1990s and deregulation of domestic financial systems at about the same time, without a compensating system of regulatory control. (4) Vast international inflows of financial assets, coming from excess liquidity in Japan and Europe being channeled through financial institutions scouring Asia for higher returns and lending at even lower nominal rates than domestic borrowers could borrow from domestic sources, creating a deep structure of *foreign debt*. [emphases in the original]

This is not the place to evaluate these rival arguments. An attempt will be made in Chapter 5 to assess both the validity of the Asian model and its sudden fall from grace. But it is significant that the Asian crisis rekindled fundamental debates about the role of governments and markets in capitalist development. Furthermore, this time the ongoing general theoretical debate has a global dimension. This last point has not always been made clear. It is one of the major arguments of this book that the global dimension is indeed critical. This will be developed throughout the volume, but particularly in the chapter on global financial architecture.

Clearly, in retrospect the East Asian financial crisis was by all accounts the most significant event in the world economy in 1997. The topic dominated the headlines, attracted worldwide attention and generated much despairing rhetoric. As we have seen, the economists naturally joined the cacophony of condemnations. Truly, the dismal science had never looked so dismal since the great depression of the 1930s. Without doubt, the speed and depth of the collapse of financial markets in East Asia caught everyone by surprise. Neither the existing surveillance mechanisms nor markets warned the euphoric investors adequately of impending calamity. The reversal of fortunes in East Asia came suddenly and surprised even the experts. The contagion spread rapidly, engulfing a number of economies in quick succession. It started as a currency crisis, and then became a financial crisis. By 1998 it had become a full-blown economic crisis. To recapitulate briefly, and anticipate a little, the actual trigger for the crisis was the 1996 export slowdown in Asia. The cyclical downturn in the demand for electronics, in conjunction with a rising dollar and a declining yen, slowed export growth, and led to some scepticism about the prospects for future growth. The initial export downturn and growing scepticism threatened the inflow of foreign capital, now badly needed to sustain the increasing current account deficits. This in turn led to market concerns about the more or less fixed exchange rates, culminating in pressure on them and their eventual collapse. Investors suffering losses started to withdraw from these markets, and the bubble in asset prices burst. Falling asset prices resulted in insolvency of financial intermediaries, resulting in a fully-fledged financial crisis.

Although the 1996 export slowdown triggered the currency crisis, the roots of the financial crisis go much deeper. It is important to note the fact that the regional crisis occurred in those countries that were more advanced and more integrated with global financial markets and, for that reason, were more successful in attracting large inflows of foreign private capital. In this sense, the crisis can be viewed as a new challenge facing the Asian developing countries as they move up the ladder of economic development. It is fair to say that the problems were not confined just to the affected economies and they can emerge in other developing countries when they reach a similar stage of economic development and integration in the world economic system. But this would be cold comfort for the economies that were so affected, at least in the short run.

Why were the affected countries so vulnerable? To begin with, there were weaknesses in financial and exchange rate management in these economies. For all practical purposes, these countries had all pegged their currencies to the US dollar for a decade or more. With good investment potential built up by past economic success, foreign capital inflows accelerated, especially since the capital accounts were liberalized. To keep the local currencies from appreciating and to curb inflation, much of the foreign capital inflow was sterilized. The sterilization led to an increase in the gap between domestic interest rates and international market rates, which, coupled with a fixed exchange rate system, further encouraged foreign capital to flow into the countries. Clearly, massive capital inflows increased the levels of investment. But the institutional capacities in the financial sectors of these countries were not sufficiently robust to manage these inflows effectively. In essence, these countries lacked the capability to allocate capital resources efficiently through a mechanism that would penalize excessively risky behaviour while rewarding productive use of capital. Poor corporate governance due to a lack of transparency as well as inadequate accounting and auditing standards also contributed to the emergence of such overly risky behaviour. Short-term external loans were often used for financing projects with long gestation periods. This led to a mismatch in maturities of financial instruments. Part of the foreign capital inflows were also invested in real estate and other non-traded sectors which are prone to speculation. Such risky behaviour in the asset markets created bubbles that had to burst eventually. Thus, in contrast to the earlier Latin American crises, the Asian crisis was mostly a private sector phenomenon.

To make the situation worse, a self-reinforcing vicious circle developed between currency and asset market declines and banking and corporate failures. The falling currency drastically increased the local currency equivalent of the foreign debt owed by local enterprises, which in turn exacerbated the currency decline. The fall of asset market prices decreased the capital of the banks which held the assets, and increased the level of non-performing loans to the corporate sector which used assets as collateral. The vicious circle contributed to the drastic depreciation of currencies and a large number of banking and corporate bankruptcies.

For all intents and purposes, the Asian financial crisis put a halt to the steady capital accumulation in Southeast Asia and South Korea for some considerable time. I have suggested here that the standard neoclassical orthodox explanations really do not offer an adequate explanation of the specificities of the crisis. The 'structuralist' explanations do somewhat better. But we are still left with the puzzle of how quickly these apparently 'sound' economies succumbed to the crises. It is also remarkable that both the post-Keynesian and the structuralist views do not have any sharp predictions regarding how adversely long-run capital accumulation prospects are affected during financial crises. The neoclassical steady-state prediction entirely ignores the path-dependent nature of accumulation and technological change. An alternative theoretical approach which is consistent with the 'structuralist' position but has a greater reach is called for. An attempt to do this, at least partially, will be made throughout this book at both the macro and sectoral levels, as well as at the microeconomic level of corporate governance. But first we need to see how sweeping the Asian crises really were. To drive this point home, three of the most important affected economics have been selected. The next three chapters consider the proximate causes of the unfolding crises during 1997–98. First we look at Thailand, where the crisis started in July 1997 as a currency crisis. Next we study the case of Indonesia, which suffered much greater turmoil – both economic and political – than any pundits had predicted in early 1997. Finally, we investigate the important (and also tragic) developments in South Korea. Initially, it appeared that all three were sudden and unexpected victims. But were the developments really so unexpected? An even better way to pose the question is perhaps to ask: Why were these crises so unexpected? What caused the blindness and what caused the insights to be shallower than they needed to be after the initial blindness was cured? The next three chapters will gradually lead us to these and other relevant questions.

It should be mentioned here that I do subscribe to the view that the Asian financial crisis was a new type of phenomenon in so far as it was the capital account that was the immediate source of the problems. However, to call it a 'capital account crisis' is not to offer an explanation, and certainly not a deep causal explanation. Therefore, to me this characterization can only be a beginning of any sustained inquiry into the causes and consequences of the crisis. Both the explorations in financial economic theory and the political economic analysis developed later will be used to substantiate this claim.

The 'structural' computable general equilibrium model in the appendix to Chapter 3 is applicable not only to Indonesia but also to all other countries. My intention here has been to show that the marriage between formal modelling based on modern economic theory and classical and modern 'ordinary language' political economy approaches need not end in an acrimonious divorce. Rather, like yin and yang, the two approaches can combine to produce a genuinely dialectical motion picture of a complex reality that is constantly changing.

Finally, the 'complexity' approach developed later in this book as an overall framework to study needs to be mentioned briefly here. The premise on which the theory presented here is based is simply that global, regional and national financial structures are complex. Intuitively, this means that characterizations of financial markets by analogy with other simple markets such as apples or oranges are inaccurate. More formally, complexity is associated with nonlinear structures, asymmetric information, different types of risk, fundamental uncertainties and bounded rationality of economic agents. In general, such an approach leads to a world of multiple equilibria and instabilities. It is the task of this book to examine these equilibria and instabilities carefully and to suggest some theoretical and practical answers to the problems of studying and containing financial crises.

2
The Beginning of the Crisis: Thailand

> There would never be any public agreement among doctors if they did not agree to agree on the main point of the doctor being always in the right.
>
> George Bernard Shaw, preface to *The Doctor's Dilemma* (1911)

Over the course of a number of years during the 1980s and 1990s the Thai monetary authorities had, with some justification, earned a reputation for sound monetary management. Likewise, the fiscal authorities had run a tight conservative budget policy throughout most of this period. A relatively open economy, Thailand had earned high praise from the IMF and the World Bank as well as foreign investors for its apparently sound economic policies. With a kind of aleatory irony that in retrospect has indeed assumed historic proportions, Thailand became the epicentre of the financial earthquake in Asia. In July 1997 the World Bank's model Southeast Asian developing economy turned out to be the weakest link in the chain of Asian finance. The devaluation of the baht triggered almost accidentally a region-wide crisis. How did this come to pass?

On the surface, the Thai financial crisis was caused by excessive investments financed by unsound short-term borrowing. As it happened, many of the investment projects undertaken with borrowed money turned out to be unproductive. The investment boom in the 1990s that was financed largely by short-term borrowings was indeed impressive. During the period 1990–96 gross domestic investment as a percentage of GDP was 40–44 per cent. One should compare this with the average figures for the same during earlier periods. When this is done – for example, during the period 1980–84 investment was 25 per cent of GDP – the acceleration of investment is nothing short of amazing.

What is equally amazing is that many of these projects in the 1990s were financed by foreign borrowing. A combination of high interest rates and a fixed exchange rate of the baht to the US dollar led to a situation in which foreign lenders were eager to lend in Thailand. Short-term interest rates exceeding 10 per cent meant a handsome return to these lenders within three to six months. Offshore borrowing was popular as the corporations discovered that the interest rates were lower compared to domestic interest rates of more than 13 per cent. The fixed exchange rate was taken to mean – correctly until the crisis hit – that there would be no exchange risk.

How did such easy borrowing and lending come to be standard practices? The answer lies in the liberalization policies pursued by the Thai government in the 1990s. In 1992, as part of a broader financial liberalization package, the Anand government deregulated the foreign exchange markets. In 1993, BIBF (the Bangkok International Banking Facility) was established in order to attract foreign funds to finance the then increasing current account deficits. The establishment of BIBF was also intended to turn Bangkok into a regional financial centre.[1] At the same time it was argued that such liberalization would increase competition in the financial sector. Clearly, this was a good idea if one followed the conventional economic logic of policy reform.

But it was too good an idea, it turned out. The BIBF did make it possible for local and foreign banks to create deposits or to borrow in foreign currencies from abroad. It also made it possible to lend money both in Thailand and abroad. However, the consequence was mainly overborrowing from offshore financial facilities. The 'animal spirits' were working only too energetically.

In the equity markets too, the same animal spirits were at work. The Securities and Exchange Act of 1992, which was promulgated to facilitate the growth of equity finance and to attract foreign portfolio capital, was seemingly succeeding with a vengeance.

Between 1988 and 1996, annual net private capital flows to developing countries jumped from about $40 billion to about $250 billion. During this period, Thailand attracted about $10 billion a year. Cumulatively, this would amount to more than 50 per cent of its 1995 GDP. The external debt of Thailand increased from a figure of almost US$40 billion in 1992 to US$80 billion in March 1997. During this period, total outstanding debt as a share of GDP increased from 34 per cent in 1990 to 51 per cent in 1996, an increase generated almost exclusively by the private sector. Of the total debt stock, 80 per cent was private debt and almost 36 per cent was short term, i.e., maturing in 12 months or less. In August 1997, the BoT (Bank of Thailand) revealed that the foreign debt was about US$90 billion, of which US$73 billion was by private companies – with US$20 billion falling due by the end of 1997. In January 1998, the Thailand Development Research Institute (TDRI) estimated that the ratio of short-term debt to foreign reserves had increased from 0.6 in 1990 to 1.0 in 1995 (and 1996), implying that the ability of the country to service short-term debt had deteriorated sharply during the first half of the 1990s. Through its access to foreign credit via the BIBF and the Eurobond market, the private sector had obtained large amounts of foreign credit. Clearly, the credit had to be utilized in some fashion.

As it turned out, an investment bubble was thus created by careless domestic lending. A substantial part of the money was channelled into already inflated assets in the *real estate sector*. Between 1992 and 1996, a total of 755,000 housing units were built in Bangkok, double the national plan estimate. Loans from financial institutions to property developers also increased to 767 billion baht, of which 45 per cent stemmed from finance companies and 54 per cent from commercial banks. By 1996, it became apparent that the supply of housing was outstripping effective demand, and in the following year, Thailand had residential vacancy rates of 25–30 per cent and vacancy rates for offices in Bangkok of 14 per cent. Moreover, many property owners artificially inflated the value of their assets and kept borrowing against them, while most real estate companies had poor cash flows. In retrospect, there can be no doubt that this was the kind of bubble that had to burst sooner rather than later.

One of the policy responses of the Thai authorities to the deluge of foreign capital was to try and retain control over domestic monetary policy. They chose to do this not by allowing the exchange rate to appreciate (as Singapore did, for example), but through sterilizing intervention (as was the case in so many other emerging markets). The combination of these two policies, however, only attracted further capital inflows, which prolonged the domestic lending boom. The policy mix kept interest rates high, and virtually eliminated exchange risk. As such, the onshore borrowers found it only too convenient to take on unhedged foreign exchange liabilities through the BIBF.

It is of course easy to criticize the policy choices of the Thai government in hindsight. The reality is that there were strong arguments in favour of sticking with a fixed exchange rate regime at the time. The fact is that Thailand is a very open economy (trade as a share of GDP was about 60 per cent in 1988 and had since risen to over 80 per cent). Exchange rate stability was therefore thought to be a legitimate policy objective to pursue, especially given that the government was pursuing other appropriately supportive macro policies. But such orthodox thinking was of little help when the economy began to teeter towards an abyss.

Finally, when the economic recession started in 1996 and the buying power of the middle and upper classes began to decline, the property bubble burst, leaving substantial bad debts on the balance sheets of the finance companies, which had financed their investments by borrowing abroad. In February 1997, Somprasong Land missed payment on a euro-convertible debenture worth US$80 million. In March 1997, the BoT had classified Bt100 billion of the loans owned by real estate developers as non-performing (i.e., not having been serviced for 12 months), but the amount of bad property loans was estimated by financial agencies at Bt300 billion (about US$7.5 billion). Regardless of which set of figures we use the situation must be seen as being close to perilous. But it was actually worse than that.

It is now well known that most of the loans – even those going to the industrial sector – were *not hedged* against currency fluctuations. What is less understood – as I have tried to show here – is that there may have been nothing irrational, according to the market logic, in this type of behaviour. Also, a *currency mismatch* arose as much of the foreign money went into non-tradable sectors of the economy, i.e., with no foreign exchange receipts. There was a *term mismatch* as well because short-term borrowing was utilized to finance long-term projects with longer-term returns. Finally, financing of equity purchases with loans that would become unrepayable if the baht lost its value, was all too common. How did the pace of financial liberalization become so rapid? In order to answer this question the background for financial liberalization needs to be investigated further.

In the period 1983–85 Thailand went through another financial crisis and severe recession. After a real devaluation of the baht by about 25 per cent and bailouts in the financial and industrial sectors Thailand emerged from the recession and showed a strong recovery – that turned into a veritable boom in 1986–87. This earlier boom resulted from a massive boost in exports and an extraordinary flow of direct foreign investments, mainly from Japan, Taiwan and South Korea. The euphoric performance of the economy increased the influence of financial technocrats in the Anand and Chuan governments in the period 1991–95. This was precisely the period of rapid financial liberalization in Thailand. In fact between 1989 and 1993 the reform process progressively accelerated. After February 1991 the BoT and the Ministry of Finance gained so much autonomy that during the 13-month term of the first Anand government as many as twenty financial reform bills were passed.

Interest rate ceilings, which had been lowered during the 1980s, were abolished on the deposits side in 1990 and on the lending side in 1992. Foreign exchange transactions were also liberalized, first with respect to current account transactions in the year 1990, and later for capital account transactions in 1991 as well, ostensibly to enhance confidence among investors and to improve Thailand's creditworthiness. The scope of business of commercial banks and finance companies was widened, and in order to promote competition and introduce a variation of universal banking, finance companies were allowed to expand into business areas that had previously been reserved for commercial banks – such as the foreign exchange business. The Anand government also decided to support the 1990 BoT plan for setting up offshore banking institutions under the BIBF in order to promote Thailand as a regional financial centre, to ensure more competition for domestic commercial banks and to enable Thai businesses to have greater and cheaper access to foreign loans. The BIBF was introduced during the Chuan government in 1993 and business in foreign currencies was unrestricted, which intensified competition in out-in lending, which had been dominated by the major Thai commercial banks before this time. Thus domestic financial liberalization interacted in a way with capital account liberalization that could be potentially destabilizing.

With respect to foreign exchange policy, the guiding principle in Thailand has always been stability, while monetary policy has been utilized to defend the exchange rate when external balance problems arose. For more than 20 years from 1963 to 1984, the Thai baht was fixed to the dollar, and monetary policies were utilized to maintain low inflation and to avoid balance of payment imbalances. In 1981, as the value of the dollar increased rapidly, two minor devaluations – totalling around 10 per cent – were carried out. During 1984, a particular political conjuncture made it possible for Prime Minister Prem to devalue the baht by almost 15 per cent and to link the baht to a basket of currencies in which the dollar remained the major component, thus leading to further de facto devaluation of the baht when the dollar fell against the yen and other currencies from 1985 following the Plaza Accord. During the post-1984 period, the baht was again fairly stable against the US dollar, pegged to the above mentioned basket of currencies. However, with the advantage of hindsight this stability seems to have been purchased at a high price.

During the early 1990s, portfolio investment and short-term private borrowing grew. Portfolio investments increased from 23.5 billion baht in 1992 to 138 billion baht in 1993, a sixfold increase. The virtually pegged exchange rate constrained monetary policy, though some economists pointed to the potentially destabilizing influence of short-term inflows. As Naris (1995) pointed out:

> While the authorities may wish to keep the Thai baht fixed to the US dollar in keeping with past practice, they will find the supply of money increasingly difficult to control. For example, attempts to

tighten the domestic money supply, leading to increases in domestic interest rates, will only induce greater capital inflows, which will eventually restore the differential between domestic and foreign interest rates. In the extreme case, monetary policy will not be able to influence domestic money supply and price levels if interest rates are exogenously determined and the exchange rate is fixed... Shielding the domestic economy from external instability and restoring the effectiveness of monetary policy can be attained only by greater willingness on the part of the Thai authorities to accept increased fluctuations in the exchange rate.[2]

In Thailand a currency crisis became a full-blown financial and economic crisis in 1997.

Loss of competitiveness and currency crisis

During 1996, it became clear that the Thai economy had lost its momentum. The economy was slowing down, recording its lowest rate of GDP growth for a decade. Thailand suddenly experienced negative export growth and export sales of labour-intensive goods such as footwear, textiles, garments and plastic products. As imports kept growing, the current account deficit increased. Meanwhile, the stock exchange lost around one-fifth of its value during the first nine months of 1996. Finally, the Board of Investment registered a downward trend in foreign investments.

It was also generally believed that the instability and incompetence of the Banharn government (1995–96) and then the Chavalit government (1996–97) repeatedly undermined the confidence of both foreign and domestic investors. The poor economic performance led to increasing widespread awareness that Thailand – due to the stronger baht, higher wages and competition from low-cost producers such as China – was losing its traditional competitiveness in labour-intensive industries (see Table 2.1). Consequently, it became obvious that a transition to more sophisticated, higher technology industries was required and that some kind of structural reform was needed to address, among other things, issues such as the low-skilled labour force, low technological capability and inadequate infrastructure.

Moreover, the technocrats in the Ministry of Finance and the BoT became worried about the large inflow of 'hot money' and the fact that Thailand's system of pegging the baht against a basket made up of US dollars, Japanese yen, and German marks made such short-term speculative investments 'too secure'. Nonetheless, the stable baht was considered

Table 2.1 Thailand's net flows of foreign direct investment classified by sectors (percentage share)

	1993	1994	1995	1996	1997
1. Industry	26.1	16.0	28.3	31.2	33.8
1.1 Food & sugar	2.2	3.5	2.0	2.0	3.4
1.2 Textiles	−0.5	2.6	1.9	2.2	1.0
1.3 Metal & non-metallic	5.5	3.4	4.6	5.0	5.4
1.4 Electrical appliances	8.2	4.5	11.7	10.6	16.0
1.5 Machinery & transport equipment	3.6	0.9	7.2	4.8	10.1
1.6 Chemicals	11.7	2.5	4.7	8.1	4.7
1.7 Petroleum products	−9.4	−8.6	−8.1	−11.0	−12.1
1.8 Construction materials	0.3	0.4	1.3	0.2	−0.6
1.9 Others	4.6	6.8	3.1	9.5	5.8
2. Financial institutions	3.7	0.5	1.3	3.2	3.5
3. Trade	12.7	25.8	22.3	24.0	30.6
4. Construction	8.8	5.3	1.8	3.1	6.2
5. Mining & quarrying	7.2	3.9	2.8	0.9	−1.0
6. Agriculture	0.8	−0.5	0.5	0.1	0.0
7. Services	1.1	4.2	4.4	5.5	7.9
8. Real Estate	40.2	33.5	42.6	33.2	19.1
9. Others	−0.5	11.2	−4.0	−1.1	−0.1
Total	100.0	100.0	100.0	100.0	100.0

Source: Monthly Bulletin, Bank of Thailand.

crucial for attracting the investments needed to finance the country's current account deficit just as there were strong vested interests (i.e., large corporations with high external indebtedness) that would lobby against a more flexible exchange rate regime.

In the second half of 1995, the US dollar began to appreciate sharply vis-à-vis the yen and other major currencies. As a result, the Thai baht and other Southeast Asian currencies pegged to the dollar followed that trend. During 1996, there were repeated rumors that the baht would be devalued. Instead the BoT continued the tight monetary policy it had already introduced in 1995, but the policy proved ineffective because of high domestic interest rates and the free flows of capital through the offshore banking facilities established in 1993. Therefore, in the middle of 1996, the BoT imposed a requirement for bank and finance companies to hold higher cash reserves on short-term deposits by foreigners. The tight monetary policy also led to a further deterioration of the quality of assets held by the financial sector. This empirical reality is consistent with the theoretical results of Stiglitz and Weiss (1981) where asymmetries of information and moral hazard are shown to lead to high risk borrowers and a high risk project portfolio with an increase in interest rates.

The currency crisis hit Thailand in early March 1997 after a speculative attack on the baht in February had driven up inter-bank rates and made liquidity tighter. Speculators realized that the Thai currency was overvalued, and there were growing reasons to believe that speculative attacks would lead to a lowering of the baht's value. Similarly, some local investors began selling baht for US dollars in order to hedge against a possible devaluation, while exporters increasingly delayed converting their export earnings into baht. As a consequence, there was a huge supply of baht in the money market. The potential instabilities alluded to earlier were now being realized.

In May 1997, with severe problems in the financial sector unsolved and with no sign of economic recovery, a new series of attacks on the baht took place and the central bank spent billions of dollars defending the baht. There were reports that international hedge funds and currency speculators were betting up to US$10 billion on a devaluation of the baht. The BoT spent US$4 billion in the spot market and, as came to light later, also accepted more than US$23 billion in forward obligations. Furthermore, the government introduced currency controls by limiting offshore trading involving the baht to deter speculation; a 50 billion baht stock market rescue fund was set up in cooperation with the banking sector. However, this would not be enough to stop the crisis.

When the property bubble burst, Somprasong Land became the first real estate company to default on an interest payment on a euro-bond in early February; soon after words, it was reported that several other property companies were having difficulty servicing their debts. Although the central bank had assured the public in mid-February that no financial institutions under its supervision faced liquidity problems it was suddenly obvious that several of Thailand's finance companies – including the largest – Finance One – were over-extended in the property and hire-purchase sectors.

The Ministry of Finance and the central bank reacted quite rapidly. Finance One was ordered to merge with Thailand's twelfth largest commercial bank, the Thai Danu Bank. Meanwhile, the Financial Institutions Development Fund (FIDF) injected 40 billion baht into Finance One. Nine other finance companies and a credit foncier (housing loans broker) with high exposure to property loans were ordered to raise their registered capital. The remaining finance companies were asked to find a further 26 billion baht as debt cover while the banks were asked to raise their provisions against bad debts.

At this juncture, the main strategy of the BoT involved the promotion of mergers among Thailand's 91 finance companies and 18 banks. In early March, the central bank also announced the setting up of a Property Loan Management Organization (PLMO) to provide 100 billion baht in five-year loans to ailing property firms. The funds were to be raised by issuing seven-year, zero-coupon bonds guaranteed by the government. Finally, the cabinet accepted a 106 billion baht downsizing in the 1996/97 budget. Through these initiatives, the Thai government seemed to have averted devaluation of the baht and a deep financial crisis. But it only turned out to be a way of delaying the inevitable.

In retrospect it is not surprising that the implementation of these initiatives was difficult. Lacking clear guidelines for the chosen merger strategy, and with Chart Pattana ministers as major shareholders in some of the worst-performing finance companies, merging and closing finance companies was difficult. When the Finance One/Thai Danu merger – considered a model for further mergers – collapsed in late May, the strategy collapsed with it. Finance One was the largest and most well-known finance company, with involvement in real estate, hire purchase and stock margin lending. The fate of Finance One was a striking indicator of the state of finance companies in general, but it was still believed that the BoT would act as a lender of last resort. However, the BoT itself had been weakened when three senior officials (including a deputy governor) were suspended because the BoT failed to act in the Bangkok Bank of Commerce (BBC) case within the 12–month limit and therefore had to drop charges against BBC executives. Finally, the PLMO initiative failed because of lack of interest in the zero-coupon bonds needed to finance the scheme. Thus instead of decisive action the country witnessed a period of dithering and indecision.

However, the time of reckoning was drawing inexorably nearer. After a month of such indecisiveness and unsuccessful implementation of measures aimed at restructuring the financial and property sectors, the new finance minister Thanong Bidaya, who was also a former president of the Thai Military Bank, investigated more deeply into the matter. When he personally looked into the arrangements of the central bank's Banking Department, he discovered that US$8 billion had been lent out to debt-ridden finance companies through the FIDF and that foreign reserves were seriously low, probably below the legally required level. Apparently it had not been noticed before that total reserves had, according to a 1940 statute, to be equal to the value of currency in circulation. That such a situation could exist led to the shocked recognition that some form of drastic action would be necessary.

Accordingly, on 27 June, 16 finance companies (including Finance One) were suspended for 30 days, and ordered to come up with merger plans or close. On 1 July, the prime minister declared, 'I will never allow the baht to devalue. We will all become poor', but the following day, the finance minister announced the introduction of a 'managed float' system, allowing the baht to slip from 26 to 32 for US$1 in just two weeks. Such avowals of inflexibility and the quick devaluation were indicative of a classic currency crisis.

As could be expected, the financial sector initiatives did not restore confidence even in the financial sector. Firstly, questions were raised as to whether vested political interests had affected the selection of the 16 suspended financial corporations, excluding some companies that were even more troubled. Secondly, the government did not stick to its own deadline – it extended the suspension. This was linked, in the press, to the presence of senior cabinet members among the major shareholders in these firms. Thirdly, the BoT sent contradictory signals as to whether it was backing the finance companies as it had done with the largest finance company – Finance One – since 1996. Finally, financial analysts did not believe the government's insistence that only the 16 suspended financial companies were unsound. As subsequent events showed, the financial analysts were right.

As the events unfolded, it became clear that more needed to be done. On 5 August, after negotiations with the IMF, the government suspended the operations of 42 more finance companies, leaving only 33 finance companies open. This time, the conditions were clear – creditors and debtors would be protected while shareholders would lose their investments. Given the rules of the game before, it was not surprising that debtors would be protected. The IMF contribution to corporate governance at this point seems to have been protecting the creditors and punishing the shareholders.

The gravity of the situation and the inadequacy of the policy responses became clear when it was revealed that the BoT had utilized a substantial part of Thailand's foreign reserves saving the baht and had committed more than US$23 billion to forward contracts defending the baht against speculators. Furthermore, it was disclosed that the BoT had extended more than US$8 billion – or, more precisely, 430 billion baht (or 10 per cent of GDP) – through the FIDF to rescue troubled finance companies. Such underwriting of bad debt must have led to a vicious cycle of moral hazard. The end of this cycle would be spectacular and tragic.

The end of this period of increasing instability, speculation and moral hazard came in July. By late July, the investor confidence – gained at great economic cost – which had kept the baht and the financial sector afloat during the first half of 1997 finally collapsed. The stable baht was history, and the BoT was no longer a safety net for the leading financial institutions, just as confidence in the BoT itself had fallen. In early August, with alarmingly low foreign reserves and a private sector weighed down with foreign debt, it was obvious that some kind of foreign assistance was needed, and when the Japanese were not willing to provide this alone, the IMF was called in. The IMF responded with its traditional stabilization package.

Actually, the IMF response was quick. On 11 August, an IMF rescue package was approved by the Fund's board. Under the umbrella of the IMF, a US$17.2 billion stand-by credit facility was made available mainly by East Asian governments for balance of payments support, and with disbursement to be made quarterly over almost three years and contingent on Thailand meeting IMF performance conditions. The total sum included US$2.7 billion from the World Bank and the Asian Development Bank to be used to enhance industrial competitiveness, improve capital markets and mitigate social problems arising from the austerity programme. It is worth mentioning that China decided to deploy US$1 billion of its foreign exchange reserves for this purpose, while the United States, in contrast, did not make any direct contribution. In contrast with the Mexican crisis (1994–95) which resulted in a US-led IMF US$50 billion bailout, the Thai crisis was left to the IMF and Japan. Initially they contributed US$4 billion each. Following the usual adjustment routine, the IMF demanded that Thailand must adopt an austerity programme, which included the following: (i) an increase in the national value-added tax from 7 per cent to 10 per cent; (ii) a 1 per cent surplus in the public budget to cover restructuring costs in the financial sector, implying a cut in fiscal spending (in all sectors apart from education and health) of 100 billion baht in the 1997–98 budget; (iii) the ending of subsidies to state companies; tight monetary policy to keep inflation at 9.5 per cent in 1997 and 5 per cent in 1998; (iv) reduction of the current account deficit to 5 per cent in 1997 and 3 per cent in 1998, as compared with the 8.2 per cent deficit in 1996; continuation of the 'managed float' system; (v) maintaining reserves at a level that would provide over three months' import cover (US$23 billion in 1997 and US$25 billion in 1998); (vi) a clean-up of the finance industry and discontinuation of the rescue of ailing finance companies. This involved acting on recommendations of the Financial Sector Restructuring Authority (FRA) regarding the future status of 58 suspended finance companies. On 8 December 1997, 56 of these companies were closed permanently. The Asset Management Corporation (AMC) assumed control of their assets for liquidation. (vii) All undercapitalized banks were to submit plans for recapitalization by 31 December 1997.[3] (viii) Revision of bankruptcy laws by 31 March 1999.

During this period, Thailand tried to follow the IMF conditions quite meticulously and, as mentioned earlier, suspended 42 more debt-ridden finance companies in addition to the 16 that had already been suspended in June. The plan for restructuring the financial sector was worked out with technical assistance from more than 15 IMF and World Bank officials and was finally announced on 15 October – two weeks after the original IMF deadline. The financial restructuring package contained the following main elements:

(i)   setting up two new agencies, the Financial Restructuring Agency (FRA) to supervise the 58 suspended fincos and to evaluate the rehabilitation plans submitted by these firms before the end of October, and the Asset Management Corporation (AMC) to buy bad assets and to then manage, restructure and sell them under the direction of the FRA;

(ii) tightening loan classification by reducing the period after which a loan is considered non-performing from 12 to 6 months and requiring higher capital-to-risk assets ratios (12–15 percent compared to the international norm of 8.5 per cent) in order to 'gradually bring the sector into line with international standards by 2000';

(iii) new rules allowing foreigners to take majority stakes in all financial institutions for a ten-year period, after which their shares have to be lowered to less than a majority through capital increases only available to Thais;

(iv) a full government guarantee to both depositors and creditors in the country's 15 local banks and remaining 33 finance companies;

(v)   acceptance of equal claims of all creditors to the collateral of finance companies, i.e., requiring that the government remove FIDF's declared preferential claim to this collateral (FIDF had extended 430 billion baht to the 58 fincos against collateral);

(vi) enactment of new laws allowing the BoT to take control of troubled financial institutions, order changes in management, and 'write down' shares to pay for losses, improve bankruptcy laws so that debtors can collect their collateral faster, and ensure that the BoT announces its forward foreign currency commitments every month.

In addition to the six royal decrees containing the financial reform package, the Thai government also announced further cuts in public spending and new taxes so that it could achieve the one per cent surplus in the 1997/98 budget as agreed to with the IMF in August 1997. The new loan classification made it almost impossible to save the troubled finance companies. The suspended companies had loan assets of 1.3 trillion baht, the majority of which were non-performing under the new classification standards, and collectively held US$16 billion in loans from foreign lenders. The new policies were not implemented promptly due to a combination of indecisiveness and government instability. A coalition partner, Chart pattana (CP), exploited Chavalit's weakness to take over responsibility for economic affairs. CP party leaders were known to have considerable interests in the financial sector, including in some of the suspended finance companies. Hence, CP was eager to gain control over the FRA and the AMC, and the issuing of the six royal decrees was delayed. Soon after, the CP party pushed for a government reshuffle, but the composition of the new government did not do enough to restore confidence. On the last day of October, the baht passed the US$1 to 40 baht threshold, and on 3 November, Chavalit announced that he would resign three days later. Politically, the events now began to move rapidly.

Under the leadership of former prime minister Chuan Leekpai, a new government took office on 15 November. Chuan installed his own economic team headed by two highly esteemed technocrats from his own party (the Democrats) – Supachai Panitchpakdi (a former central bank governor) as deputy prime minister and minister of commerce, and Tarrin Nimmanahaeminda (a former finance minister) as finance minister. The new government sent a *letter of intent* to the IMF confirming that it would adhere to the earlier IMF conditions besides specifying further measures that would be taken to re-establish confidence in the economy. The letter of intent stipulated a 1 per cent surplus in the 1997/98 budget by increasing indirect taxes, cutting the investment programmes of state-owned enterprises, raising utility prices, and lowering real wages in the public sector, just as further expenditure cuts were announced. Other measures included an accelerated and extensive privatization programme, improving the financial system's regulatory framework, which would include more liberal rules for foreign investors,and accelerated and in-depth financial restructuring following the October guidelines.

Financial restructuring was done according to the strongest possible criteria: it was announced on 8 December that only two of the 58 suspended finance companies had had their rehabilitation plans approved – the remaining 56 companies would be permanently closed. Their good assets would be transferred to one or two new banks while bad assets would be managed by the FRA and the AMC. Bad assets would be sold to the state-supported AMC for gradual market liquidation. The FRA had to complete the disposal of all of its assets by the end of 1998. Creditors (including foreigners) were assured that all creditors (i.e., also the FIDF) would be treated equally and that the assets disposal process would be orderly and fair. In August, creditors of the 42 finance companies were guaranteed by the government and could either take equity stakes in the good bank(s) or exchange their claims for negotiable certificates of deposit issued by the Krung Thai Bank at an interest rate of 2 per cent per annum over five years. By contrast, creditors of the 16 finance companies suspended in late June 1997 had to negotiate debt repayment schemes with the FRA and the FIDF. The liquidation scheme was announced in February 1998, and in the final scheme, assets were not classified into good and bad assets as evaluation of the quality of assets was left to bidders at auctions. However, assets were split into core assets (outstanding loans) and non-core assets (company assets, cars, and so on) with auctioning of the latter starting in late February. The book value of the assets was 866 billion baht, of which 30–60 per cent was expected to be retrieved from auctions and shared among creditors. In order to ensure that the asset values 'are not unduly eroded by the dumping of assets' and to 'assure bids for each asset', the AMC was also meant to participate in auctions, as was the newly established Radhanasin Bank (RAB). During the auction process, the AMC was to focus on the lowest-quality assets and to serve as buyer of last resort, while the RAB was to bid for the highest-quality assets and to be guided by commercial principles. On paper at least, this seemed detailed and competent.

Furthermore, the minister of finance announced that the government and the BoT would 'take firm action against any institutions that endanger the public interest', that legal changes in the banking account would take place in 1998, and that a committee would be set up to restore the credibility of the BoT. The committee would also investigate the role of the BoT in the events leading up to the collapse – such as the BBC scandal and the granting of 430 billion baht to the 58 suspended finance companies. These moves were also intended to demonstrate the seriousness of the Thai government to the world.

Finally, the Chuan government took radical action when it *nationalized four medium-sized banks* – Bangkok Metropolitan Bank (BMB), First

Bangkok City Bank, Siam City Bank and Bangkok Bank of Commerce – in order to prepare them for sale to foreign financial institutions. This action appeared to be inspired by the saving and loans industry bailout in the United States in the 1980s, as the BoT first wrote down shareholder capital to almost nothing and then converted short-term loans (through the FIDF) into equity, whereby the FIDF obtained almost total ownership of the banks. As a bailout arm of the BoT, the FIDF had channelled more than 500 billion baht into the banking sector by late January (in addition to the 430 billion baht that had gone to the suspended finance companies). The BMB, which had more than 43 per cent of its loans considered non-performing at the end of November 1997 and more than half its funding reported to depend on short-term liquidity provided by the FIDF, was taken over by the central bank in late January 1998. The takeover included a write-off of 11 billion baht in bad loans, while the Techapaibul family, one of the Sino-Thai families controlling private commercial banks and finance companies, had to register a 3.8 billion baht loss. The BMB model was then utilized for the three other banks subject to similar conditions. After all these, it would seem that if the standard IMF medicine was the right one, the restructuring would lead to a rapid recovery of the economy. In the case of Mexico foreign capital inflows had resumed within a few months. Would the same thing happen to Thailand and stop the panic?

However, in the case of Thailand, these measures and signals failed either to stop the large net outflow of capital from Thailand or to stabilize the foreign exchange rate. When the exchange rate passed the US$1 to 50 baht threshold in early January 1998, talk of reviewing the IMF terms resurfaced. Prime Minister Chuan Leekpai stressed that the IMF had been too optimistic about the prospects for economic recovery when it had drawn up the austerity measures, and identified the high interest rate policy and economic growth predictions as issues for discussion with the IMF. A downward revision of the latter would make it easier for Thailand to achieve the 1 per cent fiscal surplus goal in spite of an expected revenue shortfall of about 100 billion baht in 1998. Similar reservations about certain aspects of the IMF programme were expressed by Deputy Prime Minister Supachai and Finance Minister Tarrin. After a visit by Tarrin to Washington, during the second IMF quarterly review of Thailand's performance under the rescue package, the IMF Asia-Pacific Director Hubert Neiss announced that the IMF would ease the economic bailout conditions. Thailand would be allowed to run a budget deficit of about 1–2 per cent of GDP in the financial year ending 30 September 1998, instead of the previously stated 1 per cent surplus target. However, this may have been 'too little too late' as far as the living conditions of the suffering Thai people were concerned.

The adverse impact of the crisis in Thailand on the standard of living of the people was immediate. Both inflation and unemployment rose quickly. In 1998 inflation reached a double-digit level, compared with the 1997 average of about 5.7 per cent. Increases in the prices of daily necessities such as rice and vegetable oil spelled misery for poor households. The World Bank responded with a US$300 million social safety net programme. However, the cushioning effect seems to have been minimal.

Unemployment also spread quickly throughout the economy. Starting with the finance and real estate sectors, the effects of the crisis were felt in sectors as diverse as construction and textiles. As FDI stopped and some existing factories scaled down their operations, even sectors like the automobile industry announced layoffs. It is difficult to interpret the official statistics on unemployment since there is no overall national reporting system for job losses. Using a social accounting matrix for Thailand and reasonable estimates of demand contraction I have estimated that in the period 1997–98 more than a million people became unemployed as a result of the crisis.[4]

It is by now clear that the errors of the private sector in Thailand, the technocrats in BOI and MOF, and the Thai politicians were compounded by the initial knee-jerk reaction of the IMF. The wave of foreign capital that had entered Thailand in the 1990s after the financial liberalization also left hastily, thereby exacerbating the crisis of confidence and ultimately deepening the economic crisis. Falling output, declining investment, bankruptcies, reduction in real wages, increased unemployment, poverty and inequality – these were the outcomes. The verdict, harsh as it may seem, must be that in the short run the Thai government, the private sector and the international organizations all failed to respond adequately to the situation. Consequently, both the economy and the people suffered.

It is also common knowledge that the contagion spread quickly. Less than two weeks after the triggering of the Asian financial turmoil in Thailand (2 July 1997), the Philippine Central Bank was forced to allow the peso to move in a wider band against the US dollar. On 24 July the Malaysian ringgit hit a 38-month low against the dollar. However, the most dramatic economic events were still a few months away. On 14 August Indonesia announced that it was abandoning its system of managing the exchange rate through the use of a broad band. In effect, this meant that Indonesia was forced to float the rupiah. Hong Kong, with its massive reserve, was able to beat off speculators, but the Hong Kong stock market lost nearly a quarter of its value in a few days between 20 and 23 October.

On 31 October a rescue package, led by the IMF, was announced for Indonesia. With contributions from the IMF, the World Bank, the Asian Development Bank and others, the total package was US$23 billion. However, even this was not the end of the trauma for the region.

On 7 November Asian stocks nose-dived as currency jitters shook Korea, giving credence to the growing suspicion that all was not well in the country that was about to join the OECD. By 3 December Korean officials and the IMF managing director Michel Camdessus signed a letter of intent covering an international accord to provide Korea with US$57 billion to help the country recover from its financial crisis. With the Korean economy now gravely ill, Indonesia subject to daily economic convulsions and the other regional economies in financial turmoil the Asian financial crisis had now become a full-blown regional economic crisis.

The next two chapters will discuss the Indonesian and Korean crises before we turn to a general consideration of explanations in Chapter 5. Ultimately, I will offer the outlines of a somewhat novel theory of financial crisis in a developmental state and economy in the following chapters. Among other issues, the unexpectedly deep and widespread Asian crisis raises the question of the relationship between the goals of the development elite and the aspirations of the ordinary people. In the next two chapters the contradictions between the state-developmental elites and the majority of the population will become quite clear.

APPENDIX 2.1:   SOME ECONOMIC AND FINANCIAL INDICATORS FOR THAILAND

Population   60.8 million
GDP per capita   US$2,453

	1992	1993	1994	1995	1996	1997	1998F	1999F
Real GDP (yoy %)	8.2	8.5	8.6	8.8	5.5	−0.4	−7.0	1.5
CPI inflation (yoy %)	4.1	3.3	5.1	5.8	5.8	5.6	8.0	7.0
Current account (% of GDP)	−5.6	−5.1	−5.6	−8.0	−8.1	−2.0	10.0	N/A

	Mar-98	Apr	May	Jun	Jul	Aug	Sep	13 Oct
THB/US$	38.75	38.62	40.15	42.15	40.82	41.75	39.31	38.25
3-month interbank rate (%)	23.50	23.0	21.00	22.00	15.50	13.50	9.5	9.25
Prime rate	15.25	15.50	15.50	15.50	15.50	15.0	14.50	14.00

	Feb-98	Mar	Apr	May	Jun	Jul	Aug	Sept
CPI inflation (yoy %)	8.9	9.5	10.1	10.2	10.7	10.0	7.6	7.0
Exports (yoy %)	3.2	−3.3	−0.7	−12.8	−2.9	0.0	−12.5	N/A
Manufacturing products (yoy %)	−13.2	−21.2	−16.2	−17.2	−12.5	−13.8	N/A	N/A
M2 (yoy %)	18.0	15.7	14.5	13.4	13.8	13.4	11.6	N/A
Usable foreign reserves (US$ billion)	9.9	12.0	12.29	14.1	14.6	15.5	16.4	17.5
Imports cover (months)	2.9	3.3	83.4	4.0	4.1	4.3	4.6	N/A

3
The Crisis Spreads: Indonesia (with Arry Basuseno)

> ...*Sekaran kita bubaran Hari ini khotbah tak ada*
>
> ...'Now let us disperse There is no sermon today.'
>
> W.S. Rendra, *Khotbah*

Until its spectacular collapse Indonesia was advertised as a resounding success story of the twin liberalizations. These two liberalizations had to do with both the internal and external sectors of the economy. Internally, the financial liberalization that started in the 1980s and continued until the period of the crisis was hailed as a great success. Externally, both trade and capital account liberalization were held up as models for others to follow. By late 1997, the Indonesian economy lay in ruins. What went wrong?

In answering this question we will be on somewhat firmer analytical and empirical footing than in the other cases. As early as 1996 Khan and Basuseno formalized the problems of liberalization in a financial-structural computable general equilibrium (FSCGE) model. According to the analytics of the model (which are given in the appendix to this chapter), given the pace and extent of liberalization, by 1996 the Indonesian economy had already developed substantial financial fragility. It was indeed a catastrophe waiting to happen. The Thai debacle was the trigger. The question that needs to be considered is: How did an economy with a robust real sector develop such financial fragility so quickly? Much of this chapter will be concerned with addressing this question. In order to answer it properly, we need to supplement a model-type analysis of the sort given in the appendix with both historical and institutional analyses. It is to this task that we now turn.

Financial repression in the earlier period in Indonesia

Some general considerations

One of the justifications of a repressive financial system is the notion that the most important assets for a healthy and growing economy are physical assets, and that real economic decisions are independent of financial structures.[1] The accumulation of physical assets is directly related to the level of output production in the economy. In such an analysis, Money is seen as a competing asset that disturbs the creation of a healthy and growing economy. For the growth of the economy, the accumulation of money balances beyond what is the minimum necessary amount must be repressed. It is concluded, therefore, that a system of control must be installed.[2] To achieve this objective, an interest rate ceiling must be put in place to serve as a disincentive to savers. At the same time, in order to ensure adequate capital for those sectors crucial to economic growth, credit allocation must be controlled by a set of regulations. Subsidies on credit are viewed as one way of stimulating socially desirable investments. The cost of credit cannot be so high as to act as a brake on the profitability of the industrial sector. Therefore, the interest rate on loans must also be curbed.

In order to secure the growth of priority sectors government must have a direct loan operation, usually through the central bank or the state-owned banks. One straightforward way for the government to obtain the funds needed to finance the priority sectors is through the reserve requirement regulation. A high reserve requirement means the banking system must submit a large part of the money it raised to the central bank. This effectively reduces the banking sector's ability to create loans and credit, which are in effect taxed with the consequence that there is now a reduced incentive for a greater intermediation by the banking sector. Still some other regulations are believed to be needed. An exchange rate control is put in place to ensure that the funds available within the country's borders will not go to a more rewarding investment overseas. The capital market in general is underdeveloped. This is because the negative rate of interest can make the inflation hedges appear more advantageous. In the earlier period of the history of Indonesian financial development (roughly 1950–83) a certain kind of financial repression was the norm.

Inflation and interest rates

Inflation was raging in the mid-1960s due to the need to finance Indonesia's growing budget deficit. In nominal terms, government expenditures more than doubled between 1960 and 1962. Although the Indonesian saving rate was relatively high by international standards, government expenditures were more than enough to cause an imbalance. The result was a skyrocketing inflation that reached more than 1000 per cent a year.[3]

In such a situation, reducing inflation became the highest priority for the new government, which took over the country in 1965. To encourage saving, the president issued Presidential Instruction No. 2 1968. According to this instruction, incentives were given to savers in the form of a repayment guarantee from the central bank, a tax exemption for deposit interest income, and non-inquiry regarding the source of funds. The state banks' lending and deposit rates were controlled. The deposit rates were set at 6 per cent a month – equivalent to an annual rate of 72 per cent.

The state banks received subsidies to compensate for the differences in the rates. After October 1968, the state banks received a 30 per cent subsidy on the interest rate they paid on 6- and 12-month deposits. The subsidy on 12-month deposits was reduced to one per cent by 17 March 1969 and was eliminated completely on 1 May 1969 – only to reappear on 9 April 1974 at a much higher level. From that date, 18- and 24-month time deposits were given subsidies of 8 per cent and 15 per cent a year respectively. As before, the subsidies were lowered with time, so that by 1 January 1978 the subsidy for 24-month deposits was only 1.5 per cent.

At the same time, the private banks were free to set their own rates, which consequently were set much higher than those of the state banks. However, the state banks' deposits were guaranteed by the government through Bank Indonesia, the central bank. Therefore, deposits in private banks were perceived to be riskier assets. In addition, all state-owned companies were required to deposit their funds in the state banks. These factors explain the ability of state banks to accumulate much higher deposit than the private banks despite the fact that the state banks were offering much lower interest rates. In fact, the state banks were always in a position to lend in the inter-bank market while the private banks were always the ones that borrowed. The restrictions on the interest rates of the state banks created distortions in the pattern of interest rate. Not only was there a negative rate, but the gap between the state banks' rate and that of private banks increased.

The high deposit rates set for the state banks were intended to entice savers into putting their money in the banks. These high rates were needed to compensate the lenders for their loss in assets value due to the high inflation rate. At the same time, the banks were discouraged from making loans. The banks were kept in business by the government subsidy. As a result, the growth of the money supply declined from 123 per cent in 1968 to 57 per cent a year later, and to 38 per cent in 1970. With that, inflation also declined from over 600 per cent to 2.5 per cent in 1971.[4]

As we shall see, the introduction of SBI and SBPU after the deregulation package of 1983 was a step towards the development of the market mechanism. However, the way SBI and SBPU were bought and sold in the market still reflected the grip of the central bank on the domestic interest rate. The central bank set the discount rate while it should have set the amount of liquidity it wanted to draw or release to the market and let the market decide the rate.

Loans and credits

The loan policy in the mid-1960s was designed to exert control over the state banks' lending rates, to bring on tight credit policies, and to induce saving. The state banks were the targets of all of these regulations because the state banks were, by far, the biggest part of the financial sector. The other subsectors were considered negligible. Tight credit policies were necessary because of the need to slow down the inflation rate. At first, the lending rate for state banks was set at 6–9 per cent per month, or an annual rate of about 72–108 per cent. These rates were gradually reduced in the following years.

Liquidity credit, a complex system of credit rediscount facility, was introduced. The credit was allocated according to the government priority list through the Liquidity Credit Scheme. Under this scheme, the banks would be induced to provide credit to the listed priority sectors at low interest rates set by the Bank of Indonesia. Portions of the loans under this scheme would then be rediscounted to Bank Indonesia at highly subsidized rates. The permanent working capital loan (KMKP), for example, would bear an interest of 12 per cent per year. However, the bank would receive 75 per cent of the funds from Bank Indonesia at an interest rate of 3 per cent per year. Different loans would have different rediscount proportions, some as high as 100 per cent. This scheme quickly became the source of cheap funds for the state banks.

A less known deregulation package was launched in April 1974, as an effort to combat the growth in the inflation rate. Under this package every year, a ceiling for credit expansion was set. Money demand, inflation, economic growth projection, and balance of payment targets were used to determine the total amount of credit allowed for the year. Then, based on past performance, the credit was allocated to groups of banks, to individual banks within a group, and to each type of credit of each bank. The credit ceiling for each bank was continuously adjusted and became an important tool as a direct control over total credit expansion in the economy. In addition, Bank Indonesia also gave loan to priority sectors. The availability of oil funds enabled the government to create huge amounts of liquidity credit at low rates and make them available to the banking sector.

The availability of liquidity credit to state banks and at the same time the enactment of the credit ceiling enabled the central bank to facilitate economic growth while at the same time put a rein to inflation. The down side of these policies was excess liquidity on the part of the state banks, which in turn discouraged them from mobilizing private savings.

Reserve requirement

Banks are required to maintain a percentage of deposits as reserve at the Central Bank. Before the Deregulation Package of October 1988, also known as PAKTO, the required reserve was 15 per cent of deposits. There were different methods for determining the amount of reserve required depending on the type of banks, the type of deposits and so on. The Deregulation Package of October 1988 reduced the reserve requirement from 15 per cent to 2 per cent and implemented a standardized method of calculation for all banks, including non-bank financial institutions (NBFIs). In addition to the reserve requirement, from time to time the central bank has also required state banks to hold government securities (SBI). In comparison to some southern cone countries, the reserve requirement imposed on the Indonesian banking sector was quite low. Chile had required its banking sector to have 60.7 per cent in 1976 while Mexico had a reserve requirement ratio of 79.2 per cent in 1975 and Colombia had 52.2 per cent in 1979. This comparatively low requirement ratio in Indonesia was possible due to the availability of oil funds.

In 1987, there was a rush on the US dollar, which sent the interest rate on rupiah deposits up to 24 per cent a year, and the inter-bank rate soared to 40 per cent a year. The central bank reacted to this development by requiring state banks to transfer the state-owned corporation funds to the Central Bank. In return, the state banks were given a central bank's certificate, the SBI. Although the rate on SBI was increased, the action of the central bank represented another direct involvement of the government in the economy. On another occasion, when the reserve requirements were reduced from 15 Per cent to 2 Per cent through PAKTO, all state banks were again required to buy SBI. As much as 80 per cent of their liquid funds had to be placed in the SBI form with 3- and 6-month maturities. This measure was intended to curb a disturbing expansion of loan in the banking sector resulting from additional liquidity released from the previously required reserves.

Capital control and exchange rates

Government regulation No. 16/1970 abolished most direct control over exchange rates. The exchange rate control was practically removed entirely in 1971. It was believed that there was no effective means to control capital movement by the government because Singapore, as one of the major financial centres, is so close that it was impossible for the government to exert meaningful control over capital movements. Any attempt to manage the capital movements was perceived as just wasting administrative resources.

When the inflation rates were growing rapidly in the late 1950s to mid-1960s, the official exchange rate set by Bank Indonesia was not depreciated as fast. This resulted in an overvalued rupiah and therefore in an excess demand for foreign exchange. In the new order government there was a movement towards liberalizing the exchange rate.

In 1967, a Foreign Exchange Bourse was established. This establishment of the foreign exchange bourse created, for the very first time, a marketplace where rupiah could be traded against foreign exchange.[5] Government permission was no longer required to use foreign exchange, and rupiah could be traded against foreign currencies. By 1970, foreign currencies were freely traded without restriction. However, the rate was still determined by the Foreign Exchange Bourse until August 1971, when the central bank took over this responsibility.

However, it soon became apparent that the central bank was not capable of maintaining enough foreign exchange reserves to keep up with the demand and to defend the rate. In 1970, the reserves were equivalent to only six weeks of imports. Subsequently the central bank had to devalue the rupiah two times – in April 1970 and again in August 1971. The second devaluation was in part a response to the US dollar devaluation just a week earlier. After that, the exchange rate was pegged to the US dollar.

In 1978, the rupiah was devalued by 33.6 per cent in an effort to promote exports. At the same time, the rupiah was divorced from the US dollar and pegged to a basket of currencies. The effort to promote exports as a way to obtain foreign exchange continued. Another devaluation came in 1983 along with the freedom given to exporters to retain part or all of the export revenues in the form of foreign exchange. They were no longer required to surrender the foreign exchange to the central bank and could now use them freely.

The Foreign Exchange Bourse ceased to exist in 1989, and the exchange rates were absolutely free to fluctuate according to their competitive power in the markets. However, the central bank still set an indicative rate as a guide. The central bank then stood ready to intervene in the market should the rate fluctuate in an unacceptable fashion. In that sense, this system was similar to the target zone approach to foreign exchange.

The series of devaluations that took place between 1971 and 1986 were clearly in response to the general performance of the exports and imports. As is apparent from Figure 3.1, all devaluations took place when export revenues started to level off. The devaluations seemed capable of always pushing up the value of exports in the years following the devaluation, albeit with a few years of lag. There was one exception to this: the devaluation of 1983 seemed unable to achieve the intended result so that another big devaluation was mandated in 1986, a little more than two years later. In general, however, the persistently high inflation rate in Indonesia relative to those of her major trading partners (see Table 3.1) always rendered the exchange rate obsolete in a short period of time, making it necessary to implement another devaluation. This process continued until the government floated the exchange rate against a basket of currencies in 1986. It was felt by many that the devaluation should have occurred earlier – when the current account deficit was at its peak, or even before that to avoid the increase in the current account deficit.

Macroeconomic shocks, oil revenue and finance in Indonesia

After the 'oil shock' of 1973, the Indonesian economy was booming, facilitated chiefly by the influx of money from oil and other non-renewable resources. As an oil-exporting country, Indonesia benefited greatly from the dramatic rises in oil prices – first in 1974–77 and again in 1979–82. For example, in 1970, of Indonesia's total exports of $1,108.1 million, oil accounted for $446.3 million, or 40.27 per cent. One year after the first oil price increase in 1973, the oil export share had increased to 70.1 per cent of the $7,426.3 million total value of exports. The second oil price increase in 1979 pushed the share of oil and gas exports to more than 74 per cent. This trend peaked in 1982 when the oil and gas share reached 82.40 per cent of total exports. This dramatic increase in the oil and gas share in export growth was intensified by the world economic recession that began in 1980. The recession slowed demand for many of Indonesia's export commodities – which were dominated by agricultural products – but not for oil and gas. Thus the increase in oil prices and the lowered demand for agricultural products together pushed the

34

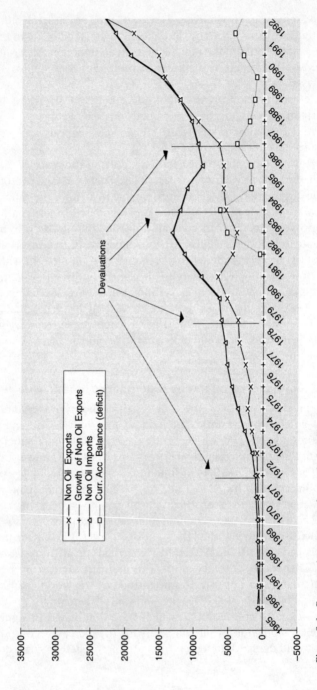

Figure 3.1 Exports, imports, and rupiah devaluations

Table 3.1 Consumer prices indexes, selected countries (1980 = 100)

Country	1983	1984	1985	1986	1987
Indonesia	137.4	151.7	158.9	168.2	285.8
Singapore	113.8	116.7	117.3	115.7	116.2
Japan	109.7	112.1	114.4	115.2	115.7
USA	120.9	126.1	130.5	133.1	137.8

oil and gas share of exports up higher than it would have been from the price increase effect alone, as is apparent from Table 3.2.

The oil and gas exports revenue fed the economy, allowing it to grow at an average rate of 7.7 per cent during the period 1970–82, and again continuing to grow at 7.4 per cent during the period 1984–94. Even while both Indonesia's structural adjustment and the global economic recession were taking place from 1982 to 1988, the economy was still growing at a steady rate of 4 per cent a year.

With this growth in income, Indonesia was able to take a more open posture in the world economy. Exports and imports grew at 32.53 per cent and 27.95 per cent, respectively during the 1970–1982 period. At the same time the degree of openness, as indicated by the sum of export and imports over GNP, grew from 61% in 1969 to 110% in 1974.

This increase in the degree of openness consequently increased the Indonesian economy's vulnerability to external shocks such as global economic recession, decreasing demand for export commodities, changes in export commodity prices, and, most importantly, a decrease in world oil prices. Unfortunately, all of these circumstances did occur and they had a great impact on Indonesia.

After 1982, the export revenue share of oil and gas began to decline, possibly as a result of one or both of the following: First, Indonesian

Table 3.2 Indonesian exports, 1970–1987 (in US$ million)

Year	Total exports	Non-oil exports	Oil and gas exports	Oil and gas exports share (%)
1970	1108.1	661.8	446.3	40.28
1974	7426.3	2214.9	5211.4	70.17
1980	23950.4	6168.8	17781.6	74.24
1982	22328.3	3929.2	18399.1	82.40
1987	17237.2	8598.9	8638.3	50.11

Source: Statistical Yearbook of Indonesia, Jakarta, BPS, 1987.

exports of non-oil commodities were growing faster than oil and gas exports; and second there was a reduction in oil and gas prices. From Table 3.3 it seems that the export revenue from oil and gas was generally declining at the same time that the exportation of non-oil commodities was increasing, thus weakening even further the oil and gas share of total exports.

Apparently, the decline in oil and gas revenues was so sharp that the increase in non-oil and gas commodities export still could not offset the decline. This is shown by the declining growth of total exports, which became negative from around 1980/82.

In terms of income, the share of income generated by the oil and gas sector also declined sharply. In 1984–85 oil generated 66 per cent of total government domestic income, but by the 1991–92 fiscal year the share of oil income in the government budget had fallen to 36 per cent.

The flow of oil revenue after 1973 had made it unnecessary to promote financial development domestically. Financial resources were abundant not only because of oil funds but also from other foreign sources who saw lending opportunities based on the projected future earnings derived from oil.

Money thus became easy to get both for the government and for the state banks. The government responded by imposing more restrictive controls over the banking system in particular and over the entire economy in general. Once again, Indonesia embarked on an ambitious development strategy, facilitated mainly by government investment in large-scale construction projects.

It is also easy to comprehend that when there is easy access to capital then there is no need for the government to entice capital flow from

Table 3.3 Growth of Indonesian exports, 1970–1987 (in US$ million)

Year	Total exports	Growth (%)	Non-oil exports	Growth (%)	Oil and gas exports	Growth (%)
1970	1,108.10		661.80		446.30	
1974	7,426.30	5.70	2,214.90	2.35	5,211.40	10.68
1980	23,950.40	2.23	6,168.80	1.79	17,781.60	2.41
1982	22,328.30	−0.07	3,929.20	−0.36	18,399.10	0.03
1983	21,145.90	−0.05	5,005.30	0.27	16,140.60	−0.12
1985	18,586.70	−0.12	5,868.80	0.17	12,717.90	−0.21
1987	17,237.20	−0.07	8,598.90	0.47	8,638.30	−0.32

Source: Statistical Yearbook of Indonesia, Jakarta, BPS, 1987.

other parts of the world. The urgent need is to 'protect (perceived) national interest' as much as possible. This could be done by restricting the flow of capital out of the country and erecting trade barriers. In order to establish a sturdy long-term foundation for national industry, it was felt that an investment policy also had to be instituted as well as more stringent foreign investment controls, and tariff and non-tariff barriers. In short, protectionist measures and a heavy dependence on oil revenues characterized the policies of the era. As the oil price declined and oil revenues decreased, the Indonesian economy came under internal and external pressure for liberalization. It is to this episode that we must now turn.

Financial liberalization in Indonesia during the 1980s

As mentioned earlier, from 1983 onwards Indonesian policy makers moved towards the reform of the financial structure and incentives. The overall emphasis in policy shifted towards market-directed accumulation and allocation of savings. Decontrolling interest rates, abandoning directed credit programmes, allowing entry of new banks (including foreign banks) and reduction of liquidity support from the central bank characterize this new approach of relying on markets. New financial instruments such as SBI and SBPU were also introduced during this period.

SBI, or *Sertifikat Bank Indonesia*, a money market instrument mainly used for contraction, was introduced in January 1984 along with a rediscount facility. In February 1985 the *Surat Berharga Pasar Uang*, a money market instrument used as an expansion tool, was introduced. In September 1986 the rupiah was devalued by 31 per cent, adding further pressure to the financial markets for adjustment.

A second series of financial reforms started in October 1988. The 27 October package (Pakto 27) allowed for new entrants to further establish new banks or branches of banks. This meant that up to 85 per cent of a joint banking enterprise could be owned by a foreign partner. A foreign bank could also issue certificates of deposit.

The Indonesian financial system consisted of the central bank, commercial banks, finance companies, insurance companies, capital market and capital market supporting institutions, and other financial institutions. With the series of deregulation measures instituted in the period 1983–93, the financial sector developments were impressive. In this ten-year period, there were 11 deregulation measures in the financial sector, eight of which were related to the banking and monetary policy. The effects of these deregulation measures are apparent in the growth of mobilized funds. The number of banks and their offices increased, as did the volume of business and the diversity of products on offer.

In 1983, there were 130 commercial banks, including seven state banks and 72 private banks, but by the end of 1993 the number had grown to 234, of which private commercial banks amounted to a total of 161 while the number of state banks remained only the same. Accordingly, the number of bank branch offices – most of them private – also grew from 1,531 offices in 1983 to 5,761 offices at the end of 1993 – a total growth of more than 276 per cent. The year 1990 alone had seen 1,358 additional bank offices, more than half of them being private banks. Thus one interesting point to note here is that the growth in the banking institution was dominated by the growth in the private banking sector. This should have led to pre-emptive thinking about appropriate regulations, including bankruptcy measures and workout procedures at a time of crisis; but no comprehensive policy measures were taken before the crisis.

During the 1980s and the 1990s the deposits also showed impressive growth. In 1990 the value of total deposits in the system was Rp. 143 trillion, growing from only Rp. 12 trillion in 1983 – a cumulative growth rate of 1,489 per cent. Strikingly, the private national banks were able to attain an even higher growth of fund mobilization, from Rp. 2 trillion in 1983 to Rp. 67 trillion in 1993 – an increase of 3,250 per cent in ten years.

The greater funds mobilized by the financial sector increased the supply of loanable funds and, consequently, increased the ability of the sector to extend credit through loan expansion. Even though the central bank's direct credit operation and the liquidity credit were decreased during the period, total bank loans had been growing by more than 1,132 per cent from Rp. 15 trillion at the end of 1983 to Rp. 189 trillion in 1994. In this growth private banks' credit increased by 2900 per cent – from Rp. 2 trillion in 1983 to Rp. 60 trillion in 1993. In addition to this the number of saving schemes increased. ATM machine and computerized banking were introduced. Credit cards and checking accounts became more commonly and widely accepted as mediums of payment. In short, the range of services offered by the banking sector and the degree of intermediation also increased.

In a complete financial system banking is only one of the sources of capital – the other is the capital market, which serves as an alternative source of funds. In the past this source of capital was in general underdeveloped. Consequently, the transaction in the capital market was minimal, with the bourse open officially two hours a day between 10:00 am and noon. In practice the market was open only for about 15 minutes.[6] To make matters worse the government imposed a regulation that would limit daily price fluctuations to 4 per cent. This situation was to be changed with Pakdes 23 1987 (December 23 1987 Package), Pakdes 20 1988 (December 20 1988 Package), and Pakdes 4 1990 (December 4 1990 Package). Through those deregulation packages, as was the case with the banking sector, the capital market was liberalized through the establishment of a private stock exchange, permission for foreign investors to buy shares, the establishment of an over-the-counter market, reductions of the controls on price fluctuation, and through the establishment of rules regarding listing, trading, and dispute settlements.

The reforms promised a rose garden, but...

By standard measures, the Indonesian financial liberalization effort could be considered a great success. The number of banks and NBFIs more than doubled in the first two years. Their repatriation or any other inflow from abroad and the decrease in reserve requirements led to an enormous increase in the size of funds intermediated in the financial system, an amount labelled 'TAFI' for 'total assets of all types of financial institutions' by the main architects of the reform programme. Both the increases in the numbers of banks and NBFIs and the growth of M1 (currency and demand deposits) and M2 (M1 plus savings deposits) increased the concentration of assets in financial institutions and the level of intermediation by them in the system.

Financial liberalization also sparked a lending boom in Indonesia, which progressively involved lending for property development and an increasing proportion of bad loans. The liberalization process left a weakened banking system and domestic capital markets that would be highly vulnerable to falls in the international value of the rupiah in its wake. The seeming success was in fact ephemeral.

To be sure, the financial reforms in the 1980s were also meant to reduce problems inherent in the state-dominated financial system. The portfolios of state banks were traditionally weaker as practices used by the state banks in evaluating projects, assessing collateral, etc. came as a legacy of the old system, i.e., state banks, with their cumbersome procedures, were not flexible enough to adjust to the new situation. Bad debts were also the result of a number of malpractices involving various fraud schemes and overall corruption in which credits were extended on the basis of personal contacts and recommendations. Therefore one needs to be cautious in assessing the role of reforms. However, the problems of poor lending practices in the public sector did not subside after liberalization. There were more resources to lend out as foreign financing became increasingly available. In 1993, the newly-appointed minister of finance Mar'ie Muhammad discovered that six out of seven state-owned banks were technically insolvent and urgently needed recapitalization of up to 8 per cent in accordance with the 1991 prudential regulations.

After all is said and done, it must be admitted – as it now is, ruefully, after the fact – that the Indonesian financial system approached the year 1997 with a very weak banking system. In particular, the system required heavy recapitalization. Much non-performing debt was not on the books; but in any serious accounting system it would need to have been written off in any case. The private sector, the banking sector and the financial sectors all had heavy external liabilities. These were usually denominated in dollars. Worst of all, these debts were often short-term and unhedged. A weak rupiah would mean an unsupportable debt burden. A policy of tightening liquidity and high interest rates – advocated in 1997 by the IMF – would create the possibility of a banking crisis. In Indonesia the aftermath of the Thai debacle led precisely to this state of affairs.

In retrospect it seems ironic that when Thailand secured IMF credit after devaluing the baht on 2 July 1997, Indonesia and South Korea both participated in the Thai rescue package, which was finalized on 5 August 1997. Each of these future victims pledged half a billion US dollars. When the Asian crisis began in mid-1997, Indonesia's macroeconomic situation was not unsound. It seemed quite sound if one compared it to the situation in Mexico before its crisis. Of course, in retrospect, it can be claimed that the macroeconomic situation could certainly be sounder, at the cost of a lower economic growth. Tables 3.4 and 3.5 show that GDP had been growing at nearly 8 per cent per year in the previous two years while the current account deficit hovered at 4 per cent. At the same time rate of growth of bank credit and of money supply were both considerably higher. The demand for money and credit, and what looks like endogenous money and credit creation, came mainly from the business sector. Some projects were legitimate, others were speculative. No distinction seems to have been made between the two types. The complexity of the Indonesian crisis should force us to probe further into the political economy of this crisis.

It seems that between 1995 and 1996 Indonesia's fundamentals did indeed strengthen. Table 3.5 suggests that reserves (measured in months of imports) improved to five months in 1996, while the ratio of M2 to

Table 3.4 Indonesia: monetary and banking data, 1992–1996

	1992	1993	1994	1995	1996
Rate of Growth Money Supply (% per year)					
M1 (Narrow Money)	7.9	27.8	23.3	16.1	21.7
M2 (Broad Money)	21.1	21.1	20.1	27.5	29.6
Rate of Growth Bank Credit (% per year)	8.9	22.3	25.7	24.2	24.9
State Foreign Exchange Banks	14.0	4.8	11.8	16.8	16.5
Private National Banks	1.2	42.8	42.8	29.4	34.3
Foreign & Joint Venture Banks	9.6	57.9	24.7	32.0	13.8
Regional Development Banks	15.3	17.9	18.2	24.8	23.2
Memorandum items					
1. Dollar deposits at DMB as % of M2	19.1	17.5	17.5	17.4	17.2
2. Credit in dollar as % of total credit	17.9	18.8	19.1	19.5	20.2
3. % of total excess liquidity of DMBs held in US$	6.9	13.6	9.3	6.8	2.7
4. The role of SBI in total market instrument (%)	88.0	94.4	79.7	73.8	78.7
5. Deposit rates (3 month, % p.a.)	19.5	14.5	12.6	16.8	17.2
6. Lending rates (working capital, % p.a.)	24.1	20.5	17.8	18.9	19.2
7. Interest differential (6 – 5) (%)	4.5	6.0	5.1	2.1	2.0

Note: DMB – Deposit Money Bank; SBI – Sertifikat Bank Indonesia.
Source: compiled from Indonesian Central Bank Statistics.

the level of reserves declined in 1996. The debt service ratio stayed steady at 33 per cent in 1996, while total external debt as a proportion of exports declined in 1996. However, one disturbing item in Table 3.5 is the increase in short-term debt, which jumped from 17.7 per cent of total debt in 1994 to 20.9 per cent in 1995 and then 24.8 per cent in 1996. As in Thailand, the increase in short-term debt was due to a complicated set of factors, most of them related to the financial liberalization process. High domestic interest rates, brought about by the authorities' efforts to maintain modest increases in money supply in the face of persistent capital inflows, encouraged further capital inflows into short-term instruments.

By July 1997, Indonesia had already begun to implement a tight credit stance, but for contrary reasons – to prevent the continued capital inflow from expanding domestic money supply. In April 1997, for example, it raised bank reserve requirements from 3 to 5 per cent. With the crisis, Indonesian authorities responded by continuing to tighten credit in order to fend off attacks on the rupiah. On 2 July 1997, banks were completely prohibited from increasing credit to property

Table 3.5 Indonesia: macroeconomic fundamentals, 1990–1996 (percentages of GDP, unless otherwise indicated)

	1990	1991	1992	1993	1994	1995	1996
Real GDP growth rate (%)	9.0	8.9	7.2	7.3	7.5	8.1	7.8
Inflation rate (CPI, %)	9.5	9.5	4.9	9.8	9.2	8.6	6.5
Fiscal balance	0.4	0.4	−0.4	−0.6	0.1	0.8	0.2
Current account balance	−2.8	−3.7	−2.2	−1.6	−1.7	−3.7	−4.0
Net capital Inflows	4.9	5.0	3.8	1.9	2.4	4.6	5.0
of which:							
Net portfolio investment	−0.1	0.0	−0.1	1.1	2.2	2.0	n.a.
Net direct investment	1.0	1.3	1.4	1.3	1.2	2.2	n.a.
Other capital	3.3	3.6	3.5	1.4	−0.9	1.3	n.a.
Net error and omissions	0.7	0.1	−1.0	−1.9	−0.1	−0.9	n.a.
Consumption	63.3	64.1	61.8	64.7	65.6	65.9	66.0
Private	54.4	55.0	52.3	55.7	57.4	57.8	58.3
Government	9.0	9.1	9.5	9.0	8.1	8.1	7.7
National savings	27.5	26.9	26.9	27.0	28.4	28.0	28.5
Private	19.1	19.8	20.5	20.4	22.0	22.4	22.8
Public	8.4	7.1	6.4	6.6	6.4	5.6	5.7
Investment	30.1	29.9	29.0	28.3	30.3	31.3	32.1
Private	23.5	21.7	20.9	20.9	24.0	25.8	26.9
Public	6.6	7.7	7.8	7.4	6.3	5.5	5.3
Reserves (in months of imports)	4.7	4.8	5.0	5.2	5.0	4.4	5.1
Ratio M2 to reserves (%)	514.0	505.7	497.4	557.1	602.9	657.4	633.3
Total external debt (percentage of exports of goods and services)	222.0	236.9	221.8	211.9	195.8	205.0	194.0
Short-term debt (percentage of total external debt)	15.9	17.9	20.5	20.1	17.7	20.9	24.8
Short-term debt (in US$ billion)	11.1	14.3	18.1	18.0	17.1	24.3	29.3
Debt service ratio (percentage of exports of goods and services)	30.9	32.0	31.6	33.8	30.0	33.7	33.0
Exports (% of GDP)	26.6	27.4	29.4	25.9	26.0	26.0	26.2
Exports (% of growth rate)	15.9	13.5	16.6	8.4	8.8	13.4	9.7
Oil price (US$ per barrel)	28.64	20.06	18.71	14.4	16.11	18.02	22.78

Source: Compiled from IMF statistics.

development except for low-cost housing. Withdrawals from rupiah-denominated assets started and soon gained strength as a result.

On 6 October, Indonesia used US$0.65 billion to defend the currency, and on 8 October it announced that it was turning to the IMF and external donors for assistance. This was generally seen as a positive, pre-emptive move. With the start of the IMF programme on 31 October 1997, 16 commercial banks were closed. Instead of improving confidence in the banking system, the closures had the opposite effect; the closures accelerated deposit withdrawals from the remaining banks and forced the central bank to provide liquidity beyond the IMF ceilings.

Doubts about the health of President Suharto and the spread of the Asian crisis to Korea contributed to the continued fall in the value of the rupiah in November and December. When Indonesian President Suharto announced a new budget, it was seen to be in defiance of the IMF because it was judged to be not at all austere. Rumours that the IMF was cutting off its programme with Indonesia were also circulating. Both were subsequently proven to be false. It was probably an error to make such an announcement, with potentially strong effects on the currency, on a Tuesday night, instead of making it at the end of the week so that market participants would have a weekend to consider its implications. Still, the precipitous plunge of the rupiah to over 10,000 to the dollar began on Wednesday as the belief spread that Indonesia would be unable to work with the IMF. This eventually became self-fulfilling as the continued fall in the rupiah made it increasingly difficult for Indonesian companies to service their external debt. Indonesia signed a new IMF programme on 15 January 1998.

This programme contained sweeping reforms, including the dismantling of state and state-enforced monopolies, the removal of consumer price subsidies, and the further liberalization of external trade. But the rupiah continued to slide as doubts spread as to whether or not Indonesian corporations and banks would be able to service the debt obligations they had accepted (from abroad) during the high tide of financial liberalization. As a feature of financial liberalization, these were debts between private parties and were not easy to consolidate. Even if the debt could be consolidated, if the government were to guarantee or accept the debt, it would create enormous moral hazard, and permanently characterize financial liberalization programmes as efforts to create private wealth from public finances for external creditors and favoured Indonesian parties. Therefore, the way out from such a hazardous situation was not clear to anybody. In a very odd way, neither the IMF nor the Indonesian policy makers really knew what they were doing.

As will be argued later (in Chapter 5), the Indonesian case more than any other demonstrates the problems of what has been called an *inconsistent developmental state*. It was not simply a matter of liberalizing without sufficient prudential regulations, as many have claimed. If this were the main problem, then among other things it is unclear why the classic tight liquidity regime after the crisis worsened the situation. The problem, it could be suggested, had more to do with the perceptions – in this case correct – of asset holders and creditors that not only was the banking sector weak but also the state was incapable (and unwilling at that point) of strengthening it. To anticipate the argument in Chapter 6 the Indonesian state became vulnerable as a result of its own internal contradictions and the contradictions in the global markets. The structure of the CGE model in the appendix captures this and some results obtained after the crisis support this hypothesis. It is important to note that such contradictions existed not only for middle-level developmental states and political economies such as Indonesia, but also for more affluent Asian countries such as South Korea. Therefore, in order to make a convincing argument, we will investigate the Korean crisis in some depth in the next chapter. Only after this has been done can we turn to examining 'the Asian Model' and constructing an analytical picture of a complex financial economy with some safeguards by looking at the concrete example of Taiwan. Chapter 6 will consider corporate governance issues related to financial controls and management. Chapter 7 addresses the issue of whether banks can learn to manage their loan portfolios better, given a certain regulatory environment. From these 'micro' issues within the national financial complexes I turn in Chapter 8 to the important international issue of global and regional financial architectures. To begin this arduous task of building towards an appropriate theory that can offer some policy guidance in the twenty-first century we need to study what was the most significant country affected by the Asian crisis – Korea.

APPENDIX 3.1: A FINANCIAL-STRUCTURAL MODEL OF LIBERALIZATION

The model was developed for applying to Indonesian financial liberalizations. However, with some modifications this can be applied to the other two cases as well. The most striking aspect of the model is the *possibility of a financial crisis* that results directly from the forces unleashed by the moves to liberalize finance quickly. This happens because of the weaknesses in the banking sector which cannot cope with the demands arising from sudden liberalization. Significantly, such crises can occur even in a flexible or 'managed float' regime. The persistence of the crisis in Asia during 1997–98 suggests that 'structural' factors rather than fixed exchange rates were the underlying causes of the crisis.

Equations of the GGE Model:

I. Households in Agriculture (HAG) – a total of seven household groups

1. $$NW_{HAG}(t) = KAS_{HAG}(t-1) + DSB_{HAG}(t-1) + DPB_{HAG}(t-1)$$
$$+ P_z(t)Z_{HAG}(t-1) + P^K_{HAG}(t)K_{HAG}(t-1) + S_{HAG}(t)$$

Household net worth at eop (end of period) is = cash + initial deposit at private, state bank + the value of stock held at eop + value of capital, which is the amount of capital at the beginning of period multiplied by price at eop to account for capital gain + saving.

NOTE: Household position is a net position. The assumption is that the households do not engage in borrowing activity. Household is a recipient of wages/salary, interest from deposit, and firm's profit. It does not borrow for consumption. A household may borrow for investment in a venture; however, once it takes a loan of this kind, then it no longer is classified as household. Depending on the type of business the household will be classified under a certain type of firm.

---

2. $$QA_{HAG}(t) = NW_{HAG}(t) - P^K_{HAG}(t)K_{HAG}(t)$$

Quantity of financial Assets of household Agriculture is equal to household net worth minus the value of physical capital at eop.

> NOTE: Physical capital of household at eop – $K_{HAG}(t)$ – includes investment made during the year. See equations 11, 22, and 33.

3.
$$q_{HAG} = A_{SB}^{HAG}(i_{sb}/\bar{i}_{sb})^{\sigma_{HAG}-1} + A_{PB}^{HAG}(i_{pb}/\bar{i}_{pb})^{\sigma_{HAG}-1}$$
$$+ A_Z^{HAG}(r/\bar{r})^{\sigma_{HAG}-1} + A_{KAS}^{HAG}$$

Agriculture households try to maximize the utility of return q_{HAG}, which is formulated using CES type harmonic mean return.

A_i^{HAG} = Distribution parameter

i_{SB}, i_{pb}, and r = interest rate at private, state bank and rate of return on capital (profit) respectively

$\bar{i}_{SB}, \bar{i}_{pb}$, and $\bar{r}$ = normal yield on bank (private and state bank) deposits and company's capital.

σ_{HAG} = elasticity of substitution

The agriculture household asset returns consist of interest from State Bank, Private Bank, the share of the firm's profit, and cash. Government security is not available for households to buy. Therefore there is no return from government security.

4. $\varnothing_{SB}^{HAG} = A_{SB}^{HAG}\dfrac{(i_{sb}/\bar{i}_{sb})^{\sigma_{HAG}-1}}{q_{hag}}$ $\rightarrow$ Share of deposit on state bank

5. $\varnothing_{PB}^{HAG} = A_{PB}^{HAG}\dfrac{(i_{pb}/\bar{i}_{pb})^{\sigma_{HAG}-1}}{q_{hag}}$ $\rightarrow$ Share of deposit on private bank

6. $\varnothing_Z^{HAG} = A_Z^{HAG}\dfrac{(r/\bar{r})^{\sigma_{HAG}-1}}{q_{hag}}$ $\rightarrow$ Share of equity

7. $\varnothing_{KAS}^{HAG} = A_Z^{HAG}\dfrac{A_{KAS}^{HAS}}{q_{hag}}$ $\rightarrow$ Share of currency

The sum of $\varnothing_{sb}^{HAG}, \varnothing_{pb}^{HAG}, \varnothing_Z^{HAG}$ and $\varnothing_{KAS}^{HAG}$ must equal one.

8. $$D_{HAG} = \varnothing_{sb}^{HAG}(QA_{HAG}) + \varnothing_{PB}^{HAG}(QA_{HAG})$$

Total agriculture-household deposit is equal to the share of household deposit in state bank multiplied by total financial assets plus the share of household deposit in private bank multiplied by total financial assets.

9.
$$Z_{HAG} = \emptyset_Z^{HAG}(QA_{HAG})$$

Total agriculture-household stock/equity is share of stock $\times$ total financial assets

10.
$$KAS_{HAG} = \emptyset_{KAS}^{HAG}(QA_{HAG})$$

Total agriculture-household cash is share of cash $\times$ total financial assets

11.
$$K_{HAG}(t) = K_{HAG}(t-1) + I_{HAG}(t)$$

Total capital owned by agriculture – household = initial capital + total investment at end of period.

II. Household non-Agriculture (HNAG) – a total of three household groups

12. $NW_{HNAG}(t) = KAS_{HNAG}(t-1) + DSB_{HNAG}(t-1) + DPB_{HNAG}(t-1)$
$$+ P_Z(t)Z_{HNAG}(t-1) + P_{HNAG}^K(t)K_{HNAG}(t-1) + S_{HNAG}(t)$$

13.
$$QA_{HNAG}(t) = NW_{HNAG}(t) - P_{HNAG}^K(t)K_{HNAG}(t)$$

14.
$$q_{HNAG} = A_{SB}^{HNAG}(i_{sb}/\bar{i}_{sb})^{\sigma_{HNAG}-1} + A_{PB}^{HNAG}(i_{pb}/\bar{i}_{pb})^{\sigma_{HNAG}-1}$$
$$+ A_Z^{HNAG}(r/\bar{r})^{\sigma_{HNAG}-1} + A_{KAS}^{HNAG}$$

15. $\emptyset_{SB}^{HNAG} = A_{SB}^{HNAG}\dfrac{(i_{sb}/\bar{i}_{sb})^{\sigma_{HNAG}-1}}{q_{hnag}}$ $\rightarrow$ Share of deposit on state bank

16. $\emptyset_{PB}^{HNAG} = A_{PB}^{NHAG}\dfrac{(i_{pb}/\bar{i}_{pb})^{\sigma_{HNAG}-1}}{q_{hnag}}$ $\rightarrow$ Share of deposit on private bank

17. $\emptyset_Z^{HNAG} = A_Z^{HNAG}\dfrac{(r/\bar{r})^{\sigma_{HNAG}-1}}{q_{hnag}}$ $\rightarrow$ Share of equity

18. $$\varnothing_{KAS}^{HNAG} = A_Z^{HNAG} \frac{A_{KAS}^{HNAG}}{q_{hnag}} \quad \rightarrow \text{Share of currency}$$

The sum of $\varnothing_{sb}^{HNAG}, \varnothing_{pb}^{HNAG}, \varnothing_{Z}^{HNAG}, \varnothing_{KAS}^{HNAG}$ must be equal to one.

19. $$D_{HNAG} = \varnothing_{sb}^{HNAG}(QA_{HNAG}) + \varnothing_{PB}^{HNAG}(QA_{HNAG})$$

20. $$Z_{HNAG} = \varnothing_{Z}^{HNAG}(QA_{HNAG})$$

Total non-agricultural-household stock/equity is share of stock× total financial assets.

21. $$KAS_{HNAG} = \varnothing_{KAS}^{HNAG}(QA_{HNAG})$$

Total non-agriculture-household cash is share of cash × total financial assets

22. $$K_{HNAG}(t) = K_{HNAG}(t-1) + I_{HNAG}(t)$$

Total capital owned by non-agriculture-household = initialcapital+ total investment at end of period.

III.   Household Total (h)

23. $$NW_h(t) = NW_{HAG}(t) + NW_{HNAG}(t)$$

24. $$QA_h(t) = QA_{HAG}(t) + QA_{HNAG}(t)$$

25. $$qh = q_{HAG} + Q_{HNAG}$$

26. $$\varnothing_{SB}^{h} = Q_{SB}^{HAG} + Q_{SB}^{HNAG} \quad \rightarrow \text{Share of deposit on state bank}$$

27. $$\varnothing_{PB}^{h} = Q_{PB}^{HAG} + Q_{PB}^{HNAG} \quad \rightarrow \text{Share of deposit on private bank}$$

28. $$\varnothing_{Z}^{h} = Q_{Z}^{HAG} + Q_{Z}^{HNAG} \quad \rightarrow \text{Share of equity}$$

29. $$\varnothing_{KAS}^{h} = Q_{KAS}^{HAG} + Q_{KAS}^{HNAG} \quad \rightarrow \text{Share of currency}$$

30. $$D_h = D_{HAG} + D_{HNAG}$$

31. $$Z_h = Z_{HAG} + Z_{HNAG}$$

32. $$KAS_h = KAS_{HAG} + KAS_{HNAG}$$

33. $$K_h(t) = K_{HAG}(t) + K_{HNAG}(t)$$

IV. Firms

34–37. $$DEF = P_i^k I_i - S_i \quad i = \text{FAG, FMIN, FTS, FI}$$

38–41. $$Z_i(t) = Z_i(t-1) + \alpha_i + \beta_i[(DEF_i(t)/P_i^k(t)] \quad i = \text{FAG, FMIN, FTS, FI}$$

42s–45. $$QL_i(t) = DEF_i(t) - P_z(t)[Z_i(t) - Z_i(t-1)] + LSB_i(t-1)$$
$$+ LPB(t-1) + LF_i(t-1) \quad i = \text{FAG, FMIN, FTS, FI}$$

Another part of the deficit must be financed through borrowing. The required amount of total borrowing at time t ($QL_i(t)$) must be equal to the amount of deficit minus the value of outstanding equity increase at the end of period plus last year's outstanding loan from state bank, private bank, and foreign loan.

The firm's total loan comes from different sources. From the State Bank, Private Bank, and from foreign loan, with distribution parameter of A_x^i, and interest rate on bank loan of i_l, interest rate of foreign loan of i_f. Using CES specification, the firms try to minimize the cost function based on capitalized borrowing cost of $\bar{i}_{xi}/i_x$.

46.–49. $$q_i = A_{sb}^i(\bar{i}_{li}/i_l)^{\sigma_i - 1} + A_{pb}^i(\bar{i}_{li}/i_l)^{\sigma_i - 1} + A_{fl}^i(\bar{i}_{fli}/i_{fl})^{\sigma_i - 1}$$
$$i = \text{FAG, FMIN, FTS, FI}$$

q_i is the average of capitalized interest rates for each type of the firm.

NOTE: It is assumed that interest rate is not the explaining factor for the firm's decision to choose between state bank or private bank. The image of the private bank as having better service, faster and easier to deal with and that of the state bank as safer, bigger, and more helpful when a firm is in trouble. Firms borrowing from the state bank are restrained by many requirements and its reputation for inflexibility must be taken into account when one tries to find out why there are certain preferences toward one or another.

The share of loan from state bank, private bank, and foreign loan of each firm is given by equation 50–61. The sum of the share must equal to 1.

50–53. $$\varnothing_{sb}^i = A_{sb}^i \frac{(\bar{i}_{Li}/i_l)^{\sigma_i-1}}{q_i} \quad i = \text{FAG, FMIN, FTS, FI}$$

54–57. $$\varnothing_{pb}^i = A_{pb}^i \frac{(\bar{i}_{li}/i_l)^{\sigma_i-1}}{q_i} \quad i = \text{FAG, FMIN, FTS, FI}$$

54–57. $$\varnothing_{lf}^i = A_{lf}^i \frac{(\bar{i}_{fli}/i_{fl})^{\sigma_i-1}}{q_i} \quad i = \text{FAG, FMIN, FTS, FI}$$

The demand for loan from each type of bank by each type of firm is given in equations 62 to 73.

62–65. $$LSB_i = \varnothing_{lsb}^i QL_i \quad i = \text{FAG, FMIN, FTS, FI}$$

Firm's demand for loan from state bank

66–69. $$LPB_i = \varnothing_{lpb}^i QL_i \quad i = \text{FAG, FMIN, FTS, FI}$$

Firm's demand for loan from private bank

70–73. $$LF_i = \varnothing_{lf}^i Ql_i \quad i = \text{FAG, FMIN, FTS, FI}$$

Firm's demand for loan from abroad

74. $$L = \sum_{i=FAG}^{FI} LSB_i + \sum_{i=FAG}^{FI} LPB_i$$

Total domestic loan = total loan from state bank and from private bank to all firms.

75–78. $$K_i(t) = K_i(t-1) + I_i(t) K_i(t) = K_i(t-1) + I_i(t)$$

Total capital stocks held by firms at the end of period equal to capital stock at the beginning plus investment at the end of period.

V. Government (G)

79.
$$FL_G(t) = FL_G(t-1) + e(\Delta FL_G^\$)$$

Foreign loan at time t (eop) = Outstanding Loan from abroad at the beginning plus New Loan from abroad in local currency. The additional loan amount is exogenous, valued at foreign currency (dollar) but converted into local currency by multiplication with exchange rate.

80.
$$QL_G = LPB_G(t-1) + LSB_G(t-1) + LCB_G(t-1) + P_G^k(t)I_G(t) \\ - S_G(t) - e(\Delta LF_G^\$)$$

Government demand for domestic credit = Govt. investment + initial borrowing from the banking system (SB, PB, and CB), less Government Saving and Loan from abroad.

NOTE: The government demand for domestic credit is a net position with loan payment included (if any). Any amount of loan repayment from the government to the banking system will appear as reduction in saving by the same amount. Government investment is exogenous.

81.
$$L_G = [\alpha_G^{SB} + \beta_G^{SB}(DEP_{SB})] + [\alpha_G^{PB} + \beta_G^{PB}(DEP_{PB})]$$

Bank credit to government = initial claims of government, certain resources in SB and PB + statutory liquidity ratio β multiplied by deposit of SB and PB.

82.
$$LCB_G = QL_G - L_G$$

Central bank loan to government; it is the government balance sheet residual i.e. the portion of total loan to government that is not fulfilled by commercial banking sector.

83.
$$K_G(t) = K_G(t-1) + I_G(t)$$

VI. Commercial State Bank Portfolio (SB)

84.
$$DSB = DSB_{HAG} + DSB_{HNAG}$$

Deposits in the state bank come from household, agriculture and non-agriculture, at a fixed rate of deposit i_d.

85.
$$RR_{SB} = u_1^{SB} + u_2^{SB}(DEP^{SB})$$

Reserve requirement in the central bank = marginal amount u_i + a fraction of deposits.

86.
$$QL_{SB} = DSB + ADVCB_{SB} - LSB_G - RR_{SB} + LIK_{SB}$$

Domestically available resources or the total loan can be given from domestic resources = deposit + advances from central bank + liquidity credit from central bank – loan to Govt. – reserve requirement.

87.
$$DCB_{SB} = RR_{SB}[1 + \theta(i_{lsb}/\bar{i}_l)^{-\gamma}]$$

The state bank reserve at the central bank is always higher than the requisite reserve requirement. The excess reserve is a function of interest rate charged by the state bank for loan. The higher the rate the lower the excess reserves.

88. $LF_{SB} = \left(L_G^{SB} + DCB_{SB} + \sum_{i=FAG}^{FL} LSB_i \right) - (DSB - REDSCNT - NW)$

The state bank resources are deposits, rediscount from the central bank and net worth. The total resources available will be used to create loans to government, commercial loans to firms and some will be used as deposits to central bank. If the available resources are less than the loan created, then foreign loan is needed.

VII. Commercial Private Bank Portfolio (PB)

89.
$$DPB = DB_{HAG} + DPB_{HNAG}$$

90.
$$RR_{PB} = u_1^{PB} + u_2^{PB}(DEP^{PB})$$

91.
$$QL_{PB} = DPB + ADVCB_{PB} - LPB_G - RR_{PB} + LIK_{PB}$$

Available resources (domestic) = deposit + advances from central bank − loans to govt − reserve requirement + liquidity credit from central bank

92.
$$DCB_{PB} = RR_{PB}[1 + \theta(i_{lpb}/\bar{i}_l)^{-\gamma}]$$

93. $LF_{PB} = \left(L_G^{PB} + DCB_{PB} + \sum_{i=FAG}^{FL} LPB_i\right) - (DPB - REDSCNT - NW)$

VIII.   Commercial Bank Total

94.
$$DEP = DSB + DPB$$

Total deposit taken by commercial bank.

95.
$$RR = RR_{SB} + RR_{PB}$$

Total reserve deposit at central bank.

96.
$$QL + QL_{SB} + QL_{PB}$$

Total resources available domestically.

97.
$$i_L = \bar{i}_L \left[\frac{L(i/i_F)^\epsilon (i_R/i_R)^\phi}{\alpha QL}\right]^{1/\delta}$$

Market clearing interest rate i_L = Loan interest rate; i_F = Foreign Loan interest rate; i_R = Rediscount Interest rate.
$\in$, ϕ, and δ = loan supply interest rate elasticities, α = loan supply intercept.

98.
$$DCB = DCB_{SB} + DCB_{PB}$$

Total deposit of commercial bank at central bank, including required reserve.

99.
$$LF = LF_{SB} + LF_{PB}$$

Total residual items. The foreign loan needed by the domestic commercial banking sector to cover excess loan over domestic resources available.

IX.   Central Bank Portfolio

100. $FL = FL_{SB} + FL_{PB} + FL_{FAG} + FL_{MIN} + FL_{IS} + FL_I + FL_G$

101. $ADVCB = ADV_{CEL} + \emptyset_4[(FL_{SB} + FL_{PB}) - FL_{CEL}] - \gamma_4(DEPCB - RR)$

Total advances available from central bank = ceiling for advances less state bank's and private bank's advances, less net deposit at central bank.

102. $KAS_{CB} = KAS_H$

103. $NWCB(t) = NWCB(T - 1) + DISCR$

DISCR = Accounting discrepancy of state-owned firms

104. $CBREV(t) = FL(t) - FL(t - 1) - SF(t) + CBRES(t - 1)$

Central Bank's reserve = net foreign loan at eop less foreign saving plus reserve at the beginning of the period.

105. $NWRES = CBLG + ADVCB + CBRES - KASCB + DEPCB - NWCB$

X.   Other Financial Balance

106. $P_Z = \dfrac{ZZ_H}{(Z_{FAG} + Z_{MIN} + Z_{FTS} + Z_I)}$

107. $INT = (A_{SB}^H + A_{PB}^H + i_L L_{SB} + i_L L_{PB}) + (A_{CB}^{SB} + A_{CB}^{PB} + i_L L_{SB} + i_L L_{PB})$

Interest payment.

XI. Production and Price Formation

108–114. $\qquad P_i^k = \xi_4 P_4 + \xi_7 P_7 \quad i = 1, 2, 3, 4, 5, 6, 7$

P_i^k = Price indexes for each sector's capital stock; capital goods come from the industrial sector and from import.

115–121.
$$P_{i0}^* = [(\Theta_{1i})^{\sigma_i^{int}} (P_1)^{1-\sigma_i^{int}} + (\Theta_{2i})^{\sigma_i^{int}} (P_2)^{1-\sigma_i^{int}} + (\Theta_{3i})^{\sigma_i^{int}} (P_3)^{1-\sigma_i^{int}}$$
$$+ (\Theta_{5i})^{\sigma_i^{int}} (P_5)^{1-\sigma_i^{int}} + (\Theta_{6i})^{\sigma_i^{int}} (P_6)^{1-\sigma_i^{int}}$$
$$+ (\Theta_{7i})^{\sigma_i^{int}} (P_7)^{1-\sigma_i^{int}}]^{1/(1-\sigma_i^{int})}$$

$i = 1,2,3,4,5,6,7$ P_{i0}^* = cost indexes for sectoral intermediate uses, input output coefficient = a_{ji}^* and constant elasticities of substitution among intermediate inputs = σ_i^{int}

122–128. $\qquad a_{ji}^* = \left[\dfrac{P_i^* \Theta_{ji}}{P_j} \right]^{\sigma_i^{int}}$ $\quad$ j = Sector; i = Market participant HAG – FI

a_{ji}^* = Input Output Coefficient.

129–135. $\quad P_i^c = [(\Theta_{Li})^{\sigma_i^{FIN}} (W_i)^{1-FIN} + (\Theta_{Ki})^{\sigma_i^{FIN}} (r_i + \delta_i)(P_i^K)^{1-FIN}]^{1/(1-\sigma^{1-FIN})}$
$$+ (\Theta_i^*)^{\sigma_i^{FIN}} (P_i^*)^{\sigma_i^{FIN}}$$

CES Cost function = labor cost + fixed capital cost + cost of intermediate goods used i = sector/commodity 1–7
σ_i^{FIN} = Elasticities of substitution

136–142. $\qquad L_i = (P_i^c \Theta_{Li}/W_i)^{\sigma_i^{FIN}} X_i$ $\quad$ i = Hag – FI

Level of employment.

143–149. $\qquad r_i(t) = \dfrac{1}{P_i^K(t-1)} \left[P_i^c(t) \Theta_{Ki} \left(\dfrac{X_i(t)}{K_i(t-1)} \right)^{1/\sigma_i^{INT}} \right] - \delta_i$

Sectoral rates of profit are determined by output level X and incoming capital stocks $K_i(t-1)$
i = HAG – FI

150. $$r(t) = \frac{r_{HAG}(t)P^K_{HAG}(t)K_{HAG}(t-1) + \cdots r_{FI}(t)P^K_{FI}(t)K_{FI}(t-1)}{P^K_{HAG}(t)K_{HAG}(t-1) + \cdots P^K_{FI}(t)K_{FI}(t-1)}$$

Average rate of profit (used for household portfolio decisions) depends on sectoral rate of profit

151–157. $$X_{ji} = a^*_{ji}\left[\frac{P^c_i\Theta^c_i}{P^c_i}\right]^{\sigma^{FIN}_i} X_i \qquad j = \text{commodity } 1\text{--}7$$

$$I = \text{mkt participant HAG} - \text{FI}$$

Intermediate goods flow using a^*_{ji} coefficient of input output defined with regard to the intermediate aggregate. (Flow of goods j (sector j) to market participant i; i.e. demand of good j by market participant i.)

158–164. $$Mi = \left[\frac{P_i\Theta_{0i}}{e(1+t_0)P_0}\right]^{\sigma^{FIN}_i} X_i$$

i = Sectors 5, 6 & 7 (Import Mining and Import other)
Mi = Derived demand for import

165–171. $$P_i = P^c_i(1 - t_i) \; i = 1\text{--}7$$

After-tax prices for each sectors/commodity

XII.   Income Generation and Saving

172. $$W = w_{HAG} L_{HAG} + \cdots w_{FI}L_{FI} + W_{fh} - W_{hf}$$

173–179. $$\Pi_i(t) = r_i(t)P^K_i(t)K_i(t-1) + \Pi_{fi} - \Pi_{if}$$

i = HAG, HNAG, SB, PB, FAG, FMIN, FTS, FI.
Profit income flows.

180–185. $$OS_i = (1 - \nu_i)\Pi_i + SUB \quad i = \text{SB, PB, FAG, FMIN, FTS, FI.}$$

Operating surplus of firms i is part of profit after the household share of ν
Government-owned firm (Bank) receives subsidy *SUB*

186–191. $$S_i = (1 - d_i - t^{dir}_i)OS_i \qquad i = \text{SB, PB, FAG, FMIN, FTS, FI}$$

Saving of the firm, equal to operating surpluses less dividend d payment less direct taxes t_i^{dir}.

192.
$$Y_{HAG} = W_{HAG} + d_{SB}^{HAG} OS_{SB}^{HAG} + \cdots d_{FI}^{HAG} OS_{FI}^{HAG} + \nu_{SB}^{HAG} \Pi_{SB}^{HAG}$$
$$+ \cdots \nu_{FI}^{HAG} \Pi_{FI}^{HAG} + TRAN_{gHAG} + TRAN_{fHAG}$$

Household AG income = wages + dividend + share of profit + transfer from G and abroad.

193.
$$Y_{HNAG} = W_{HNAG} + d_{SB}^{HNAG} OS_{SB}^{HNAG} + \cdots d_{FI}^{HNAG} OS_{FI}^{HNAG} + \nu_{SB}^{HNAG} \Pi_{SB}^{HNAG}$$
$$+ \cdots \nu_{FI}^{HNAG} \Pi_{FI}^{HNAG} + TRAN_{gHNAG} + TRAN_{fHNAG}$$

194.
$$Y_h = Y_{HAG} + Y_{HNAG}$$

Total HH income is the sum of HAG income and HNAG income

195.
$$D_{HAG} = D_0^{HAG} + (1 + s_{HAG}) Y_{HAG} - TRAN_{HAGf} - t_{HAG}^{dir} Y_{HAG}$$
$$- (A_5^h + i_L L_5) + Y_{HAG} NW_{HAG}$$

Consumption demand = initial / basic consumption + consumption − transfer abroad − direct taxes

196.
$$D_{HNAG} = D_0^{HNAG} + (1 + s_{HNAG}) Y_{HNAG} - TRAN_{HNAGf} - t_{HNAG}^{dir} Y_{HNAG}$$
$$- (A_5^h + i_L L_5) + Y_{HNAG} NW_{HNAG}$$

197.
$$D = D_{HAG} + D_{HNAG}$$

198.
$$S_{HAG} = Y_{HAG} - TRAN_{HAGf} - t_{HAG}^{dir} Y_{HAG}$$
$$- (A_f^{HAG} + i_L L_5) - D_{HAG}$$

199.
$$S_{HNAG} = Y_{HNAG} - TRAN_{HNAGf} - t_{HNAG}^{dir} Y_{HNAG} - (A_f^{HNAG} + i_L L_5) - D_{HNAG}$$

200.
$$S_h = S_{HAG} + S_{HNAG}$$

201.
$$Y_g = \sum_{i=1}^{4} t_i P_i^c X_i + et_0 P_5 M_5 + et_0 P_6 M_6 + et_0 P_7 M_7 + t_h^{dir} Y_h + \sum_{i=SB}^{FI} t_i^{dir} OS_i$$
$$+ \sum_{i=1}^{4} t_i^{exp} P_i^c E_i t$$

Government income consists of the sum of indirect taxes from all sectors + domestic currency of import indirect taxes + direct taxes from household + the sum of direct taxes of firms + export taxes.

202.
$$S_g = Y_g - \sum_{i=1}^{7} P_i G_i - TRAN_{gh} - (A_5^g + i_l L_g)$$

203.
$$S_f = \sum_{i=1}^{7} \Pi_{if} + W_{hf} + \sum_{i=5}^{7} e P_i M_i + TRAN_{hf} + TRAN_{gf} - \sum_{i=1}^{4} (1 + t_i^{exp}) P_i^c E_i$$
$$- W_{fh} - \sum_{i=1}^{4} \Pi_{fi} - TRAN_{fg} - TRAN_{fh}$$

Current Account Deficit in foreign currency terms is converted to domestic currency, with export tax rate of t_i^{exp}.

XIII.   Final Demand Determination

204.
$$\tilde{D} = \sum_{i=1}^{7} \Theta_i^{dem} P_i \qquad i = 1-7$$

205–211.
$$C_i = \Theta_i^{dem} + (\alpha_i^{dem}/P_i)(D - \tilde{D}) \quad i = 1-7$$

212–215.
$$I_i(t) = [I_{0i} + \omega_i \{r_i(t) - i_i(t)\}] K_i(t-1) \quad i = \text{firms; FAG} - \text{FI.}$$

Investment demands of firms depend positively on rate of profit r_i and negatively on loan interest rate i_l. The firm investment parameter is ω_i.

216–217.
$$= I_i(t) = [I_{0i} + \omega_i \{r_i(t)\}] K_i(t-1) \qquad i = \text{SB and PB}$$

State bank and private bank demand for investment depend positively on the rate of profit. The Investment demand, loan rate and deposit rate is negative and positive respectively. However, a simultaneous increase in the loan and deposit rate will net a zero effect. The decisive factor in this case is the spread between loan and deposit rate. But the spread will correlate with rate of profit thus the spread effect on investment demand has been reflected through the inclusion of r_i.

218. $$I_{HAG} = I_{0HAG} + \omega_{HAG}^i i_l + \omega_{HAG}^y (Y_{HAG}/P_{HAG}^k)$$

219. $$I_{HNAG} = I_{0HNAG} + \omega_{HNAG}^i i_l + \omega_{HNAG}^y (Y_{HNAG}/P_{NHAG}^k)$$

220. $$I_h = I_{HAG} + I_{HNAG}$$

Household demand for investment is a function of interest rate (with investment parameter ω^i and real income (investment parameter W^y).

221. $$I_g = I_{0g}$$

222–225. $$E_i = E_{0i} \left[\frac{eP_f^E}{(1 + t_i^{Exp})P_i^c} \right]^{\eta}$$

Export depends on the ratio of price of foreign goods and domestic border price, the elasticity is η. $i = 1-4$

XIV. Commodity Balances

226–232. $$X_i = \sum_{j=HAG}^{FI} X_{ij} + C_i + G_i + \xi_i \left(\sum_{j=HAG}^{FI} I_j \right) + p_i \left[\sum_{i=1}^{7} \delta_i K_i(t - 1) \right]$$

$i =$ Commodity 1–7; $j =$ HAG – FI
$p_i =$ sectoral composition of depreciation

XV. Saving–Investment Balance

233. $$SI = \sum_{i=HAG}^{FI} S_i + S_f - \sum_{i=HAG}^{FI} P_i^k I_i$$

Saving of all sectors (excluding the G) plus foreign saving less investment of all sectors (foreign saving not included) will be zero if overall macroeconomics balance is to be maintained.

4

The End of the South Korean Miracle

You can predict things only after they have happened.

Eugène Ionesco, *Rhinoceros*

Over a two-month period from October 1997 to December 1997 South Korea was reduced from being the eleventh largest economy in the world to one that had to go cap in hand to the international financial institutions in order to survive. This sudden shift took even the IMF by surprise. As late as October 1997 the IMF mission visiting Seoul had given South Korea a clean bill of economic and financial health. So what went wrong?

The best approach to answering this question is historical. In order to understand the recent crisis we need to go back several years and from there trace our way towards the crisis.

Prelude to the crisis: financial liberalization and investment growth

During the few years preceding the crisis, Korea did not experience the kind of double-digit growth that it had during an earlier period, but the average economic growth from 1993 to the beginning of 1997 was still a respectable 7.6 per cent per annum. It peaked in 1996 at nearly 9 per cent, as shown in Table 4.1.

During this period the Korean economy was, as in the past, fuelled by exports. However, growth during this period was accompanied by unusually high levels of investment. As a matter of fact, investment was so high that it outstripped Korea's high savings rate, which itself stood at well above 30 per cent. In many respects, this high investment was a positive development as the economy was coming out of a mild recession during the 1991–92 period, but it was also partly responsible for a sharp increase in the current account deficit. There were two major reasons for this high investment: the strengthening of the yen

60

Table 4.1 Major indicators of the Korean economy, 1991–1997 (percentage)

	1991	1992	1993	1994	1995	1996	1997[1]
GDP[1]	9.1	5.1	5.8	8.6	8.9	7.1	6.1
Non-agricultural	10.0	5.0	6.5	9.1	9.3	7.4	6.3
Domestic demand[2]	10.5	3.9	5.3	8.7	8.8	7.9	2.4
Consumption	9.3	6.8	5.3	7.0	7.2	6.9	5.0
Private	9.5	6.6	5.7	7.6	8.3	6.9	4.8
Public	8.5	7.6	3.0	4.2	1.0	7.1	6.5
Fixed investment	12.6	−0.8	5.2	11.8	11.7	7.1	−2.1
Construction	13.0	−0.6	8.9	4.5	8.7	6.3	0.9
Equipment	12.1	−1.1	−0.1	23.6	15.8	8.2	−5.9
Commodity exports	12.2	10.9	9.7	14.6	25.3	14.5	24.2
Commodity imports	19.4	4.0	5.6	21.8	221.3	13.9	6.5
Increase in stocks/GDP	0.5	0.0	−0.9	0.3	0.5	1.4	—
Compensation of employees/NI	60.2	61.0	60.4	60.0	61.2	63.3	—
Gross savings/GDP	35.9	34.7	35.1	35.2	35.9	34.3	34.2
Gross investment/GDP	38.9	36.6	35.1	36.1	37.0	38.2	36.1
Current account/GDP	−2.8	−1.3	0.3	−1.0	−1.8	−4.8	−1.9
Terms of trade	0.6	0.0	4.4	1.2	−3.6	k−12.3	−10.3
Unit export price	0.5	−1.6	0.4	1.7	5.0	−13.4	−14.9
Unit import price	0.0	−1.6	−3.8	0.5	8.9	−1.2	−5.3
Consumer price index	9.3	6.2	4.8	6.3	4.5	4.9	4.4
Producer price index	4.7	2.2	1.5	2.8	4.7	2.7	3.8

Notes: 1. The figures under GDP are averages from the first quarter to the third quarter.
2. Domestic demand = consumption + fixed investment.
Sources: The Bank of Korea, *National Income*, various issues.
The Bank of Korea, *Balance of Payments*, various issues.
The National Statistical Office, *Consumer Price Index*, various issues.

and the financial liberalization and market opening. Both of these factors increased the availability of foreign credit.

Until the spring of 1995, when the yen hit a level of 79.5 to the US dollar, the Japanese currency appreciated continuously. Consequently, the East Asian countries were becoming increasingly competitive vis-à-vis Japan in exports of manufactures, and increasing even further their export earnings. This resulted in a great deal of direct foreign investment and domestic capital formation throughout East Asia. Korea benefited more than any other East Asian country from the high yen because it competed directly with Japan in many industries where Japan was the leading exporter.

The second factor which led to the investment boom was the accelerated deregulation of domestic markets and the relaxation of restrictions on capital account transactions. The market deregulation greatly reduced the scope of industrial policy, while financial market opening facilitated capital inflows. These changes were also responsible for the massive increase in investment. From the 1960s and throughout the 1980s, there were many restrictions on foreign capital inflows. Through its industrial policy, the government regulated the inflow of foreign capital and coordinated many of the investment decisions of the large conglomerates (chaebols) that were – and still remain – the backbone of the Korean economy.

By the early 1990s it was thought that the national political economy had become too complex for the government to make sound investment decisions for the chaebols. Korea had also come under increasing pressure from developed countries demanding that the policy makers should liberalize Korea's financial sector. Liberalization began in earnest in 1993, immediately after the inauguration of the administration of Kim Yon Sam, and was accelerated by Korea's accession to the OECD as its 29th member. The upshot of all this was that the government lost much of its control over investment activity, and the domestic financial institutions were allowed greater freedom in borrowing from the international financial markets and in lending to domestic enterprises. Table 4.2 lists the major financial liberalization measures taken by Korea in the 1990s. The irony of the situation was that Korean financial institutions were not adequately prepared for financial market liberalization and market opening because they had

Table 4.2 Major financial liberalization measures in Korea during the 1990s

---

1 Interest rates deregulation (in four stages: 1991 to July 1997)
  –By 1997, all lending & borrowing rates except demand deposit rates, were liberalized

2 More managerial autonomy for the banks and lower entry barriers to financial activities
  –Freedom for banks to increase capital, to establish branches, and to determine dividend payments (1994)
  –Enlargement of business scope for financial institutions (1993); continuous expansion of the securities business of deposit money banks (1990, 1993, 1994, 1995).
  –Freedom for banks and life insurance companies to sell government and public bonds over-the-counter (1995).
  –Permission for securities companies to handle foreign exchange business (1995)
  –Abolition of the limits on maximum maturities for loans and deposits of banks (1996)

3 Foreign exchange liberalization

–Adoption of the Market-Average Foreign Exchange Rate System (1990)

–Easing of the requirement for documentation providing 'real' (i.e., non-financial) demand in foreign exchange transactions (1991)

–Setting up of foreign currency call markets

–Revision of the Foreign Exchange Management Act (1991): changing the basis for regulation from a positive system to a negative system

–Introduction of 'free Won' accounts for non-residents (1993)

–Allowance of partial Won settlements for the export or import of visible items (1993)

–Foreign Exchange Reform Plan (1994): a detailed schedule for the reform of the foreign exchange market structure

–A very significant relaxation of the Foreign Exchange Concentration System (1995)

4 Capital market opening

–Foreign investors are allowed to invest directly in Korean stock markets with ownership ceilings (1992)

–Foreigners are allowed to purchase government and public bonds issued at international interest rates (1994), equity-linked bonds issued by small and medium-sized firms (1994), non-guaranteed long-term bonds issued by small and medium-sized firms (Jan. 1997), and non-guaranteed convertible bonds issued by large companies (Jan. 1997)

–Residents are allowed to invest overseas securities via beneficiary certificates (1993)

–Abolition of the ceiling on the domestic institutional investors' overseas portfolio investment (1995)

–Foreign commercial loans are allowed without government approval in so far as they meet the guideline established in May 1995

–Private companies engaged in major infrastructure projects are allowed to borrow overseas to pay for domestic construction cost (Jan. 1997)

–Liberalization of borrowings related to foreign direct investments (Jan. 1997)

5 Policy loans and credit control

–A planned termination of all policy loans by 1997 is announced (1993): a step-wise reduction in policy loans to specific sectors (e.g., export industries and small and medium-sized firms)

–Simplifying and slimming down the controls on the share of a bank's loans to major conglomerates in its total loans

Source: Chang, Ha-joon, et al. (1998), p. 3.

not developed sufficient expertise in credit analysis, risk management, due diligence, and international finance in general. The supervisory authorities were also pressured to overhaul their regulatory system in order to make it more compatible with a liberalized system. In the process, many restrictions and control measures were eliminated or relaxed. At the same time the authorities did not install the new system of prudential regulation that was needed to safeguard the stability and soundness of financial institutions. In these developments lay the potential for a serious financial crisis.

During the 1990s, all of the large chaebols also expanded their investment in Korea's major industries in an attempt to maintain their respective relative positions. Their management system, with decision making concentrated at the top, made it difficult for the chaebols to adjust their investment and output to rapid changes in market conditions. The chaebols were reluctant to issue equities, since doing so could lead to a loss of control by the major controlling families. Therefore the chaebols became highly leveraged. One survey has revealed that the average debt/equity ratio of the 30 largest chaebols was more than 380 per cent in 1996, four times as high as that recorded in Taiwan.

Between 1993 and 1996, there was a net foreign capital inflow of $46.3 billion, more than ten times the total net inflow for the whole of the 1980s. For the most part, these inflows were induced by large interest rate differentials between the domestic and foreign financial markets and consisted of short-term portfolio investment, as shown in Table 4.3. Most of this new capital was used to finance investment in Korea's major export-oriented industries, such as electronics, automobiles, iron and steel, shipbuilding, and petrochemicals. Many Korean chaebols participated in a major direct investment effort in foreign countries, especially in Europe and Southeast Asia. In 1993, Korea's total foreign direct investment was about $13 billion. Only a year later it had jumped to $23 billion. The mode of financing of this FDI was mainly through foreign credit. Needless to say this also made Korea more vulnerable to adverse financial shocks.

The shock finally came in late 1996, when the Japanese yen began to fall in value. With the depreciation of the yen, Korean exporters found themselves suddenly losing competitiveness in their traditional export markets of North America and Europe. To make matters worse, the terms of trade also moved against Korea at this time. Table 4.3 shows quite clearly how inventories of exporters started to increase and were financed by costly short-term credit from the merchant banks. The government refused to come to the aid of chaebols that were heavily indebted. Corporate bankruptcies began to occur rapidly – soon there was a cascade of them. At the same time, the volume of non-performing loans at financial institutions also began to skyrocket. The twin burdens of non-performing loans and corporate bankruptcies precipitated a full-blown financial crisis.

Table 4.3 South Korea's capital account balance (US$ billion)

	1992	1993	1994	1995	1996	1997 First Half	1997 July to Nov.
Liabilities	8.8[1]	8.4	13.4	20.0	26.4	13.8	2.5
Loans and foreign investment	5.2	8.7	7.4	9.4	13.4	8.8	5.3
Public	−0.6	−1.8	−0.3	−0.5	−0.5	−0.2	−0.1
Commercial	−0.5	−1.1	−0.3	−0.2	−0.2	0.1	0.8
Direct investment	0.6	0.5	0.8	1.2	2.0	1.1	0.8
Portfolio investment	5.8	11.0	7.3	8.9	12.1	7.7	3.8
Trade credit	0.9	−0.4	2.2	3.6	6.6	2.1	−0.1
Others[2]	2.7	0.1	3.8	7.0	6.4	2.9	−2.6
Assets	0.5	1.5	4.4	6.6	9.4	3.1	0.3
Direct investment	1.0	1.1	2.1	3.1	3.9	1.8	0.4
Portfolio Investment	0	0.3	0.5	0.4	0.9	0.7	0.3
Export on credits	−1.7	−0.7	−0.1	0.9	0.6	0.1	0.5
Others	1.2	0.9	2.0	2.2	3.9	3.4	−0.9
Balance (liabilities − assets)	8.3	6.9	9.0	13.4	17.0	10.6	2.3

Notes: 1. A positive balance indicates capital inflow. A positive figure under liabilities or assets means an increase.

2. Others include the change of the liabilities of merchant bank corporations and development institutions, such as the Korea Development Bank, Korea Long-term Credit Bank, and Korea Export and Import Bank.

Source: Bank of Korea, *Balance of Payments*, various issues.

The crisis unfolds

The crisis unfolded with unexpected speed. The first major victim was the Hanbo group. A large producer that specialized in iron and steel, Hanbo was Korea's 14th largest chaebol. It was unable to meet the payments of the principal and interest on its borrowings. The intention was to restructure it through a workout programme organized by its credit banks. As it turned out, Hanbo was placed under court receivership because the workout programme failed. Thus began a series of corporate debacles in one of the most successful Asian economies.

The Hanbo collapse revealed that many loans to this group had been made under political pressure. The pervasiveness of corruption discovered in Korea was one of the major factors in foreign investors' loss of confidence in the government and the economy in general. Even in retrospect it seems amazing to hear the claim that informed participants did not know about these events. It is more likely that the market participants did know – the full extent of knowledge may, however, be debatable – but believed that the government would bail out the firms.

Most astonishing among the developments that followed, and the one that caused the government to lose a great deal of its credibility, was the near-bankruptcy of the Kia Group in July. At first, the Kia Group, the nation's eighth largest chaebol, was also to be covered by a workout programme, but this too proved unworkable.

By the first week of September, six chaebols, including Kia, had been placed either under a workout plan or become insolvent. These chaebols accounted for about 10.4 per cent of the total assets of the 30 largest chaebols. But the damage to credibility in asset markets was already done. By September foreign investors were ready to stampede out of Korean equities. By October foreign investors had moved out of the stock market in droves, and Korean banks were increasingly unable to roll over their short-term foreign loans. In order to avoid default, they were forced to turn to the Bank of Korea for liquidity or to resort to the foreign overnight loan markets. On 19 November, the government announced a reform package which included measures for disposal of non-performing loans and the widening of the exchange rate fluctuation band. This, however, did little to stop the panic. It was too little, too late.

At this stage, the Korean government finally announced to the public its decision to approach the IMF in order to ask for assistance. The negotiations between the Korean government and the IMF were completed in a record time of only ten days on 3 December. The IMF agreed to provide a total of $21 billion to be disbursed in 11 instalments over a three-year period from its emergency financing and other facilities. It also secured financial commitments totalling $36 billion from the World Bank, the Asian Development Bank, the United States, Japan, Germany, Canada, the United Kingdom, Australia, and other international organizations and countries, which would serve as a second line of defence. The IMF conditionalities required tight monetary policy, a fiscal surplus, sweeping financial reform, further liberalization of the financial markets, and also two conditionalities which were unusual for an IMF programme – greater flexibility in the labour market and restructuring of the chaebols. On closer examination one discovers that these really were standard measures, forced to fit an unprecedented situation. It is not surprising that the IMF measures did little to allay fears and stabilize the financial markets and the foreign exchange market. The won/dollar exchange rate continued to depreciate. Bankruptcies and business closures proceeded apace.

Rumours had begun to circulate among foreign investors that Korea might have to declare a debt moratorium. The IMF and the US Treasury must have both realized that stronger measures would be required to shore up confidence and boost the Korean economy. Finally, on Christmas Eve, the IMF and the G-7 countries came up with a $10 billion emergency financing programme. It appears that this emergency finance did succeed in turning market sentiment around by demonstrating the resolve of the IMF and G-7 to rescue Korea from financial collapse. In retrospect it is now clear that the IMF served as a lender of last resort in the East Asian financial crisis. This was especially true during the Korean crisis.

The predictable effects of the IMF programme were a sharp increase in domestic interest rates and a substantial depreciation of the won/dollar exchange rate. The monetary contraction dried up the availability of bank credit, especially to small and medium-sized firms. This led to further contraction in the real economy. A genuine debt-deflation type of economic crisis humbled one of the most successful Asian economies. Such an experience has led some observers to ask if the crisis could have been avoided. Let us look at both the macroeconomic and microeconomic evidence to see if this question can be answered adequately.

Growth and inflation

Table 4.4 compares the macroeconomic performance of the Korean economy for three periods: (i) the early 1980s, when Korea experienced its first large-scale currency crisis; (ii) the late 1980s, when it enjoyed strong growth; and (iii) the 1990s until the onset of the current crisis. It

Table 4.4 Macroeconomic indicators of Korea (%, US$ billion)

	1980–85	1986–91	1992	1993	1994	1995	1996
Real GDP growth	6.3	9.9	5.1	5.8	8.6	8.9	7.1
CPI inflation	10.9	6.1	6.3	4.8	6.2	4.5	4.9
Corporate bond yield	19.0	15.1	16.2	12.6	12.9	13.8	11.9
M2 growth rate	20.6	18.8	18.4	18.6	15.6	15.5	16.2
Fiscal balance/GDP	−2.5	−0.2	−0.7	0.3	0.5	0.4	0.3
Current account/GDP	−3.8	3.0	−1.5	0.1	−1.2	−2.0	−4.9
Foreign reserves	7.1	12.2	17.1	20.3	25.7	32.7	33.2

Sources: Bank of Korea, *MonthlyStatistics*, various issues; Ministry of Finance and Economics, *Financial and Monetary Statistics*, various issues.

appears that the Korean economy continued solid growth performance into the 1990s.

Although not as high as the average growth rate of the late 1980s, the growth rate still exceeded 8 per cent in both 1994 and 1995. The annual inflation rate measured by CPI stayed relatively low, between 4 and 6 per cent since 1992. Price stabilization and lower inflation expectation led to a gradual decline in nominal interest rates. The benchmark interest rate, the three-year corporate bonds yield, declined from 16.2 per cent in 1992 to 11.9 per cent in 1996. Thus the macroeconomic conditions were basically sound. It also appears that monetary and fiscal policies were conservative. The annual M2 growth rate, which used to be more than 18 per cent in the early 1990s, came down to around 15 per cent. The fiscal deficit was about 2.5 per cent of GDP in the early 1980s, but it turned into a surplus in 1993 and remained in surplus thereafter. Therefore, profligate fiscal and monetary policies are in all likelihood not the real culprits.

Only in the external sector can one discern some signs of trouble. The current account deficit kept growing from 1994, amounting to 2.0 per cent of GDP in 1995 and 4.9 per cent in 1996. Despite the current account deficits, a steady inflow of foreign capital boosted by the liberalization of the financial market kept the overall balance in surplus.

Current account, exchange rate and external liabilities

The fact that current account deficits have grown sharply since 1995 led many to believe that the Korean economy was already on an unsustainable path. This argument implies that the overvalued Korean won was at the root of her currency crisis. Certainly, it cannot be denied that increasing current account deficits could have been a background factor in undermining foreign investors' confidence. But, as can be seen in Table 4.5, the current account deficit and the degree of currency overvaluation were not large enough to provoke a crisis.

First, there was good reason to believe that the current account deficit in 1996 and 1997 was a temporary, cyclical phenomenon. The growing current account deficit was mainly due to the drastic fall in the international prices of Korea's major exports such as semiconductors, steel, and petrochemical products. The export price index and terms of trade fell by 13 per cent in 1996 alone.

Since the sharp drop in export prices was regarded as temporary, the current account was expected to improve soon. Saving and investment rates reinforced this interpretation of events. As mentioned earlier, between 1994 and 1996, Korea's saving rates increased but investment rates

Table 4.5 Terms of trade and real exchange rates

	1991	1992	1993	1994	1995	1996	1997
Export price index	94.2	93.2	93.6	95.2	100.0	86.6	75.0
Import price index	96.4	94.9	91.3	91.8	100.0	98.8	93.4
Terms of trade	97.7	98.2	102.5	103.7	100.0	87.7	80.3
Saving rate (%)	36.1	35.0	35.3	36.3	37.3	37.4	36.4
Investment rate (%)	38.9	36.2	35.1	37.5	38.0	38.8	33.3
Real exchange rate vis-à-vis the yen	90.9	91.6	100.0	104.3	94.7	87.9	92.6
Real exchange rate vis-à-vis the US dollar	98.4	100.5	100.0	95.0	91.3	98.3	101.3

Note: The terms of trade are calculated by dividing the export price index by the import price index and multiplying the result by 100. Saving rate is defined as 1 − {households and government consumption GDP} and investment rate as gross capital formation/GDP. Real exchange rates are calculated as the multiples of nominal exchange rate and the CPI of the foreign country divided by the CPI of Korea. It is normalized so that the real exchange rate in December 1993 is equal to 100. 1997 data are for the first half of 1997.
Source: Bank of Korea, *Monthly Statistics*, various issues.

increased even faster. As a result, the current account deficit worsened. Thirty years of high growth performance had led Korean policy makers to believe that investment is always a virtue and that current account deficits due to an investment boom would not be a serious problem.

Secondly, Korea's current account deficit was not large compared with other countries in the region – or compared to Mexico before the crisis. In Mexico and Thailand, current account deficits had reached more than 5 per cent of GDP for several years prior to their currency crises. On the other hand, Korea's current account deficit at its greatest amounted to 4.9 per cent of GDP in 1996 and by the second quarter of 1997 it had even started to decline. In sum, in any examination of the nature and the extent of the current account deficit in Korea, denouncing it as the main reason for the crisis does not seem to be convincing.

Whether the Korean won was significantly overvalued prior to the crisis is also a very controversial issue. The Korean won depreciated against the US dollar by 8.6 per cent in 1996 and 5.8 per cent during the first quarter of 1997. As can be seen in Table 4.4, thanks to this nominal depreciation, the real exchange rate vis-à-vis the dollar increased significantly in 1996, returning to the early 1990s level. The yen also depreciated against the dollar and the Japanese inflation rate was very low during this period. As a result, between 1993 and 1996, the Korean won actually appreciated against the yen by 12.1 per cent in real terms. By the end of the first quarter of 1997, the real exchange rate index returned to the 1993 level – when Korea's current account was largely in balance. This is in contrast with the cases of Thailand whose currencies were significantly overvalued prior to the beginning of the Asian crisis. However, the structure of external liabilities of Korea should have given pause even at this time.

After the out break of the crisis, the existence of excess foreign borrowing and the mismatch between short-term debt and foreign reserves in Korea came sharply into focus. The total external debt grew by 300 per cent from 1992 to 1997 and reached US$ 121 billion at the end of 1997. However, the growth of debt was seriously underestimated. The amount of debt was estimated following the World Bank definition and did not include offshore borrowing of domestic financial institutions, overseas borrowings of foreign branches and subsidiaries of domestic enterprises. This discrepancy between the actual liabilities and the announced figures rendered the foreign exchange market more speculative and volatile at the end of 1997. For transparency, the Korean government and the IMF agreed to use a new definition of total external liabilities, which added the offshore borrowing of Korean banks and their overseas branches and subsidiaries to the external debt as defined by the World Bank. Under this new definition, the actual external liabilities were shown to have been underestimated by almost $50 billion, amounting to $1,610 and $1,970 billion dollars at the end of 1996 and 1997, respectively. The difference would have been even larger had the borrowings of overseas branches and subsidiaries of domestic enterprises been included.

As has already been alluded to, it is not just the size of Korea's external debt that underwent dramatic changes at this time. There was also a notable change in the maturity structure of the external debt. The proportion of short-term debt to total external debt rose from 43 per cent to 58 per cent between 1994 and 1996. If we use the new definition of external liabilities, the proportion of short-term debt becomes 62.2 per cent in 1996. Clearly, this implies that most offshore borrowings of domestic banks were short term in nature. In fact, the proportion of short-term debt in offshore borrowings of domestic banks and their overseas branches and subsidiaries was 78.0 per cent as of December 1996 and 75.4 per cent as of September 1997.

If we consider the changes in debt-related indicators of currency crises it seems that most of them had been deteriorating since the mid-1990s. For example, Korea's debt to GNP ratio increased from 13 per cent to 22 per cent between 1990 and 1996. But it is still true that Korea's debt to GNP ratio was low compared with those of other countries that have recently been experiencing currency crises. In 1996 the debt to GNP ratios for Indonesia, Malaysia, the Philippines, and Thailand were 47, 39, 54 and 46 per cent respectively, and in 1994 that of Mexico stood at 35 per cent. However, if we compare other indicators such as the ratio of foreign reserves to short-term debt and the ratio of foreign debt to monthly import, Korea was in no better shape than the other crisis-hit countries. In hindsight, one may argue that these debt-related indicators strongly signalled the possibility of a currency crisis. However, at least until mid-1997, these indicators were not taken seriously by either foreign investors or domestic policy makers.

Table 4.6 gives a list of selected leading indicators of banking and currency crises compiled by Goldstein and Reinhart (1997). The list

Table 4.6 Selected leading indicators of banking and currency crises

Indicator	Transformation	Data frequency
Real output	12-month growth rate	Monthly
Equity prices	12-month growth rate	Monthly
International reserves	12-month growth rate	Monthly
Domestic/foreign real interest rate differential	Level	Monthly
Excess real M1 balances	Level	Monthly
M2/international reserves	12-month growth rate	Monthly
Bank deposits	12-month growth rate	Monthly
M2 multiplier	12-month growth rate	Monthly
Domestic credit/GDP	12-month growth rate	Monthly
Real interest rate on deposits	Level	Monthly
Lending interest rate/deposit interest rate	Level	Monthly
Real exchange rate	Deviations from trend	Monthly
Exports	12-month growth rate	Monthly
Imports	12-month growth rate	Monthly
Terms of trade	12-month growth rate	Monthly
Moody's sovereign credit ratings	1-month change	Monthly
Institutional investor sovereign credit ratings	Semi-annual change	Semi-annual
General government consumption/GDP	Annual growth rate	Annual
Real credit to the public sector/GDP	Level	Annual
Short term capital inflows/GDP	Annual growth rate	Annual
Foreign direct investment/GDP	Annual growth rate	Annual
Current account imbalance/GDP	Annual growth rate	Annual
Current account imbalance/ investment	Annual growth rate	Annual

Source: Goldstein and Reinhart (1997).

includes both real and financial indicators and covers both domestic and external sectors. Kaminsky and Reinhart (1996) and Goldstein and Reinhart (1997) have also arrived at a list of 'best and worst' performing indicators of currency and banking crises. Table 4.7 reproduces this list. From this, it would appear that some of the 'best' predictors – such as real exchange rate, exports, equity prices, real output, etc. were not 'alarming' in the case of Korea. Furthermore, even the debt-related indicators mentioned previously did not cause much consternation for several reasons.

First, the Korean government believed that the deterioration of these indicators was a temporary phenomenon. As explained earlier, the sharp increase in the external debt in 1996 was largely due to a huge current account deficit, which was believed to be caused by the temporary deterioration in export prices. In fact, the current account was showing signs of improvement in the second quarter of 1997. Furthermore, the debt to GNP ratio of the 1990s was not unprecedented.

Secondly, the shortening of the maturity structure could be interpreted as a sign of an enhancement in Korea's credit standing in the international financial markets. Considering the term structure of interest rates in the international financial markets where long-term rates are typically higher than short-term rates, it is natural for countries with a higher credit rating to rely more on short-term financing. As mentioned

Table 4.7   Currency and banking crises: best versus worst performing indicators

	Currency crises indicator	Banking crises indicator
BEST	Real exchange rate	Real exchange rate
	Banking crisis	Equity prices
	Exports	M2 multiplier
	Equity prices	Real output
	M2/international reserves	Real interest rate on deposits
	Real output	Exports
WORST	Terms of trade	International reserves
	Domestic/foreign real interest rate differential	Terms of trade
	Imports	Excess real M1 balances
	Bank deposits	Lending interest rate/deposit Interest rate
	Lending interest rate/deposit interest rate	Imports

Sources: Kaminsky and Reinhart (1996); Goldstein and Reinhart (1997).

earlier, government regulation also contributed to the shortening of maturity, since long-term borrowing was more heavily regulated than short-term borrowing. Short-term borrowing was loosely regulated because the government believed that most short-term debt would be trade credits that would automatically vanish with time.

Thirdly, the short-term borrowing of Korea consisted mainly of inter-bank loans. Since financial institutions usually maintain steady long-run relationships with one another, it was believed that these short-term debts could be rolled over without difficulty. This was in sharp contrast to the Indonesian case, where most of the short-term borrowing was arranged by individual enterprises rather than by banks. In addition, as we have seen, Korea's external debt was mostly private debt without explicit government guarantee. Therefore, its increase was not expected to affect sovereign risk directly. In Mexico, by contrast, a sharp increase of Tesobonos, the dollar-denominated government debt, was the main reason for the downfall of its country credit rating. However, in retrospect we know that the private nature of debt in Korea failed to make any different at the end.

Microeconomics: the financial market's expectation of the crisis

During the first half of 1997, the forward exchange rates in the won–dollar market closely followed the spot exchange rate. However, from July 1997 the non-deliverable forward exchange rate began rising faster than the spot rate, indicating that the market was anticipating a depreciation of the won. On the other hand, the domestic forward exchange rate continued to move in line with the spot rate. This might have been due in part to the thinness and inefficiency of the domestic market, but was mostly attributable to active forward intervention by the Bank of Korea.

Both forward premiums began rising after July 1997, when the crisis erupted in Thailand. However, the one-month premium never exceeded 20 won per dollar, nor did the three-month premium exceed 50 won per dollar. Therefore, what investors anticipated was not a currency crisis but a smooth depreciation of the won. Only in late October did the international capital market begin to anticipate the upcoming crisis in Korea – at this point the forward premium took a big jump. The bankruptcies of several big corporations and the outbreak of the Southeast Asian crisis contributed to this increasing trend. As the Asian crisis gathered momentum short-term loans were being called in and marginal calculus could no longer predict what would happen. In terms of the complex dynamics of the system, a point of bifurcation has been reached. From here on there would be a headlong plunge into crisis. Thus the question of whether the crisis could have been avoided really became irrelevant. The really important issue is what made such a *steep* descent inevitable.

What is particularly tragic about the Korean situation is that the economy was on the verge of a technological take-off. Earlier studies (Khan 1998, 1999a) have shown that South Korea and Taiwan were the two Asian tigers which could perhaps have moved into the phase of creating a positive feedback loop innovation system (POLIS). This could have refuted the Krugman–Lau–Young claims that their growth was largely due to factor accumulation rather than productivity growth through innovation and technical change. However, earlier studies (Khan, 1998, 1999a, 1999b) found evidence of an emerging POLIS that was quite fragile in South Korea in particular. After the tremendous beating that the economy has taken it is doubtful that innovators such as Samsung will be able to regain their prominent position in the race to innovate. Clearly, the chaebols were affected adversely. However, what is also true is that, on the whole, the workers lost a great deal more than the capitalists in this crisis. The Korean crisis had adverse distributional consequences as well, as the history of the 'social pact' after the crisis shows.

On 15 January 1998, the Tripartite Committee of representatives of business, labour, and government was established to find ways to increase the South Korean labour market's 'flexibility'. The committee formulated a 'Social Pact' supposedly aiming to share the costs of overcoming the ongoing crisis in an equitable manner. Initially, the committee had 16 members: five representatives of labour unions, five representatives from corporations (management), and six representatives of the government (two from government, and four from the political parties). The major objectives of the committee were: (i) to ensure the sharing of the burden of restructuring the Korean economy; (ii) to guarantee compliance with the economic reform programme prescribed by the IMF; and (iii) to restore foreign investors' confidence in Korea.

On 20 January 1998, the Tripartite Committee reached a compromise agreement on a burden-sharing plan. It issued a five-point agreement:

1. The government should investigate the causes of the economic crisis and, by the end of January 1998, it should draw up effective measures to protect the jobless, restore price stability, and ensure job security.
2. Business firms should carry out sweeping restructuring, but they should make every effort to minimize layoffs. They should also make their business operations transparent.

3. Labour unions should actively cooperative with management in adjusting wages and in setting work schedules.
4. Management and labour should cooperate with one another to prevent disputes from erupting into major conflicts or strikes.
5. The Tripartite Committee should complete the formulation of the agenda in time for the February special session of the National Assembly.

The Tripartite Committee announced the 'Social Pact' and its concrete action plans at the end of January. It is doubtful whether in the end the burden-sharing was really all that equitable. In spite of the so-called 'social pact', layoffs and unemployment became widespread. President Kim Dae-Jung acted in good faith to effect a genuine corporate restructuring; but the limits of what could be done became evident even before the end of 1998. The contraction of the Korean economy and its subsequent restructuring extracted a heavy price from the Korean workers, while the big corporations suffered minimal disruption. Even a determined president with popular backing could not undo the unholy alliance between powerful bureaucrats and big business.

Therefore, in terms of the distributional consequences of the crisis it is ironic that distributional conflicts were fundamentally solved in favour of Korean capital by a populist government led by Kim Dae-Jung. Kim's election was made possible by the popular dissatisfaction with the economic management of the previous regime, among other things. His election had held out hope for the realization of a genuinely progressive political and social agenda. Unfortunately, the economic crisis preoccupied the aged leader and his advisors. Unemployment rose, poverty increased and incomes and social status became more polarized. This is by now a sad and familiar litany. What remains to be done is to ask seriously why all this had to happen. We must ask further if there are general lessons to be drawn from these debacles. And last but not least, we must understand the role of global capital in these crises. Out of this understanding may emerge the vision for a new and more humane world economic order. This is the task of the remaining chapters.

5
Finance in a Complex Capitalist Economy: Failures of Global Markets and Developmental States

> Asia is a state of disordered mind full of paradoxes.
>
> Unknown Asian writer

1 The Asian financial crisis and the Asian model of development

In this chapter the key question raised is: how can we conceptualize finance in a complex capitalist economy in the aftermath of the Asian financial and economic crises? I start the discussion of this and related issues by posing a simpler empirical question: have the Asian financial and economic crises proved that the Asian model of development (AMD) was wrong? The implications of answers to this question are far-reaching. In the end, the theoretical issues raised by the problem of finance in a complex capitalist economy and the political economy of developmental states will both be implicated in what is an apparently empirical investigation.

Clearly, the Asian financial crisis imposed a huge economic cost on the high growth Asian economies. In terms of both economic growth and income distribution, the crisis has extracted a heavy toll. But how are these economic and welfare costs to be interpreted? Before we judge them to have invalidated the AMD, we must ask: Did the crisis stem primarily from basic domestic institutional weaknesses which can be attributed to the generic character of the AMD? If the answer to this question is yes, then the AMD can be held culpable. On the other hand, if the fundamental causes of the crisis are to be located outside of the AMD then a different type of analysis is called for. It has even been suggested that the reason for the crisis may have to do with the abandonment of the AMD by countries such as South Korea.

In this chapter I will argue that, on balance, the care for the abandonment of the AMD thesis has more empirical support. Yet, this conclusion will only raise a further, vexing question: Does the AMD need to be

76

abandoned at a certain stage of development by those very countries that have followed it hitherto as a relatively successful development strategy? And, if so, what is the optimal transition strategy out of the AMD? What kind of non-AMD-type institutional setting is necessary in the short and intermediate terms? From our analysis it will emerge that these questions have both empirical and theoretical dimensions. A more precise formulation of these questions can lead to an attempt to formulate a prologomenon to a theory of integration of an AMD-type economy into the global economy. Such a preface to a theory of a transition towards economic integration will be presented later. To anticipate a little, a part of the preliminary aspects of the theory, as developed in the course of the next few chapters, tackles the problem of globally increasing risk when capital accounts are liberalized with no regard to the weaknesses of the domestic financial system. It will also need to address the theoretical relevance and the practical problems of creating a new global financial architecture. But first we need a more precise formulation of the AMD than has been offered here to date.

Prior to the Asian financial crisis there were several contending interpretations of the East Asian development experience. At the risk of ignoring some specific nuances of particular writers on the subject, these various interpretations can nevertheless be divided into two broad categories. In order to clearly distinguish between the two versions in the subsequent discussion and for ease of reference I will call the first version the AMD–market version, or AMDM for short. The second interpretation will be called the AMD–structural, or AMDS in the abbreviated form. The reasons for these designations will become clear in the following paragraphs.

The first interpretation is connected most prominently with a World Bank study (1993). In particular, this study emphasizes the market-friendly aspects of the East Asian economic system. Such an interpretation stresses that AMD embodies only reluctant interventions that are subject to checks and balances and are transparent. On the whole, AMDM claims that the key factors behind the success of AMD are getting prices right and adopting an export-oriented trading regime. According to this analysis, openness, free trade and competition are the fundamental aspects of this model.

The World Bank's East Asian Miracle study of 1993 acknowledged a number of policy interventions. These included targeted and subsidized credit to selected industries, low deposit rates and upper limits on borrowing rates. All of these policy measures helped to increase and sustain profits and retained earnings. The report even acknowledged that domestic import industries were protected; that government banks were established and played a key credit and capital allocation role; that these banks were supported through active policy intervention; that public investment supported applied research; that there were firm- and industry-specific export targets; that export marketing boards and other supporting institutions were developed; and that there was widespread sharing of information between the private and public sectors. In short, various sorts of industrial and other policies promoted and even protected certain key industries while some others were ignored.

At the same time the Bank study concluded that those interventions were not in fact necessary. Nor were they sufficient for promoting growth. While the sufficiency part of the claim may be accepted for the sake of argument, and is possibly true, the necessity part will be insisted upon by the second school of thought on the interpretation of AMD. I now turn to this.

There are a number of economists who stress the important role played by the state in East Asian development. Beginning with Japan after the Meiji restoration, there seems to be a historical trajectory that is telescoped even more rapidly after the Second World War by the Asian tigers. In particular, in spite of differences in detail, South Korea, Taiwan and Singapore were all heavily state-guided economies. In the AMD-structural interpretation, the state is viewed as an active agent of development. Even in Hong Kong, where orientation towards the free market is most prominent, the role of state-subsidized housing etc. have been emphasized in a Ricardian context by researchers such as Peter Ho.

Of course, it should be clearly stated at this point that both AMDM and AMDS are 'ideal types'. However, for the sake of bringing out the important differences for theory and policy, it may be useful to present the major aspects of the second interpretation quickly below.

First is the close relationship between the government and business. According to many observers (Johnson, 1982; Amsden, 1989; Chang, 1994; Wade, 1998a,b; Stiglitz, 1994; Khan, 1983, 1997, 1998) the close consultation between government and business and the guidance of business by the government has been a key ingredient of high growth performance. In explaining Japanese high speed growth Murakami and others have pointed to *Gyosei Shido* (administrative guidance) as a major institutional feature. After the 1997 crisis, of course, many critics have characterized such government-business relations as crony capitalism.

Secondly, and following on from the above, is the system of informal – and quite often unwritten – guidance to business. Lacking formal legislation, such procedures do not seem to have the form of the universal 'rule of law' that is usually associated with developed capitalism in the West.

Thirdly, both the capital and the labour markets seem to be largely 'internal'. In the capital market the domestic banking system finances businesses in a long-term, relational setting. This can be contrasted with the mainly arm's-length dealings with formal procedures in the Anglo-American system. Hostile takeovers as corporate governance mechanisms are also not encouraged. This last point is important in that it leads to the problem of comparing and evaluating the performances of different types of corporate governance systems. I will have more to say on this in Chapter 6.

In the labour markets, a dual labour market situation can be observed. For small firms a relatively more classical type of flexible labour market is the norm. Such markets can be modelled with classical labour demand and supply schedules. The other type of labour market is 'internal', the so-called lifetime employment model. In either case, wages and salaries rose as the economies developed and productivity increased.[1]

In the areas of international trade and financial relations the East Asian economies practiced a form of integration that may be called 'strategic'. The strategy was to open trade along with selective industrial policies while emphasizing the role of competition. Capital account liberalization was not openly advocated until the 1980s and 1990s.

2 The failure of the Asian model, the global markets and the developmental states

Our review of the role of the fundamentals, the capital supply shocks, various structural and institutional factors and the history of financial liberalization in the three economies discussed so far shows that even an initially successful developmental state such as South Korea could not contain the crisis of the late 1990s. What we have here, judging by the evidence submitted, is a situation of triple failures. Although the word 'failure' sounds harsh and dramatic the word is appropriate in underlining the historical contingencies of both the Asian model and the globalization moves of the 1990s. Therefore I will use the word in this historically contingent sense while underlining the fact that the Asian model was also a real success in many ways. However, here I want to focus on the triple 'failure' in this carefully hedged and historically contingent sense.

First, the Asian model itself, which was a product of historically contingent factors during the Cold War period, failed. Second, the global capital markets also failed – for reasons of moral hazard, adverse selection and herd behaviour. Markets failed to assess risks properly and to function smoothly for a number of reasons discussed in specific cases. Finally, the Asian financial crisis brought to the fore the failures of developmental states such as Thailand and Indonesia. In this sense, proper governance does seem to matter. But so do the other two previously-cited factors. In the larger picture, these developmental states can be fairly described as not just weak or strong – qualifiers that are time-specific even for a particular state, and usually misleading – but as inconsistent. They have been inconsistent with regards to the monitoring of financial markets, to follow a sequence of liberalization where prudential and other necessary regulatory structures are developed first, and to understand the risk of volatility and short-termism in the capital markets in the age of 'globalization'.

If the above characterization is correct then discussion should focus on both the weakness of domestic institutions and the fragilities of global markets. In other words, both developmental states and global markets must be reassessed. Each of these tasks would require a multi-volume study. In the rest of this book, I will discuss two particular aspects of the economic and political economic problems identified here. In Chapter 7, I discuss the role of banks and consider whether they can manage default risks better in the future. This discussion is motivated by the problems of corporate governance of banks in Asia and what can be done to resolve them in the near future; but the problem of monitoring is also a general issue. In Chapter 6, I discuss the more general issues related to the role of corporate governance in both the financial and the nonfinancial sectors. In particular, I raise the question of how to look at the governance problems of family-based businesses in Asia. Here, the main theoretical conclusion is to show the limits of the principal–agent framework, and to suggest a 'realist' approach to corporate governance that emphasizes the role of the fiduciary responsibilities of firms. In Chapter 8, I take up the issues related to global market failures that lead us directly to the question of 'governance' of global markets. My analysis shows that a more modest goal of managing international monetary and financial relations is, perhaps, the only realistic option. Yet even this poses enormous theoretical challenges and practical difficulties. I follow an evolutionary approach in general, and offer what I call an *'extended panda's thumb'* argument to advance the case for a hybrid global financial architecture that would combine a reformed IMF with regional financial architectures.

The key lesson to draw from the Asian financial crisis and the demise of the Asian model is that complex capitalist economies are hard to manage – for both governments and firms. The first of these propositions has been recognized for a long time. The second may come as a surprise, especially to the proponents of the first. But in complex economies with multiple equilibria reflecting problems of information, incentives, and imperfections of other sorts that lead to various nonlinearities and nonconvexities we can expect both governments and markets to fail – sometimes on a massive scale. A partial resolution of the many complex problems involved here is the best we can hope for at the moment. The next few chapters will attempt to do so. For the moment I want to contrast, from an evolutionary perspective, the sudden liberalization of capital markets in the crisis economies with the relatively gradual liberalization pursued in Taiwan. Taiwan operated in a much more competitive, free market mode in goods markets than South Korea; but whereas South Korea took the plunge into capital account liberalization in the 1990s, Taiwan has been following a gradual evolutionary path towards full convertibility at its own pace with a flexible exchange rate. A historical account of the evolution of Taiwan's financial system can therefore be expected to throw some light on the problems of financial market regulation in a developing economy as it grows into an institutionally complex real and financial economic environment.

3   A path-dependent account of Taiwan's development into a complex economy: a short financial economic history through the 1980s and early 1990s

Figure 5.1 gives a snapshot of the financial system in Taiwan during its evolution up to the early 1990s. The Ministry of Finance (MOF) and the Central Bank (CB) are the two major government institutions responsible for maintaining orderly markets. Within the general financial system there is a preferential subsystem that, among other things, finances some aspects of constructing a modern technological infrastructure.[2] Thus, in contrast to the relative laissez-faire industrial institutions, the financial system relies more on controls and directives.

The existence of a dual financial system has a historical background. The formal financial system has always been subject to strict control, and, with the exception of a few private banks established by overseas Chinese or those that were transformed for specific political reasons, banks were regulated directly by being government-owned. Bank

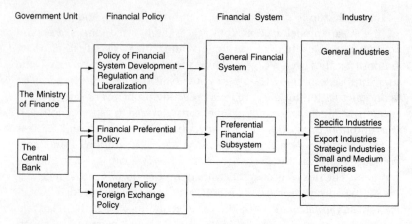

Figure 5.1   Systemic view of the political economy of Taiwan's financial structure

interest rates were controlled by the Central Bank and official interest rates usually adjusted more slowly than the market-determined rate through demand and supply. These regulations were maintained for decades until 1989, when a new Banking Law was promulgated and bank privatization and interest rate liberalization were adopted. The long-regulated banking system could not meet the rising market demand for funds. One problem is that government banks tend to operate conservatively. Those firms which can afford to present collateral more easily have an edge in receiving bank loans. Usually big firms have more easy access to credit compared to small and medium-sized businesses, which have difficulty obtaining funds from government commercial banks. Those businesses have to pursue underground capital, and an informal financial market has grown accordingly. As a result, formal and informal financial markets coexist. This is a central characteristic of Taiwan's financial markets.

The formal financial system is composed of two subsystems: (i) financial institutions and (ii) financial markets (Figure 5.2). Financial institutions include two groups – namely, the monetary institutions which create credit money, and other financial institutions, which cannot do so because of legal restrictions.

The first group of financial institutions includes the Central Bank of China (CBC), commercial banks (domestic banks and local branches of foreign banks), specialized banks, and cooperatives (credit cooperative associations, credit departments of fishermen's associations). Specialized banks include the Export–Import Bank of China (dealing with

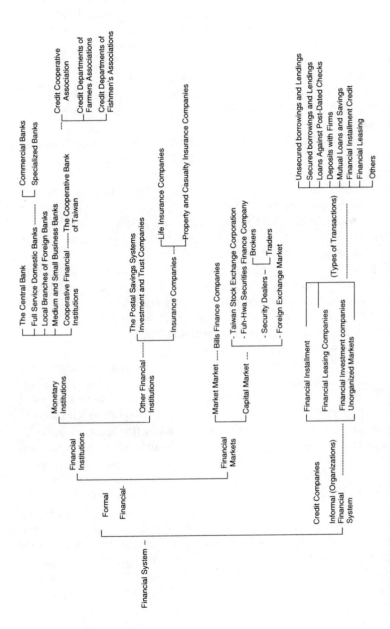

Figure 5.2 The financial system in Taiwan

trade financing activities), the Farmers Bank of China (farm financing activities), Land Bank of Finance (real estate financing activities), the Cooperative Bank of Taiwan (cooperative-related financing activities), and the Central Trust of China (dealing with government-purchase-related financing activities).

Other financial institutions cannot create money, but they are permitted to mobilize idle money in order to finance investments. These include the postal savings system, investment and trust companies, and insurance companies.

Financial markets include the money market and the capital market. Broadly speaking, the foreign exchange market can also be included. The money market is the short-run fund market. Financial instruments in the money market include treasury bills, commercial paper, bankers' acceptances and negotiable certificates of deposits. These instruments are usually exchanged in the three local bills finance companies. The central bank often enters this market to execute open-market operations for the purpose of controlling the money supply.

The capital market is a place for long-term bill transactions. Financial instruments in the capital market include stocks, government bonds, corporate bonds and bank debentures. The stock market grew dramatically in the 1980s. The Taiwan Stock Exchange Corporation is the exchange centre, and Fuh-Hwa Securities Finance Companies deal with finance demand for funds and securities.

The operation of foreign exchange activities is executed by the central bank and authorized foreign exchange banks. The authorized banks are where foreign exchange transactions take place – this section includes some major domestic banks plus the local branches of foreign banks.

The informal financial markets include all of the financial activities which are not approved by the Ministry of Finance. Financial instalment credit companies, financial leasing companies and financial investment companies are registered companies under the Ministry of Economic Affairs. However, they conduct their activities as financial institutions. Any financial intermediation activities performed by a business not approved by the Ministry of Finance are illegal. Therefore, these companies are classified as informal financial markets. There are many kinds of transactions in this market. Unsecured borrowings and lendings, secured borrowings and lendings, and loans against post-dated checks are popular informal financial activities. 'Deposits-with-firms' means that some businesses collect funds from their employees, or even from the general public. 'Mutual-loans-and-savings' is commonly used as a way to pool savings of relatives and friends.

Given the above structure of the financial system, there are four kinds of financial sources for the business sector: financial institutions, the money market, the capital market, and the curb market. Table 5.1 shows the shares of these financial sources from 1964 to 1991. The money market did not appear until 1976. Table 5.1 shows that financial institutions are the most important financial source – on average, from 1976 to

Table 5.1 Evolution of Taiwan's financial sector: the financial sources for the business sector during the development into a complex economy, 1964–1991 (Unit: NT$ Million, %)

End of year	Financial institution		Money market		Capital market		Curb market		Total
	Amount	%	Amount	%	Amount	%	Amount	%	
1964	13, 708	47.81			7,410	25.84	7,555	26.35	28,673
1965	16,940	48.33			9,190	26.22	8,922	25.45	35,052
1966	20,889	50.40			8,180	19.74	12,377	29.86	41,446
1967	30,250	61.24			5,930	12.01	13,213	26.75	49,393
1968	37,021	61.12			7,450	12.30	16,102	26.58	60,573
1969	40,267	60.18			8,150	12.18	18,490	27.64	66,907
1970	48,886	61.04			8,930	11.15	22,267	27.80	80,083
1971	75,837	62.98			9,100	7.56	35,468	29.46	120,405
1972	95,138	67.20			10,590	7.48	35,842	25.32	141,570
1973	127,716	65.30			16,843	8.61	51,034	26.09	195,593
1974	175,311	67.83			24,964	9.66	58,188	22.51	258,463
1975	217,673	66.64			32,797	10.04	76,191	23.32	326,661
1976	252,236	64.48	2,207	0.56	48,714	12.45	88,050	22.51	391,207
1977	277,295	59.34	9,949	2.13	63,085	13.50	116,976	25.03	467,305
1978	342,513	57.40	17,373	2.91	81,166	13.60	155,707	26.09	596,759
1979	428,490	55.90	46,687	6.09	104,789	13.67	186,596	24.34	766,562
1980	573,574	53.51	65,464	6.11	131,867	12.30	301,978	28.09	1,071,983
1981	637,622	53.67	109,769	9.24	158,080	13.31	282,576	23.78	1,188,046
1982	755,500	54.47	133,288	9.61	186,622	13.45	311,601	22.47	1,387,011
1983	821,159	54.14	159,425	10.51	201,999	13.32	334,103	22.03	1,516,686
1984	852,272	51.60	195,908	11.86	232,801	14.09	370,819	22.45	1,651,800
1985	866,343	47.81	195,423	10.79	252,536	13.94	497,613	27.46	1,811,915
1986	989,694	47.88	154,510	7.47	287,471	13.91	635,558	30.74	2,067,233
1987	1,185,375	50.60	138,066	5.89	338,976	14.47	680,352	29.04	2,342,769
1988	1,458,643	55.89	129,308	4.95	395,663	15.16	626,114	23.99	2,609,728
1989	1,822,109	57.81	191,768	6.08	466,729	14.81	671,103	21.29	3,151,709
1990	2,103,235	56.89	347,112	9.39	558,025	15.09	688,663	18.63	3,697,035
1991	2,475,989	58.07	344,554	8.08	680,825	15.97	762,497	17.88	4,263,865
Ave. of 1976–1991	990,128	54.97	140,051	6.98	261,834	13.94	419,338	24.11	1,811,351

1991 they contributed 54.9 per cent of the total financial sources for businesses. The curb market is the second biggest financial source for firms, contributing 24.11 per cent of total financial sources. The capital market provides only 13.94 per cent of financial sources for firms. The money market has provided only 6.98 per cent on average since it was established. In other words, the level of direct finance is rather small and the market has not been popular. The indirect finance market is comparatively larger, and has provided most of the funds.

Table 5.2 shows the level of assets of various financial institutions. Taking 1993 as an example, in terms of assets, the central bank processed about 15 per cent of total financial resources, while depository institutions account for 67.99 per cent. Among depository institutions, domestic banks have the largest share – 44.07 per cent. Other financial institutions have smaller market shares. The market shares of assets for other financial institutions in 1993 can be ranked in descending order as follows: the postal savings system, life insurance companies, investment and trust companies, property and casualty insurance companies, securities finance companies, and the smallest, bill finance companies. The postal savings system grew rapidly after the 1970s because of the convenience provided by its widespread units.

The number of units for each type of financial institution can be observed from Table 5.3. In 1991, there are 17 domestic banks, running a total of 773 branches. Each domestic bank is allowed to open a maximum of three branches every year. A new bank can open only five branches when established. Foreign banks were allowed to open only one branch until 1987. Credit cooperatives and credit departments of farmers' and fishermen's associations have more units and more branches, but most of these are small, so that their market share of assets is comparatively low. What deserves mention at this point is that the number of branches in the postal savings system has been the largest. However, the number of domestic banks has risen sharply to 34 banks, since the introduction of banking privatization under the 1989 Banking Law.

The market share of loans and deposits can be seen in Table 5.4. In 1991, domestic banks accounted for 44.45 per cent of total deposits, and 63.45 per cent of total loans. Obviously, domestic banks have constituted the major portion of Taiwan's financial system. If we include local branches of foreign banks and medium-sized business banks in this classification, then the market share for banks increases. Other financial institutions, although they provide different services and have grown quickly in terms of number of branches, have less than 10 per cent of the market share.

Table 5.2 Evolution during the 1980s and early 1990s: total assets of financial institutions in Taiwan (units: NT @ million, %)

Items (End of Year) Institutions	Total assets			
	1981	1986	1991	1993
Central Bank	523,199 (21.67)	1,749,414 (27.73)	2,253,616 (18.46)	2,651,884 (14.87)
Depository institutions				
1. Domestic banks	1,138,614 (47.17)	2,596,284 (41.16)	5,830,846 (42.66)	7,828,474 (44.07)
2. Local branches of foreign banks	120,253 (4.98)	142,449 (2.26)	293,098 (2.14)	370,117 (2.08)
3. Medium business banks	78,610 (3.26)	250,337 (3.97)	847,609 (6.20)	1,196,629 (6.74)
4. Credit cooperatives	136,619 (5.65)	336,470 (5.33)	1,030,168 (7.54)	1,556,681 (8.76)
5. Credit department of farmers' and fishermen's Associations	105,926 (4.39)	328,598 (5.21)	775,889 (5.68)	1,124,925 (6.33)
Subtotal	1,580,022 (65.46)	3,654,138 (57.93)	8,777,610 (64.22)	12,076,826 (67.99)
Other financial institutions				
1. Investment and trust companies	81,513 (3.38)	118,838 (1.88)	523,640 (3.83)	443,557 (2.50)
2. Postal savings systems	182,812 (7.57)	738,173 (11.70)	1,274,640 (9.33)	1,714,125 (9.65)
3. Life insurance companies	29,765 (1.23)	18,904 (0.30)	448,638 (3.28)	699,479 (3.94)
4. Property and casualty insurance companies	9,221 (0.38)	16,710 (0.26)	36,643 (0.27)	56,029 (0.32)
5. Bills finance companies	5,110 (0.21)	7,511 (0.12)	34,702 (0.25)	44,008 (0.25)
6. Securities finance companies	2,350 (0.10)	4,577 (0.07)	48,843 (0.36)	86,070 (0.48)
Subtotal	310,771 (12.87)	904,713 (14.34)	2,367,106 (17.32)	3,043,268 (17.13)
Total	2,413,992 (100.0)	6,308,265 (100.0)	13,668,332 (100.0)	17,761,978 (100.0)

Source: The Central Bank of China, *Financial Statistics Monthly*, various issues.

The foreign exchange market is the place where the foreign reserve exchanges take place. The central bank and the foreign-exchange-authorized banks exchange foreign reserves mutually. Foreign-exchange-authorized banks include domestic banks and local branches

Table 5.3 Evolution of finance – 1980s and early 1990s: number of units of financial institutions in Taiwan

Year Institutions	1961 December		1971 December		1981 December		1991 December		1993 October	
	Firms	Branches	Firms	Branches	Firms	Branches	Firms	Branches	Firms	Branches
Total	409	1,369	431	1,897	441	3,060	495	4,196	526	4,388
Domestic banks	10	260	14	417	15	580	17	773	34	1,145
Local branches of foreign banks	1	1	6	6	24	24	36	47	37	32
Credit cooperatives	80	153	78	228	74	286	74	499	74	522
Credit departments of farmers' and fishermen's associations	291	385	294	394	284	784	311	1,096	312	851
Medium business banks	8	84	8	118	8	195	8	298	8	402
Investment and trust companies	1	1	6	6	8	31	8	70	6	49
Insurance companies	17	34	24	80	23	167	36	181	50	156
Postal savings system	1	451	1	648	1	1,023	1	1,121	1	1,258
Bills finance companies	—	—	—	—	3	5	3	20	3	22
Securities finance companies	—	—	—	—	1	1	1	1	1	2

Source: MOF, *Yearbook of Financial Statistics of the Republic of China*, 1986.
Notes: 1. Data do not include the Central Bank of China, and Central Deposit Insurance Corporation.
2. The number of branches includes head offices.

Table 5.4 Outstanding deposits and loans of financial institutions in Taiwan, 1961–1993 (NT$ million, percentage)

Items (End of Year)	Deposits				
Institutions	1961	1971	1981	1991	1993
Domestic banks	14,120	76,288	633,456	3,725,216	5,122,308
	(75.57)	(65.21)	(53.48)	(42.90)	(44.79)
Local branches of	6	157	5,104	75,736	122,456
Foreign banks	(0.03)	(0.13)	(0.43)	(0.87)	(1.07)
Medium business	915	5,858	56,713	679,028	971,010
banks	(4.90)	(5.01)	(4.97)	(7.82)	(8.49)
Credit	1,892	12,983	126,301	988,339	1,493,538
cooperatives	(10.13)	(11.10)	(10.66)	(11.38)	(13.06)
Credit department	1,105	6,557	89,964	726,331	1,058,591
of farmers' and fishermen's association	(5.91)	(5.60)	(7.60)	(8.36)	(9.26)
Postal savings	632	11,812	165,751	1,242,914	1,607,323
systems	(3.38)	(10.10)	(13.99)	(14.31)	(14.05)
Investment and	—	1,167	78,398	494,780	376,609
trust companies		(1.00)	(6.62)	(5.70)	(3.29)
Life insurance	15	2,167	28,838	451,983	685,669
Companies	(0.08)	(1.85)	(2.43)	(8.66)	(5.99)
Total	18,685	116,989	1,184,525	8,684,327	11,437,504
	(100.0)	(100.0)	(100.0)	(100.0)	(100.0)

(End of Year)	Loans				
Institutions	1961	1971	1981	1991	1993
Domestic banks	14,358	92,289	885,035	4,742,106	6,722,477
	(82.15)	(75.54)	(66.94)	(63.45)	(62.83)
Local branches of	70	4,743	107,753	235,704	279,349
foreign banks	(0.40)	(3.88)	(8.15)	(3.15)	(2.61)
Medium business	659	5,506	68,750	727,231	1,044,710
banks	(3.77)	(4.51)	(5.20)	(9.73)	(9.76)
Credit cooperatives	1,235	8,719	88,028	582,911	926,602
	(7.07)	(7.14)	(6.66)	(7.80)	(8.66)
Credit department	817	4,972	66,464	395,002	702,295
of farmers' and fishermen's associations	(4.67)	(4.07)	(5.03)	(5.29)	(6.56)
Postal savings systems	56	479	1,873	24,918	104,701
	(0.32)	(0.39)	(0.14)	(0.33)	(0.98)
Investment and	277	3,746	78,210	448,780	407,154
trust companies	(1.59)	(3.06)	(5.91)	(6.00)	(3.81)
Life insurance	5	1,721	26,085	317,360	512,249
companies	(0.03)	(1.41)	(1.97)	(4.25)	(4.79)

Total	17,478	122,184	1,322,198	7,474,012	10,699,537
	(100.0)	(100.0)	(100.0)	(100.0)	(100.0)

Source: Central Bank of China, *Financial Statistics Monthly, Taiwan District, the Republic of China*.
Note: Outstanding loans includes loans, investments and holdings of real estates.
Deposits = Deposits held by enterprises and individuals + government deposits.

of foreign banks. In 1992, there were 55 authorized foreign exchange banks, composed of 17 domestic banks (247 branches) and 38 foreign banks (48 branches).

Policies for financial system development

Since the Second World War, Taiwan's financing system has been strictly controlled. Although financial liberalization has been on the agenda for some time, the speed of reforms did not accelerate until the 1980s.

The major component of the financial system is the banking system. Therefore, when we discuss the development of the financial system, we always take the development of the banking system to be representative. The regulations on the establishment of new banks, regulations on foreign banks, and the activities of bank operations have been historically significant. These restrictions have been gradually eased, but they have not been completely removed.

1   Interest rate regulation and deregulation

The purpose of the regulation of interest rates in the early stages of economic development is to provide low-cost capital to entrepreneurs. After the economy has grown to some extent, interest rate liberalization is pursued largely with the aim of improving efficiency of the financial markets.

The government in Taiwan has controlled bank interest rates for a long time. Only in recent years have they been decontrolled. Prior to 1975, the government-prescribed interest rates for loans and deposits were set at uniform rates. In 1975, the government required that uniform interest rates for deposits would be prescribed by the Central Bank of China, and that the ceiling and floor interest rates for bank loans would be fixed by the Interest Rate Recommendation Committee of the Banks Association and would be subject to the approval of the central bank. The financial institutions can be further classified into several subsystems according to their functions and activities. Besides the commercial financing system, there is the trade financing system, the small and medium-sized business financing system, and the strategic industries financing system, among others. These subsystems can be termed the financial preferential system. This is because they can engage in preferential financing for specific industries.

Subsequently, several adjustments were made which have gradually enlarged the range between the ceiling and floor interest rates for bank loans. The interest rates for banks debentures and negotiable call loans were allowed to fluctuate freely in 1980. In 1985, the ceiling limit for interest on loans was abolished, with only the floor limit being retained.

With the introduction of the new Banking Law on 19 July 1989, both the ceiling and floor limits for interest rates on deposits and loans were abolished, and the process of interest rate liberalization was finally completed. The interest rate recommendation committee was dissolved at the same time. Before private commercial banks started operations, although interest rates could technically be decided by each bank, market interest rates remained relatively stable over a period of time. The costs of capital for the three major commercial banks were similar so that their interest rate structures were also broadly in line. After interest rate liberalization, they acted as the price leader for a while in a Stackelberg fashion. The interest rates of the three major banks were identical most of the time. In effect, they collusively monopolized the market. However, when the new private banks began to prepare for establishment in late 1991, the variances of the prime rate of different banks widened, from 0.24 per cent before August 1991 to more than 0.45 per cent after September 1991. This trend continued through the rest of the 1990s.

2 Deregulation of private banks

In order to completely secure the stability of financial markets and control the flow of funds, the government still favours government-owned financial institutions over private banks. However, the efficiency of government banks is considered to be much lower than that of private banks. Yang's (1993) study on their relative efficiency supports the above assertion. However, private banks have also been known to engage in risky lending.

Banking privatization is one of the most important financial reforms in Taiwan's financial history. The deregulation of private banks was allowed by the Banking Law of 1989. In June 1991, 15 new banks were authorized. By April 1993, 17 banks were established and operating, creating better service attitudes and more competition across the whole of the banking industry. However, Taiwanese authorities have become convinced of the need for prudential and other regulatory structures for private banks in the aftermath of the Asian financial crisis.

3 Control and deregulation of ownership of banks

Owning the banks allows the government, but also councilmen, to determine the direction of funds. From the viewpoint of public policy, the government can execute industrial policy through government banks more easily than it can through private banks. From the viewpoints of vested groups, councilmen can influence loan decisions by manipulating their political power.

Banks in Taiwan were not allowed to be privatized until the Banking Law of 1989. Although there were four private banks, three of them were owned by overseas Chinese, and the fourth was recast from the Bank of China for political considerations. Government banks have been criticized because their operations restrict efficiency, and their attitudes are believed to be much too conservative.

In order to increase its ability to self-manage, some measures were attempted. In 1990, the three major commercial banks attempted to sell their share of stock to the public. However, this action was not successful because the stock market was in recession at this time and few people purchased the stocks. The proposal of selling shares was then delayed further. In addition, several drafts of 'The Law on the Management of Government Banks' were proposed, written and modified, but they were not approved by the Legislative Yuan. As alluded to earlier, both privatization and regulation continue to be policy objectives in Taiwan.

4 Restrictions on foreign banks

In order to attract foreign capital, local branches of foreign banks were welcomed. On the other hand, in order not to put too much pressure on local financial institutions, foreign banks are restricted to some extent. However, although restricted, the activities of foreign banks did create some competition for local banks. Facing the global tide of financial internationalization, the regulations on foreign banks operating in Taiwan were gradually eased.

The number of local branches for each foreign bank is clear proof of the restrictions. Foreign banks were allowed to open only one branch before 1986. From 1987, they could open two branches, and from 1991 three. By the end of 1989, government banks had 55.7 branches on average, while foreign banks averaged just 1.2 branches.

5   Broadening of bank activities

Following the declared trend of financial liberalization and financial internationalization, approved activities for banks were gradually broadened. For example, in the past, bills transactions were allowed to be conducted only by bills finance companies. However, these activities were opened to some private banks in 1992. The Ministry of Finance seems to be planning to develop the banking industry into a universal banking system. But going slow has been the standard procedure while the declared policy is to liberalize and deregulate.

6   Path towards financial internationalization

Several steps have been taken to move towards financial internationalization. These include the following: 1. The establishment of foreign financial institutions. 2. The establishment of foreign branches of domestic banks. 3. The creation of an inter-bank call market for foreign reserves. 4. The release of control on capital movement. The government-set limit on capital outflow per capita each year was $5 million, and capital inflow per capita each year was $50,000. This restriction has been adjusted to a $5 million ceiling for both capital inflow and outflow. 5. A plan to establish Taipei as an Asian financial centre as part of the APROC plan. The government of Taiwan wants to follow the lead of Singapore, Japan, and Hong Kong and become one of the Asian financial centres. Abundant savings, foreign reserves, and highly-educated human resources can be advantages. However, some other features still need to be improved: free capital movement, a preferential tax system, information systems, and internationally-accommodating financial regulations and affiliated financial services. It will take time for Taipei to reach the appropriate standards and become a financial centre with global credentials, if it indeed ever succeeds.

7   Financial preferential policy

In order to stimulate industrial development and fulfill specific purposes, financial preferential policies were and still are often adopted by the government. Some financial subsystems were specifically established for this function. One can think of examples such as an export financing system, the small and medium-sized business financing system, and the financing system for strategic industries. In addition, some selective credit policies were and still are occasionally executed.

The special loans give some privileges to some selected customers. Such privileges include low interest rates and easier access to funds.

Some special loans, such as strategic industry loans, are executed by particular specialized banks. Some other loans are executed by domestic general banks and foreign banks. A good example would be loans for export. Others, such as small and medium-sized enterprises loans, are executed by a combination of both specialized banks and general banks.

The preferential financial subsystems have clearly been important in financing industrial development and, more recently, the building of a POLIS. A brief description and analysis can reveal the broad contours of this process.

1   The export financing system

General commercial banks offer loans for exports at preferential interest rates, and provide easier financing terms for exports. The Export–Import Bank of China also plays an important role, providing insurance, loans, and guarantees for exports.

Ever since export promotion was proposed in the 1960s as Taiwan's economic development strategy, export financing policy has taken on a crucial role.[3] To some extent, Taiwan's excellent economic performance during the 1960s and early 1970s can be attributed to its outward-oriented development policies which were supported by an inward looking financial system.

Export industries received high priority in credit rationing, and were granted low interest loans to provide financing for reshipment, production and the import of raw materials. After the 1970s, as a continuous trade surplus led to increased foreign exchange reserves, the authorities gradually reduced the interest rate difference. This preferential policy lasted for many years until 1989.

In the trade financing system, the Export–Import Bank of the Republic of China (Eximbank) still plays a significant role. This bank was established on 11 January 1979, and is a state-owned specialized bank which provides specific medium- and long-term export–import credits and guarantee services under the supervision of the Ministry of Finance. Starting on the first of April of its founding year, Eximbank also took over the responsibility for the export insurance services from the Chung Kuo Insurance Corporation.

In accordance with the 'Export–Import Bank of the Republic of China Act', the objectives of the Bank are to support government economic and trade policies and to assist local firms in expanding external trade and engage in overseas investments, with the aims of promoting national economic development and further enhancing international economic cooperation.

2 Small and medium-sized business financing system

Small and medium-sized businesses are the most active sector of the Taiwanese economy in terms of the number of firms and employees, the value of products, and other relevant criteria. However, they still have difficulties obtaining loans from formal financial markets. In order to solve this problem, a small and medium-sized business financing system was established within the formal financial system. This system is composed of banks, i.e., commercial and special banks (medium business banks), Medium Business Credit Guarantee Funds (MBCGF) and the Small Business Integrated Assistance centre. The following functions are provided by this system.

1 Financing

In addition to commercial banks, the medium-sized business banks are the specialized banks which do SME financing. These specialized banks were transformed from mutual savings companies after 1975 when the Law of Banking was revised. Only one of them, the Medium Business Banks of Taiwan (MBBT), is government-owned. All others (regional) are private. Each bank has its own channel for its source of funds. The MBBT accepts transfer deposits from the postal savings system and the support of the government Development Fund of the Executive Yuan. Special loans in various programmes are usually lent out through government banks. Furthermore, the credit cooperative associations and credit departments of farmers' and fishermen's associations are not directly connected with SMEs, but they may provide part of the funding demand of SMEs.

2 Guarantees

The establishment of the SMBCGF, a non-profit organization, provides vital assistance to SMEs that usually do not have healthy financial structures or sufficient collateral. The SMBCGF not only provides credit guarantees to SMEs that are rich in development potential and lack collateral, assisting them to obtain finance from financial institutions for sound development, but also simultaneously shares the financing risk with the financing institutions in order to enhance the institutions' confidence in SME financing.

3 Assistance

In July 1982, seven provincial banks funded the establishment of the Small Business Integrated Assistance centre to provide assistance to

SMEs that encounter difficulties in applying for financing through provincial banks or have poor financial management. Financing diagnosis and financial management assistance are two of the primary services offered by the centre.

The functioning mechanism of the entire SME financial system can be described as follows: SMEs apply to banks directly for financing. If the bank is sceptical about the SME's ability to repay the loan, the bank may apply to the SMBCGF to guarantee a certain per centage of the loan. The SME may also ask for diagnostic assistance of its operation, management, technology and marketing in order to prepare a report as a reference to encourage the bank to approve the loan.

4 Strategic industry financing system

This is perhaps the most crucial for our purposes, since the building of a POLIS would have been impossible without it. Preferential policies for strategic industries were introduced in 1982 and six criteria were adopted which the selected strategic industries must meet to be so designated: high linkage effect, high market potential, high technological intensity, a high degree of value-added, a low energy coefficient, and a low level of pollution emissions. Within these strategic industries, certain products are designated to be actively promoted, most of which are in the mechanical engineering products, and information and electronics sectors. The list of selected products has been amended several times and after 1986 a few products from the biochemical and material industries were included. In the Six-Year National Development Plan, some new key industries were added, mainly from sectors such as the biochemical and material industries. The recent policy affirms this trend and tries to deepen it.

Taiwan's government offers two preferential measures for the purpose of subsidizing strategic industries – (i) preferential loans, and (ii) technology and management guidance. Preferential loans are administered both by a pool of funds administered by the Bank of Communications, and by a pool of funds administered by the Medium Business Bank of Taiwan. Funds for both pools are supplied in part by the government's Development Fund. Yang (1993) evaluated the costs and benefits of this policy empirically and found that the ratio of financial support does not seem to play an important role in the technology improvement and management improvement activities of firms. However, re-estimating Yang's relationships using more recent and detailed data shows both an absolute as well as a ratio effect. On both counts the preferential policies have successfully directed credit to strategic industries with positive effects.

In 1992, the Six-Year National Development Plan was promulgated. Originally, the plan targeted total expenditures of NT$8 trillion. This amount would require a great deal of domestic savings and foreign capital to accommodate the investment. In 1993, the plan was reduced in scale. However, the need for funds is still very acute. In order to solve the funding problem, the government designed several methods for collecting funds, such as the issuance of government bonds, an increase of tax bases, and even the setting-establishment of a 'Japanese-style fiscal investment and loan programme' to pool postal savings and pension funds. The appropriateness of these approaches was widely discussed domestically. In the aftermath of the financial crisis in Asia domestic investment rose still further.

One may look at the lengthy description of the monetary and financial controls and simply conclude that these are inappropriate instruments for a complex economy making its transition to a special niche in the emerging knowledge-based global economy. However, such a conclusion would be hasty for at least two main reasons. First, Taiwan has shown itself capable of reforming the financial system slowly while creating a complex economic structure. Secondly, the plight of Korea shows that the hubris believing oneself to be a member of the club of privileged countries that led to deregulation can lead to disaster. However, this is not to say that gradual reforms are not necessary. In fact, they are both necessary and inevitable.

The contrasting examples of Korea and Taiwan show that the construction of a complex economy requires a healthy financial system. In turn, the health of the financial system depends upon a deft combination of market and non-market institutions. Overregulation can cripple an economy, but so can a sudden and inappropriate rush towards financial liberalization. The old-fashioned virtues of prudence and caution seem attractive all of a sudden after the economic tragedies in South Korea and, more recently, in Argentina.

6

Corporate Governance: a New Theory and Reform of the Family-Based Corporate Governance System in Asia

> A: I play it the company way
>   Where the company puts me, there I'll stay.
> B: But what is your point of view?
> A: I have no point of view!
>   Supposing the company thinks...I think so too!!
>
> Frank Loesser, *'The Company Way'*

In this chapter I want to probe the question of corporate governance not only in the context of post-crisis Asia, but also as a general problem that exists in any complex capitalist economy. The scandals that erupted in the United States, beginning with the notorious Enron affair in 2002 are reminders, if such reminders are necessary, that complex problems of governance are more ubiquitous than both big business and most economic theorists have acknowledged hitherto.

At the same time I want to emphasize that both the proximate and the underlying causes of the Asian and other recent financial crises were macroeconomic in nature. They had more to do with premature capital account liberalization than so-called 'crony capitalism'. This is not to suggest, however, that governance issues are entirely irrelevant. Far from being irrelevant, they are crucial for efficient growth and distribution. Thus, in contrast with most conservative and radical analyses of financial crises and their aftermath, this book attempts to adopt a rather more holistic approach without blaming bad governance per se for financial crises that were largely macroeconomic phenomena. While understanding the economics and the political economy at both the macro and micro levels are crucial they should not be confused, and a wrong causal analysis can have drastic consequences for growth and welfare. My claim is that good corporate governance must be the foundation of a sound economy in the future. Hence just as the conservatives were wrong in their thesis that 'crony capitalism' was the main cause of the Asian crisis, it will be a mistake to ignore the real and serious problems of corporate governance in Asia and elsewhere. By itself good corporate governance will not always prevent large-scale macroeconomic shocks in an open economy, but the transparency and accountability of corporations can make the job of macroeconomic policy makers much easier – in addition to the benefits it will have for shareholders, workers and consumers.

Corporate governance in a narrow sense addresses the fundamental microeconomic issue of how the managers of the firm are induced by banks, equity markets, or other mechanisms to act in the best interests of its shareholders and hence to maximize the discounted present value of the firm. In a wider sense, corporate governance can or should address a whole host of issues for multiple stakeholders – ranging from efficiency and equity to the promotion of economic and political freedom. Recently, Iwai (1999) has created a framework that distinguishes between the realist and nominalist approaches and can address many of the meta-questions about corporate governance.

The present chapter tries to present a preliminary conceptual framework consistent with the realist approach within which to frame the salient issues regarding Asian corporate governance. An attempt is also made to address some significant issues for reforming corporate governance in East Asia.[1] Finally, the limits of the most popular theoretical approach based on agency costs are also explored. It is argued that a complete explanation for the successes and the failures of the family-based system of governance requires a somewhat different model than that starting from the assumption of atomistic, utility-maximizing agents. This alternative approach should also be able to explain the persistence of different corporate governance structures – often within the same country.

It appears that the standard approaches that consider the firm to be simply a nexus of contracts cannot completely account for the particularities of the relationship types of corporate governance found in East Asia. Therefore, this chapter extends Berglöf's (1997) twofold classification of corporate governance structure to a threefold one by analysing family-based corporate governance structures.[2] Since large family business groups are prevalent in the East Asian crisis economies, their corporate governance structures would seem to be of immediate relevance in our analysis. The challenge, however, is to link this structure analytically to the two other types that can be labelled bank-led[3] and equity market-based corporate governance systems.[4] Only by making these analytical links clear can one begin to consider the policy issues raised by the Asian crisis as well as by transition from one type of governance to another. This chapter is organized as follows. The following section presents a new conceptual framework and typology, including family-based corporate governance. Some important aspects, including financing, monitoring and performance of family businesses, are discussed in section 3. Then, in section 4, the transactions costs related to the institutional environment in which the family businesses operate are considered. In particular, the existence and enforcement of property rights laws are examined in order to see how these contribute to the incentive structures and performance of family businesses in East Asia. The final section presents some tentative conclusions and some suggestions for areas of future analytical and empirical research.

1 A new conceptual framework and typology: family-based corporate governance

Even before the crisis in Asia extensive debate was taking place in Europe, the United States and Japan about the relative merits of different types of corporate governance systems. Broadly speaking, two general types of corporate governance structures have been discussed.

The first type can be called a shareholder or equity market-based governance model of the Anglo-American type (hereafter EMS). This is usually contrasted with the continental European or Japanese-type stakeholder or relationship model. In the second type (for example, the Japanese main bank system) banks play a key role in monitoring the performance of corporations. Therefore, this type of governance structure could be called a bank-led governance system (or BLS). Note that BLS can either be a Japanese-style main bank system as mentioned above, or the German-style universal banking system.[5] However, the BLS and EMS are not the only two possible types of corporate governance systems.

In both Northeast and Southeast Asia there is a preponderance of family-based firms that are not necessarily controlled by banks or by equity markets. Nevertheless they do operate as economic entities within the context of a relationship-based system. Thus family-based corporate governance system (FBS) can constitute a third type of corporate governance.[6]

Given this threefold division,[7] we can now ask: what are the relevant dimensions in which these systems can be compared and contrasted? Berglöf (1997) developed a set of criteria to answer this question for comparing EMS and BLS types of corporate governance. In addition to Berglöf's original criteria for comparing the BLS and EMS, I have introduced here two additional features that relate specifically to corporate governance. The first is the monitoring of non-financial enterprises by the system, i.e. how the managers of corporations are monitored by outside financiers such as banks and shareholders. This type of governance is intimately associated with how corporations are financed, i.e., corporate finance. Such monitoring by the firms' financiers is clearly an important function of the financial system. Secondly, and more generally, the issue of self-monitoring needs to be addressed. This issue is particularly relevant to family business groups in which ownership and management are not clearly separated. This applies equally to both financial and non-financial firms. Table 6.1 compares and contrasts the BLS and EMS styles of corporate governance. For reasons explained in the next paragraph we consider FBS in a separate setting in Table 6.2.

Before presenting the characteristics of the FBS type of corporate governance in Table 6.2, it may be useful to define family businesses more carefully. According to Suehiro (1993), the family business can be thought of 'as a form of enterprise in which both ownership and management are controlled by a family kinship group, either nuclear or extended, and the fruits of which remain inside that group, being distributed in some way among its members' (p. 378).

Suehiro draws his inspiration from Chandler (1977) who defines family business as follows:

> In some firms the entrepreneur and his close associates (and their families) who built the enterprise continued to hold the majority of stock. They maintained a close personal relationship with their managers, and they retained a major say in top management decisions, particularly those concerning financial policies, allocation of resources, and the selection of senior managers. Such a modern business enterprise may be termed an entrepreneurial or family one, and an economy or sectors of an economy dominated by such firms may be considered a system of entrepreneurial or family capitalism. (p. 9, quoted in Suehiro (1993, p. 378))

In discussing family business in East Asia in this chapter our emphasis will be on control and de facto control rights more than formal

Table 6.1 Comparing equity market-based and bank-led systems of corporate governance

	Type of corporate governance system	
	Equity market-based System (EMS)	Bank-led system (BLS)
Share of control-oriented finance	Low	High
Financial markets	Large, highly liquid	Not necessarily small but less liquid than EMS
Share of all firms listed on exchanges	Large	Not necessarily small
Investor orientation	Large	Concentrated
Investor orientation	Portfolio-oriented	Control-oriented
Shareholder rights	Strong	Weak
Creditor rights	Strong	Strong for close creditors but applied according to a 'contingent governance structure' (Aoki)
Dominant agency conflict	Shareholders vs management	Banks vs investors Workers may be important stakeholders as in Aoki's model of the Japanese firm
Role of board of directors	Important	Limited, but less so than in the case of FBS
Role of hostile takeovers	Potentially important	Quite limited
Role of insolvency	Potentially important	Potentially important; but possible systemic crisis may postpone bankruptcies
Monitoring of non-financial enterprises (NFE)*	Can be done through interlocking directorships, but equity market and threat of takeovers are the most important mechanisms	Mixed; with adequate regulations that are enforced and stable intra-group shareholding monitoring can be effective [Aoki's contingent governance]
Self-monitoring	Possible; but the mechanisms above apply for the most part	Possible, with oversight by government and members of the group Potential for abuse

Note: *NFE is clearly a large but special category. However, frequently in the literature on corporate governance the governance of non-financial firms is the focus. In addition to NFE, the financial firms (who are sometimes the monitors) themselves need to be monitored.

Table 6.2 Description of family-based systems of corporate governance

Share of control-oriented finance	High initially, but may vary as family groups get bank and equity financing from outside
Financial markets	Small, less liquid
Share of all firms listed on exchanges	Usually small
Ownership of debt and equity	Concentrated
Investor orientation	Control-oriented for family groups
Shareholder rights	Weak for outsiders
Creditor rights	Strong for close creditors Weak for arm's-length creditors
Dominant agency conflict	Controlling vs minority investors
Role of board of directors	Limited
Role of hostile takeovers	Almost absent
Role of insolvency	Potentially important
Monitoring of non-financial enterprises (NFE)	Mixed; in the presence of strong regulations and government vigilance monitoring could be efficient. However, the presence of moral hazard and possibility of bail-outs could lead to lax monitoring.
Self-monitoring	Initially, self-monitoring is effective. At later stages there is a strong tendency for insiders to be predatory towards outsiders. Could still be efficient but efficiency depends on the performance of owner-managers.

ownership. Claessens, Djankov, Fan and Lang (1998, 1999) and Claessens, Djankov and Lang (1998, 1999) have pointed out in their recent studies of corporate control in Hong Kong, Indonesia, Korea, Malaysia and Thailand two important features of industrial organization in East Asia. These are:

(i) families have control over the majority of corporations;
(ii) such control is also magnified 'through the use of pyramid structures, cross-holdings and deviations from one-share-one-vote rules' (Claessens, Djankov, Fan and Lang, 1999, p. 3)

In Appendix 6.1 the ownership structure for Thai corporations illustrates the first point. In Appendix 6.2 the immediate control/ultimate cash flow rights diagram of the Lotte Group, as calculated by Claessens et al., illustrates point (b) above.

The evidence gathered so far demonstrates that the ultimate control of the corporate sector in East Asia is, on the whole, family-based. One study shows that '16.6% and 17.1% of total market capitalization in Indonesia and the Philippines respectively can be traced to the ultimate control of a single family (the Suhartos and the Ayalas)'.[8] It goes on to point out that the top ten families in Thailand, Indonesia and the Philippines account for more than 50 per cent of the market capitalization.

In Table 6.2 a qualitative description of the FBS system is given. The reader should note that the relevant categories for comparison across the rows in this table are exactly the same as for BLS and EMS. In the next section a more detailed analysis of FBS is attempted with the help of some quantitative information and specific references to family-based corporations and corporate groups (for example, the CP Group in Thailand and the Lucky - Goldstar Group in Korea).

The reader should note that both BLS and EMS are closely associated with the dominant mode of corporate finance by banks and equity markets respectively. In the case of FBS in East Asia, the financing can come from three different sources. First, FBS, especially in the initial stages of development of family businesses, could be financed internally to a large extent. Second, as the enterprise grows over time, the role of banks becomes more prominent. Third, at some stage – perhaps overlapping with the second, that of bank financing – outside equity may become the most significant source of corporate finance. However, the key difference between FBS as a governance system and BLS and EMS lies in the fact that neither the banks nor the equity markets ultimately control the family business groups. In the final analysis, the control resides with the family (or families). As we shall see, this may be an economically rational decision, but ultimately FBS can run into trouble as well, as has been demonstrated graphically by the Asian crisis.

As alluded to above, Table 6.2 is only a qualitative description of the FBS corporate governance system. Although it facilitates comparisons and contrasts with the other systems, we need to go into more detail with the help of as much quantitative information as is available at this point. Bearing this in mind, the following section presents some important aspects, including the financing, monitoring and performance of family businesses with special emphasis on asymmetric information and monitoring aspects of the FBS type of governance system.

2   Financing, monitoring and performance of family businesses

Without being exhaustive, the essential aspects of the family-based system can be discussed under the following five headings:

1. The extent of family-controlled corporations in East Asia.
2. The dominant modes of financing.
3. The key information asymmetries and agency conflicts.
4. The problems of monitoring family businesses.
5. Investment and capital accumulation by the corporations.

These five aspects have been chosen because they are the most significant from the point of view of determining the problem of corporate governance in East Asia for family-controlled corporations in practice. The first four are the most important elements of corporate governance structure, while investment and capital accumulation can be seen as the most important performance indicator for a late industrializing economy.

1   Ownership and control

1.1   The overall picture of ownership and control

Although empirical evidence is not widely available, at least for those companies covered in the World Scope data base, it is possible to calculate the percentage of total market capitalization controlled by families in East Asia.

According to a recent study by Claessens et al., for the World Bank, the share of top ten families in the total market capitalization in Indonesia in 1996 was 57.7 per cent. For Philippines and Thailand this share was 52.5 and 46.2 per cent respectively. For Korea the share of top 15 families was 38.4 per cent and for Malaysia 28.3 per cent.

This picture of concentrated ownership of corporations by a few (usually between five and 10) family groups is supported by individual country studies by Suehiro for Thailand, Sato for Indonesia, Taniura for Taipei, China and Korea and Koike for Philippines.

1.2   Ownership and control in the financial sectors

Most of the private commercial banks and finance companies in Thailand are controlled by family business groups. For example, the top bank in Thailand, Bangkok Bank Limited, is controlled by the Sophompanitch family. The Farmer's Bank, which is the second-largest bank, is controlled by the Lamsum family. Of the 15 private domestic commercial banks and 53 finance or security companies that were operating before the crisis in Thailand, the overwhelming majority were controlled by family groups. In Philippines and Indonesia a similar system also prevailed. In Indonesia before the crisis, of the 144 private commercial banks many were controlled by combinations of family groups. In Korea, there are explicit, fairly low limits (15 per cent for regional banks and only 4 per cent for all other banks) on the ownership of stocks by a family or chaebols in a particular company. Hence the formal degree of ownership is low, but control can still be exercised through member companies who own stocks, deviation from the one-share-one-vote rule, and other related practices. It is not known to what extent this is true in the financial sector, but Table 6.3 showing the extent of overall control by insiders for the top chaebols is revealing.

2 Financing

After an initial period of internal financing (Koike, 1993), many East Asian family-based businesses developed into highly leveraged firms. In 1996, Korea was the economy with the highest debt/equity ratio of 3.54. Thailand was next, with a ratio of 2.36. In some sectors such as construction the debt/equity ratio was double the national average. What is significant is that despite high levels of debt, the BLS type of governance did not come into play. The lack of effective bank monitoring in the face of such seemingly high levels of debt, much of which is owed to the banks, is indeed a puzzle. Some plausible explanations are discussed in the subsection on monitoring.

Table 6.3 Ownership of Korean business groups by insiders (percentage of common shares held)

Business group	Founder	Relatives	Member Companies	Total
Hyundai	3.7	12.1	44.6	60.4
Samsung	1.5	1.3	46.3	49.3
LG	0.1	5.6	33.0	39.7
Daewoo	3.9	2.8	34.6	41.4
Sunkyong	10.9	6.5	33.5	51.2
Sangyong	2.9	1.3	28.9	33.1
Hanjin	7.5	12.6	18.2	40.3
Kia	17.1	0.4	4.2	21.9

Source: The World Bank, *East Asia: The Road to Recovery*, 1998, p. 60.

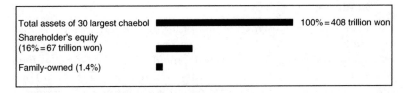

Figure 6.1 The average equity of chaebols
Source: Yuji Akaba, Florain Budde Jungkiu Choi, 'Restructuring South Korea's Chaebol', *The McKinsey Quarterly*, 1998, number 4.

Furthermore, in the case of Korea, the overall share of family-owned equity is formally quite small as figure 6.1 shows. The share of equity outside of families is also small (16 per cent), but much larger than that of the families. It is surprising that seemingly there is no control by outside shareholders. Table 6.3 suggests a plausible hypothesis. Actual control by the family groups far exceeded the formal ownership of chaebols, preventing monitoring by outside shareholders or their representatives.

3 Information asymmetries and agency issues

In the case of FBS, initially the family members act as owner-managers. Then, as the firm grows and is professionalized, there is still close monitoring of managers by the owners. When the family business is almost entirely financed 'internally' (including financing from relatives and other informal networks, as in the case of overseas Chinese), and remains limited in scope and scale, the asymmetry of information and the consequent problem of adverse selection and moral hazard between the owners and managers is usually not very severe. This is true largely because there is no effective separation between ownership and management.

However, as family business grows there arises a conflict between the owner-managers and the financiers (whether banks or outside shareholders). This can give rise to the possible failure of FBS due to private risk taking not validated by market results (moral hazard) – for example, investment in the wrong projects. It could also lead to the selection of the more risky (wrong) borrowers (adverse selection). Therefore, the FBS system works well when self-monitoring is present, or when banking and security market (prudential and other) regulations and an effective legal system make the misuse of finances less likely.

4   Monitoring

As mentioned previously, the self-monitoring incentives for FBS may exist only at an earlier phase of growth. As Suehiro (1993) points out, following Nakagawa, 'the development of family business could be the result of a rational choice by an entrepreneur in a backward or a latecomer nation, where the government had intentionally promoted industrialization'.

In all of the East Asian economies this apparently had been the case. Many family enterprises, particularly under their founder-owners, showed tremendous flexibility during the period of accelerated growth. It is likely that family enterprises succeeded in economizing on scarce managerial resources. It must have been nearly impossible to function flexibly and effectively without constant self-monitoring, both ex ante and ex post, at this stage.

In general, the problem of monitoring really arises once the firm acquires a large element of external financing. It may become particularly acute when firms develop into conglomerates, investing in areas where they do not have much experience or expertise. It is also difficult to monitor such activities from outside because expertise may also be lacking on the part of the external financiers. Even with a market for corporate takeovers this problem may persist (Hikino, 1997). In the case of banks acting as monitors there is also the problem of who monitors the monitors.[9] In fact, this last question brings us back to the problem of understanding the origins of the banking crisis and corporate governance problems in Asia with which this chapter began. Further research must help us to understand better whether banks failed to monitor effectively because of state interference, or rapid deregulation, or influence from family businesses, or a combination of all of these factors.

5   Corporate investment, accumulations and growth

If the aim of corporate governance is to enhance efficiency, then the right quality and quantity of investment in the appropriate sectors should be the right strategy for the firm. In these regards, East Asian corporations have registered impressive quantitative growth rates. For example, between 1988 and 1996 the median growth rate for a large sample of listed companies in Korea was 13.6 per cent. Thailand's mostly family-based corporations showed an even more impressive rate of capital accumulation over the same period at 13.8 per cent per year. Indonesian corporations were close behind at 12.7 per cent. The sample includes both financial and non-financial firms. It would appear that mainly as a result of massive accumulation of capital, both types of firms grew rapidly. The earlier studies of family business groups such as Salim Group in Indonesia (Sato, 1993), Lucky Goldstar Group in Korea (Koike, 1993), Samsung in Korea (Khan, 1998, forthcoming) and CP Group in Thailand (Suehiro, 1993) have indicated how family firms rapidly grew and diversified.

However, quite often the motive for diversification was to protect and enhance family fortunes, rather than to build up productive capacity (Suehiro, 1993). Suehiro further pointed out that in the case of Thailand, much of the diversification was carried out in order to take advantage of existing tax shelters as well.

To summarize the argument so far, it is clear that family-based corporations have played a major role during the boom period of the 'East Asian Miracle'. What went right during this period at the firm level, as documented by the studies cited above, is the economically efficient use of the flexibility of family-based management. The owner-managers, together with the professional managers they hired (e.g. the CP Group in Thailand, the Ayala Group in the Philippines, or Samsung and Lucky Goldstar in Korea among others), met the challenges of late industrialization in many sectors by exploiting profit opportunities as they arose. These ventures were certainly helped by government policies, including policies to build infrastructure. Finally, the family and kinship networks, especially among the Southeast Asian overseas Chinese, made 'internal' (in the broad sense of the word) financing a source of expansion for a reasonable length of time initially. Self-monitoring may also have been effective during this period to a large extent. In addition, the family members in leading positions probably monitored the hired management closely as well.

Part of what went wrong – at the micro level – certainly came when the family enterprises expanded beyond the point where they could be financed primarily from the internal resources of the family groups. This resulted in highly leveraged debt-financing. At the same time the control of the firm – through means discussed earlier – was not shared with outside shareholders. As a result, neither the BLS nor the EMS type of governance could be exercised efficiently.

An important area of ongoing and future research will examine the broad hypotheses advanced in the previous paragraphs in the context of late industrialization at the level of family-based corporate systems. It is possible, in principle, through further empirical work to ascertain whether FBS should be replaced completely by BLS or EMS (or some combination of both – a hybrid form of governance perhaps) or whether FBS can still be a viable form for some East Asian economies, particularly those at a lower stage of development (perhaps with a GDP/capita of US $3000 or below). Even if this hypothesis can be demonstrated to be true for the low-or middle-income economies in the aggregate, there is still the further question of whether diversification has reached beyond the economies of scope allowed by the level of development of the economy. If this is true, then diversification is now a drag on scarce managerial and financial resources of the corporations. In addition, the monitoring problems may also have become increasingly severe, leading to a failure of FBS. These significant issues require further empirical research using and building upon the conceptual framework presented in this chapter. Given the limited scope of the present chapter only some rudimentary analysis can be carried at this stage. Accordingly, in the rest of the chapter I examine briefly the relation between transaction costs and the family-based system of governance by interpreting the existing evidence on the legal environment and diversification in the relevant Asian economies. Even this very preliminary investigation reveals some surprising features with regards to the relationship between different stages of development, legal systems and FBS. Furthermore, the relationship between FBS and diversification also turns out not to be as simple as is usually assumed in the literature. In particular, diversification seems to be more closely related to the internal management structure and the expertise of the firm, on the one hand, and the external industrial organization on the other, than to some formal structure of corporate governance per se. These issues are discussed in greater detail in the next section.

3   FBS at different stages of development: legal systems, transactions costs and diversification

One way to make the hypothetical relationship between the level of economic development of a particular country and the form of corporate governance for a family-based business more concrete is to think in terms of transactions costs. In particular, underdevelopment may be associated with not only incomplete markets but also imperfect legal systems where property rights are not well-defined nor the court system well-developed. In such circumstances, the enforcement of such laws as may exist may also be haphazard. This latter phenomenon is related to the weakness of governance in a broader sense. Given this type of weakness – both legal and institutional – firms may be able to minimize transactions costs by using a flexible, relationship-oriented form of organization. Historically and culturally, in East Asia this form has generally been identified with family businesses. Therefore, it is possible that FBS may be the paradigmatic form of corporate governance for the Asian countries at various stages of development. Such a conclusion is not intended to deny that Asian economies at different stages of development will have to address different problems with respect to their systems of family-based corporate governance.

In order to clarify whether this is indeed the case, it is instructive to consider some common measures of how the legal systems perform in various Asian countries. Table 6.4 gives some quantitative measures used specifically to assess the quality of legal environments (La Porta et al. 1998). Using exactly the same measures as La Porta et al. have introduced in the literature through their pioneering study of law and (corporate) finance, but applying them in the specific context of Asian economies at different stages of development, we can draw a number of interesting conclusions.

Table 6.4 measures the quality of the legal environments that firms face in selected Asian countries. The relevant information is summarized in this table for the Asian economies that are of particular interest to us. Five measures of the quality of legal environment are used in Table 6.4, namely efficiency of the judicial system, rule of law, corruption, risk of expropriation by the government, and probability of contract repudiation by the government. In addition, an assessment of the quality of

Table 6.4 Stages of development and the legal environment in selected Asian economies

Country	Enforcement variables				Accounting		GNP per capita (US$)	
	Efficiency of judicial system	Rule of law	Corruption	Risk of expropriation	Risk of contract repudiation	Rating on accounting standards	1996	1997
Hong Kong	10.00	8.22	8.52	8.29	8.82	69	24,290	25,280
Malaysia	9.00	6.78	7.38	7.95	7.43	76	4,370	4,680
Singapore	10.00	8.57	8.22	9.30	8.86	78	30,550	32,940
Thailand	3.25	6.25	5.18	7.42	7.57	64	2,960	2,800
Indonesia	2.50	3.98	2.15	7.16	6.09	na	1,080	1,110
Philippines	4.75	2.73	2.92	5.22	4.80	65	1,160	1,220
South Korea	6.00	5.35	5.30	8.31	8.59	62	10,610	10,550
Taipei, China	6.75	8.52	6.85	9.12	9.16	65	13,310	14,069

Definition of variables

Variable	Description	Sources
Efficiency of judicial system	Assessment of the 'efficiency and integrity of the legal environment as it affects business, particularly foreign firms' produced by the country-risk rating agency *Business International Corporation.* It 'may be taken to represent investors' assessments of conditions in the country in question'. Average in the period 1980–1983. Scale from 0 to 10, with lower scores signifying lower efficiency levels.	Business International Corporation
Rule of law	Assessment of the law and order tradition in the country produced by the risk-rating agency *International Country Risk* (ICR). Average of the months of April and October of the monthly index between 1982 and 1995. Scale from 0 to 10, with lower scores for less tradition for law and order. (Scale has been changed from its original range going from 0 to 6.)	International Country Risk Guide
Corruption	ICR's assessment of the corruption in government. Lower scores indicate 'high government officials are likely to demand special payments' and 'illegal payments are generally expected throughout lower levels of government' in the form of 'bribes connected with import and export licenses, exchange controls, tax assessment, policy protection, or loans'. Average of the months of April and October of the monthly index between 1982 and 1995. Scale from 0 to 10, with lower scores for higher levels of corruption. (Scale has been changed from its original range going from 0 to 6.)	International Country Risk Guide
Risk of expropriation	ICR's assessment of the risk of 'outright confiscation' or 'forced nationalization'. Average of the months of April and October of the monthly index between 1982 and 1995. Scale from 0 to 10, with lower scores for higher risks.	International Country Risk Guide

Repudiation of contracts by government	ICR's assessment of the 'risk of a modification in a contract taking the form of a repudiation, postponement, or scaling down' due to 'budget cutbacks, indigenization pressure, a change in government, or a change in government economic and social priorities'. Average of the months of April and October of the monthly index between 1982 and 1995. Scale from 0 to 10, with lower scores for higher risks.	International Country Risk Guide
Accounting standards	Index created by examining and rating companies' 1990 annual reports on their inclusion or omission of 90 items. These items fall into seven categories (general information, income statements, balance sheets, fund flow statement, accounting standard, stock data and special items). A minimum of 3 companies in each country were studied. The companies represent a cross-section of various industry groups where industrial companies numbered 70 percent while financial companies represented the remaining 30 percent.	International Accounting and Auditing Trends, Center for International Financial Analysis & Research, Inc.
GNP and GNP per capita	Gross National Product and Gross National Product per capita in constant dollars of 1996 and 1997.	World Bank

Source: Modified from La Porta et al. (1998) pp. 1122–6 and 1142–3.

a country's accounting standards is presented since accounting can play a crucial role in corporate governance.

Scrutinizing Table 6.4 it can be seen that, in general, countries with a low GDP per capita – such as Indonesia, Thailand and the Philippines – have relatively underdeveloped legal systems and an uneven enforcement of laws. This would seem to imply that, ceteris paribus, firms in these economies face high transactions costs. NIEs such as Hong Kong and Singapore show scores on all the relevant variables that indicate a more developed legal structure and its enforcement. Among the NIEs, South Korea and Taipei, China both rank lower in these respects than Singapore and Hong Kong. Surprisingly, Malaysia, which is closer to the lower-income countries in terms of GDP/capita, actually has a higher standing in terms of the efficiency of its judicial system than either South Korea or Taipei, China.

Another interesting finding from Table 6.4 is that the transparency and efficiency of accounting standards show little variation from one economy to another. For example, Thailand, with a score of 64, is in the same category as Taipei, China, which receives a score of 65. Even Hong Kong has a score of 69, only slightly ahead of Thailand. One popular explanation for the failure of corporate governance in East Asia attributes it, among other factors, to the lack of transparency in accounting standards. The available evidence, however, raises doubts about the validity of this assertion. How is it possible that economies such as Hong Kong and Taipei, China can have FBS styles of governance that are seemingly successful, given that their accounting systems are no more transparent than that of Thailand?

The data presented in Table 6.4 with respect to specific factors such as the rule of law and efficiency of the judicial system are also consistent with the hypothesis that at a lower stage of development the legal systems are less efficient, and, other things being equal, present higher transactions costs. While more developed economies such as Hong Kong and Singapore score 10 out of 10 in terms of efficiency, less developed countries like Indonesia, the Philippines and Thailand score much lower (2.5, 4.75 and 3.25 respectively). Therefore, it seems plausible that FBS can economize on transactions costs – given the inefficient legal systems – in these lower-income countries.

What is really surprising is that some economies with efficient legal systems such as Hong Kong also have a family-based system of corporate governance.[10] How can FBS function successfully in these economies? Are there features of FBS that remain relevant even at higher levels of income in Asia? It could be conjectured that there may be *specific* factors in each case that can explain the continuing relevance of FBS. For example, in Hong Kong the government and banks hold a negligible portion of the shares of the companies, making a system of family control inevitable. However, competition in a more or less laissez faire environment, where corporate and other laws are interpreted clearly and enforced reasonably well, might explain why FBS is still a workable form of corporate governance in Hong Kong. Another interesting case is Singapore which has some large family-controlled firms and business groups, but a system of corporate governance that is influenced by the government through the government-linked corporations. In the case of Singapore, the close guidance from government in a competitive environment might explain the relatively better performance of its family businesses. These are, of course, conjectures that would require more careful formulation and further verification.

Finally, both South Korea and Taipei, China have similar levels of development and family-based systems of corporate governance. Yet South Korean chaebols are undergoing restructuring after the crisis while Taipei, China's system continues to work relatively well. We need to ask what can explain the different performances of FBS in these two cases.

The upshot of the whole discussion is that concrete case studies of corporate governance of these economies must be carried out in order to assess the workability of the FBS in each particular case. Among other things, this should also help focus attention on the feasible policies for making the transition from FBS, if necessary, in economies such as South Korea.

4 Development of family businesses, transactions costs and diversification

A significant factor that may at least partly explain the differential performances of FBS is the diversification between Asian economies. How should we test the various formulations of what may be called the diversification hypothesis?

One way to formulate the diversification hypothesis that directly addresses the concerns of this chapter is to consider the relationship between diversification and family-owned firms.[11] At a low level of development, diversification may be a way to lower transaction costs by diversifying in order to create internal factor markets. We can call this the 'internal market hypothesis' (Claessens et al., 1999).[12] Here, internal factor 'markets' can refer broadly to within-firm allocation of raw materials, labour, and financial capital.[13]

Existing empirical work on the reasons for the diversification of family-owned firms leads to the conclusion that at low levels of development, diversification increases profitability. However, as legal systems become more transparent and efficient with increasing Asian economies is the extent of corporate diversification. What is the relationship GDP/capita there is actually a 'diversification discount'. In other words, further diversification actually leads to a loss of value.

Claessens et al. (1998) present some interesting econometric evidence regarding the relationship between different stages of development in Asian economies and corporate diversification. They find a positive effect of diversification on corporate performance at an earlier stage of development. They also try to estimate the influence of family group membership on diversification. One of their main findings is that family group membership can be linked to excessive diversification. They also find diversification at an earlier stage of development adding value to the firm, while at a later stage there is a negative impact of diversification on the value creation. Their overall estimate of this so-called 'diversification discount' is about 5 per cent on average.

Here again looking at seemingly successful FBS governance in Hong Kong, and Taipei, China raises the question of whether diversification discounts really exist for these economies as well. Since the study cited uses cross-section data from a limited sample this question cannot be answered without further careful econometric work. Single country studies using time-series data are needed to determine if and to what extent diversification discount exists in each case.

However, it can be conjectured prima facie that the diversification discount, if it exists at all in the above cases, must be much smaller than that operating in the crisis economies. A hypothesis that can explain the seemingly better performance of firms in these economies through concentration in general, in their core competencies would emphasize the greater professional expertise and internal efficiencies of these firms together with the industrial organization aspects, particularly the existence of a higher level of market competition. For the present let us call it the influence of industrial organization (or IIO) hypothesis, keeping in mind that factors internal to the firm – such as managerial and professional expertise – are also included. According to the IIO hypothesis, diversification is less a function of corporate governance per se than these other strategic efficiency-driving factors. Without competent management with strategic vision and market competition corporate governance by itself may have little influence. Of course, to the extent that good corporate governance creates incentives to develop a competent, professional management structure it will be of particular relevance as well. In addition to the commonly expressed concerns with corporate governance IIO should usefully focus the attention of policy makers on the nature and extent of managerial expertise and incentive structures within the firm. It should also direct the policy makers' attention to the extent of competition in the markets in which the family businesses participate. Therefore, it will be important to test a suitable formulation of this hypothesis for various Asian economies at different stages of development on a case-by-case basis. One particular form that can be called the (governance) parity hypothesis would attribute equal importance to both corporate governance and to factors included under the rubric of industrial organization above. Specifying the parity hypothesis as a null hypothesis and testing this against various alternatives statistically could throw more light on the relative importance of corporate governance in determining corporate performance in Asia.

5   A mathematical model of corporate governance and financing of an entrepreneurial firm: the limits of the principal-agent model

In this section, I discuss a model of corporate finance and show the limits of the principal-agent framework in the Asian context. The model is presented in several steps as follows:

1. In a private ownership economy consider the owner's choices regard-ing investing in projects. At the initial period (called period 0) a fixed amount I has to be invested. Let e denote the personal effort expended for the project. Let the unit cost of e be equal to 1. Consider two more periods and the dynamic choices as follows with two possible states of nature, Good and Bad, denoted as G and B respectively.

Period 0	Period 1	Period 2
Investment I made	State realized	Payoff in good state $= x$
Effort E after the	In good state the project	Payoff in bad state $= y$
investment	can continue	with probablity P_B and
	In bad state the project	Zero with probablity $(1 - P_B)$.
	is liquidated	Assets become worthless
	For $L \leq I$	

2. Banks enter the market in each period to acquire information and make loans. By making loans, a bank gains access to the internal records of the firm. The bank monitors the firm's accounts. Information is 'soft' and cannot be communicated to the outsiders even if the firm wishes to do so. The costs of monitoring are assumed to be negligible.
3. Equity market, or arm's-length investors, lend in period zero and collect payments in period 2. Even if they lend they do not examine the books, either because the private cost of monitoring is high or because the size of the loan is small.
4. Information asymmetries: Everybody in period zero knows about the state of the project at the time. However, once the project starts only

the owner knows the effort *e*. The owner also learns about the state before deciding to continue with the project. The 'inside' bank is also informed. It learns about the effort provided and the state at the same time as the owner. 'Outside' banks and equity holders can only have public information.

5. Contracts: Following Diamond (1991) and Gale and Hellwig (1985), without loss of generality, it is sufficient to consider only pure discount debt contracts (see also Rajan (1992) which is followed closely here). The firm borrows an amount A_t at period t and is required to make one paymentfor D_{t+i} convenience and to add some realism contracts over only one period would be called 'short-term contract'. Contracts longer than one period are called 'long-term contracts'. Any debt contract can be written as a convex combination of both short-term and long-term contracts.

In this model the borrower decides both what type of lender to select and the length of the debt contract. He must also decide on the level of effort *e*. After writing the contract in period 1, the borrower must decide whether to continue or quit (and liquidate).

The lender in this model offers the contract at period zero under given terms and conditions. In period one the lender must decide whether to renegotiate, stop the supply of credit, keep the old contract, or offer a new contract in the next period.

6   Optimal contracts

Expected surplus to the owner at period zero:

$$q(e,\ y)(X - I) - (1 - q(e,\ y))(I - L) - e$$

where $y =$ common knowledge information about project quality in period zero and $q(.)$ is the probability of the good state. This is a function that is increasing in both its arguments.

It is clear that the project should be financed only if the surplus is positive for some effort level. The effort level which maximizes the surplus can be found by solving:

$$\text{For } e^* = e$$

$$q_1^*(e,\ y) = \frac{1}{X - L} \tag{A1}$$

The optimal contract must possess the following features:

(1) The owner should receive the incentive to quit voluntarily in the bad state. The same purpose will be served if the lender has the ability and the incentive to coerce the owner to do the above.
(2) The incentive structure and the environment should be such that the owner will get all the surplus in G and bear all the losses in B.
    It is a deep result of the contracts literature that no rational contract can simultaneously achieve objectives (1) and (2) above.

6.1 Arm's-length contract

An amount I is borrowed at period 0. It is promised to be repaid in period two as a sum D_{02}.
The owner chooses the optimal effort level by solving

$$\max_{e} \quad q(e, y)(X - D_{02}) + (1 - q(e, y))(P_B(X - D_{02})) - e \qquad \text{(A2)}$$

Let e_a^* solve the corresponding FOC.
The lender must conjecture that the (ex-post) effort level will be (say)e_a. He will lend, as long as

$$D_{02} \geq \frac{I}{[q(e_a, y) + (1 - (q(e_a, y)]P_B} \qquad \text{(A3)}$$

In a rational expectations equilibrium the lender's conjecture must be self-fulfilling. Hence

$$e_a = e_a^* \qquad \text{(A4)}$$

If the credit market is competitive (A3) holds with equality. If an optimal contract exists, it is defined implicitly by the following equation when $e = e_a^*$

$$q_1^*(e, y) = \frac{1}{[X - I - \dfrac{(1 - q(e_a^*, y))(1 - P_B)I}{q(e_a^*, y) + (1 - q(e_a^*, y)P_B}](1 - P_B)} \qquad \text{(A5)}$$

However, $e_a^* < e^*$. The reason is simple. The owner continues in the bad state. This forces the lender to demand a higher face value, thereby reducing the amount of surplus available to the owner in the good state.

The inefficiency arises from the inability of the owner to commit to quit in the bad state.

Also for low values of y (reflecting the intrinsically poor quality of the project) the face value demanded could be too high. Generally, the returns to the lender could also decline with an increase in face value because this would reduce the incentive to provide effort (minimize e_a in equation (A3)). Credit will then need to be rationed.

6.2   Bank contracts

6.2.1   Short-term bank contract

Here in period one if the state is B the project can be liquidated. The bank recovers L. In state G the bank can use discretion and demand a share of the surplus in return for further lending. There is thus a bargaining game to be solved. In equilibrium the owner gets $r(X - L)$ and the lender gets $(1 - r)(X - L) + L$ where $0 \leq r \leq 1$. Here, r denotes the share of the unallocated surplus going to the owner after bargaining. Although assumed to be exogenous here it can be made endogenous. However, at this stage of our analysis this will only make the model more complicated without providing much illumination. We can think of r as the 'bargaining power' of the owner. Let q^*_{SG} denote the probability of reaching the good state.

$$q_1(e, y) = \frac{1}{r(X - L)} \tag{A6}$$

is the FOC for the owner's 'best' effort decision at period 0.

When $e = e^*_{SG}$ and the condition for individual rationality holds we have,

$$\left[1 - \frac{I - L}{q^*_{SG}(X - L)}\right] - r \geq 0 \tag{A7}$$

This is the non-negative profit condition for the bank. With a value of r close to 1 the bank may not be able to cover the depreciation losses. On the other hand, if the value of r is low (i.e. close to 0) then the owner, facing poor incentives, will not exert much effort. In either of these two extreme sets of cases the rational bank will not lend. For intermediate values, the bank may lend; but there will be suboptimal effort.

It is to be noted, however, that by constraining bargaining sufficiently by means of an external nonrenegotiable mechanism the incentives for providing optimal effort can be restored. One possibility is for the bank to commit lending at a particular interest rate. At the same time the bank should have the option to pull out whenever the effort observed is lower than optimal. Aghion, Dewatripont and Rey (1994) and Hart and Moore (1988) discuss various constraining options of this type.

6.2.2 Long-term bank contract

In this case in period 1 the loan can be renewed automatically and in period 2 the required repayment is D_2. Let us see what may happen in between. In period 1 if the state is B it is best to abandon the project. However, the bank cannot do this when the contract is long-term. During renegotiation the surplus from closing down is $(L - P_B X)$.

The owner will get $\quad P_B(X - D_2) + r(L - P_B X)$

The bank will get $\quad P_B D_2 + (1 - r)(L - P_B X)$

The first term in each expression is the amount specified in the initial contract.

The feasibility condition here is:

$$X \geq \frac{I - (1 - q_{LB}^*)(1 - r)(L - P_B X)}{q_{LB}^* + (1 - q_{LB}^*)P_B} = D_2$$

The R.S. gives the face value demanded by the bank so that it can break even. The inequality says that the project return should be enough to meet this requirement in the good state.

It is now time to ask how far this type of models can take us in evaluating governance. Clearly, monitoring aspects come out as crucial, and this is a major insight of this approach in understanding the agency problem of capitalist organizations and finance. Yet, there are several aspects in the Asian context that are overlooked by this approach. In particular one can make the following three observations:

(1) In the Asian context the owner may not have much of a chance to choose between contracts.
(2) International environment may give firms incentives to borrow on a short-term basis.
(3) Most importantly, in order for this stylized framework to be relevant, an enabling environment of supporting network of institutions and administrative apparatus for enforcing contracts must exist.

It should also be emphasized that a 'realist' view of the corporation would recognize the contextual nature of the problems of Asian corporate governance. At the same time, it would highlight, as I have done here, historically and logically, the problem of fiduciary responsibilities of the corporate form of capitalist organization. Clearly, such responsibilities can and should be discussed in a larger domestic and international socioeconomic context that includes the evolution of legal institutions and international economic relations as well.

7 Conclusions and suggestions for future research

In this chapter I have tried to analyse some basic issues related to corporate governance systems in East Asia. The threefold division of corporate governance systems presented in this chapter seems appropriate from the perspective of a realist approach to the nature of the corporation and its governance. According to this view, the 'historic mission' of the corporation as the site of capital accumulation may require different types of governance structures at different historical stages. In particular, in the East Asian context, the FBS structure has played an important role in the initial phase of capital accumulation in the East Asian countries. Indeed, its prevalence in Asian economies at all levels of development makes FBS almost a paradigmatic feature of corporate organization and governance in Asia. Complex questions, however, arise over how appropriate this system is currently in both Northeast and Southeast Asia. At present, one proposal is that it should be replaced by BLS. For instance, the new bank-based governance could be modelled on either the Japanese or the German type of corporate governance. For this to happen, however, bank restructuring and recapitalization and an improvement of prudential regulation, accountability and transparency will be essential. A competing proposal is that the transition should be towards an EMS style of corporate governance. It should be recognized that the problems here are even more formidable. The thinness of both bond and equity markets is one problem. In addition, there are the usual problems of a lack of adequate regulatory structures, transparency and accountability. The proposal for self-monitoring by the Stock Exchange of Thailand (SET) is an example of how difficult it is to have an EMS style of governance in Southeast Asia. In particular, the limited expertise and other institutional resources make the implementation of such proposals (which should ideally be self-enforcing) problematic. Still, future empirical work should focus on the appropriateness of each one of these structures, using whatever systematic quantitative and institutional information is available.

Another important aspect of family business in East Asia is their ability to adapt and reform. As Suehiro (1993, 1997) has pointed out, one rationale for the FBS system is their flexibility in terms of the managerial decision-making process and their efficiency in capital accumulation in the context of latecomer industrialization. The question that arises in the context of the crisis in East Asia is whether, for the Southeast Asian economies in particular, the process of 'catch-up' growth is still continuing. If that is the case, the transition process from FBS to either BLS or EMS may need to be slowed down. In Northeast Asia, however, as some researchers have shown (Khan 1997, 1998, forthcoming), the period of 'catch-up' growth has largely ended and global competitiveness must be based increasingly on organizational and product and technical innovations. Here the transition from FBS may need to be effected more speedily. However, as emphasized earlier, much more empirical research using detailed micro data sets with country-, sector- and firm-specific information is necessary before any definitive conclusions can be reached. In this context, the suggestion that the firms' managerial expertise as well as the industrial organization can be just as important as the form of corporate governance in determining their performance should also be taken seriously.

An important area of investigation for such future research should be those Asian economies with strong family-based corporate groups that weathered the AFC relatively well. Economies such as Hong Kong seem to have a large presence of family-based corporations and yet they have managed to maintain their economic vigour. What explains the seemingly better performance of FBS in these economies? This is the subject of ongoing research. Following a methodology that combines fieldwork, statistical analysis of existing data bases and an examination of the legal and institutional environment will lead to a better understanding of corporate governance and performance. Contrasting findings of this type of research with the findings about corporate governance in the crisis economies is a necessary condition for discovering the right road to reforming corporate governance in Asia. It is also clear that there is no single royal road to reform. Rather, a case-by-case approach that takes the institutional histories and their path dependence in each economy seriously is necessary.

In a critical approach to reform, an intriguing question is how relevant from a perspective of long-run growth corporate governance will be in the future. Such a question is motivated by the need to distinguish between a 'normal', growth-inducing macro-institutional environment and periods of crisis. It may be that during normal periods of growth, when many institutions and policies are creating opportunities for growth, a few badly managed firms would be of little significance. An extreme form of this hypothesis, of course, is that even with systemic bad corporate governance, under favorable aggregate macroeconomic and other institutional conditions growth is not hindered. A counter-hypothesis is that prior to the crisis some economies, such as Korea, had a reasonably well-functioning corporate governance system; but matters changed some time prior to the crisis. From this perspective, in the particular case of South Korea it may be hypothesized that the early 1990s were one such watershed period when the external environment of chaebol regulations changed, making bad governance inevitable. If this is true then internal reforms of governance on their own may not be sufficient to induce the corporations to produce efficiently. On the other hand, the first hypothesis does not see such reforms as being even a necessary condition for future Asian growth. Clearly, given the different implications of these various hypotheses it is important to test them fully before recommending appropriate policies for corporate governance reform in East Asia.

Finally, the analysis presented in this chapter shows both the scope and the limits of the principal–agent approach to corporate governance. Given multiple stakeholders and longer time horizons for at least some of these principals, the agency problem needs to be recast in terms of more explicit social goals. Such an approach does not start from the atomistic agents, but rather from the concept of the firm as a socially embedded hierarchical system. Bounded rationality, uncertainty and transactions costs can then be modelled quite naturally. For normative analysis, such a theoretical approach can also use a non-utilitarian approach to welfare such as Sen's (social) capabilities approach.[14] In this context, the issue of the fiduciary responsibility of the corporation assumes the utmost importance. The recent Enron and other scandals in the United States show that this is an issue of positive and normative salience not just in post-crisis Asia but in every economic system with corporate forms of organizational structure.

APPENDIX 6.1:   FAMILY-BASED BUSINESSES IN THAILAND

Table A6.1.1   Characteristics of top shareholders in large Thai corporations, 1979 and 1988

Top Stockholders/Equity Percentage	**1979**(%)	**1988**(%)
(1) Individual:	72 (33.0)	74 (29.7)
1–9%	3	4
10–29%	35	43
30–50%	29	23
51–100%	1	4
Foreigner	4	0
(2) Family investment company:	26 (11.9)	16 (6.4)
1–9%	3	5
10–50%	17	9
51–100%	6	2
(3) Thai corporation:	37 (17.0)	67 (26.9)
1–9%	3	5
10–29%	15	24
30–50%	10	19
51–100%	9	19
(4) Foreign corporation:	78 (35.8)	81 (32.5)
10–48%	32	26
49–50%	10	11
51–98%	10	13
99–100%	26	31
(5) Government bureau	3 (1.4)	8 (3.2)
(6) Crown Property Bureau	2 (09)	3 (1.2)
Total	218 (100.0)	249 (100.0)

Sources: Calculated by Suehiro (1993, p. 388) using the following directories: for 1979, Pan Siam Communication Co., *Million Baht Business Information Thailand, 1980–81* (Bangkok, 1981); for 1988, International Business Research Thailand Co., *Million Baht Business Information Thailand, 1989* (Bangkok, 1989).
Notes:
1. Large corporations indicate firms with 0.3 billion baht (1979) and 1 billion baht (1988) in terms of total annual sales.
2. Public corporations have been excluded.

Table A6.1.2   Top three stockholders in large Thai corporations, 1979 and 1988

Top Three Stockholders	1979 %	1988 %
(1) Individuals (Thai):	60 (27.5)	61 (24.5)
Belonging to the same family	21	33
Belonging to multiple families	39	28
(2) Individuals plus corporations:	38 (17.4)	32 (12.9)
With group companies[a]	14	13
With non-group companies	24	19
(3) Thai corporations:	22 (10.1)	48 (19.3)
Belonging to the same group	4	17
Among different groups	15	19
Holding-company type[b]	3	12
(4) Foreign corporations:	90 (41.3)	97 (39.0)
Exclusively foreigners[c]	33	38
With Thai corporations	43	51
With Thai individuals	14	8
(5) Government bureau	8 (3.7)	11 (4.4)
Total	258 (100.0)	249 (100.0)

Source: Calculated by Suehiro (1993, p. 389) same as Table A6.1.1.

Table A6.1.3   Family stockholders and management control in large Thai corporations, 1988

Top Management	Equity Percentage of Largest Stockholder			Total	%
	1–9	*10–49*	*50–100*		
Presidents/general managers:					
(1) Same family with the largest stockholder	3	33	55	91	59.5
(2) Same families with 2nd or 3rd stockholders	2	8	1	11	7.2
(3) Different families[a]	4	22	11	37	24.2
(4) Foreigners	2	11	1	14	9.2
Sub-total	11	74	68	153	100.0
(5) No data available	—	3	2	5	
Chairmen of board:					
(1) Same family with the largest stockholder	1	21	34	56	62.9
(2) Same families with 2nd or 3rd stockholders	1	4	—	5	5.6
(3) Different families	7	13	5	25	28.1

Table A6.1.3   Continued

Top Management	Equity Percentage of Largest Stockholder			Total	%
	1–9	*10–49*	*50–100*		
(4) Foreigners	1	2	—	3	3.4
Sub-total	10	55	39	89	100.0
(5) No data available	—	39	31	71	
Presidents (P)/chairmen (C):					
(1) Both of P/C belonging to the same family with top three stockholders	2	14	29	45	50.0
(2) Either of P/C belonging to the same family with top three stockholders	2	19	8	29	32.2
(3) Others	6	8	2	16	17.8
Sub-total	10	57	39	90	100.0
(4) No data available	1	38	31	70	

Sources: Survey by Suehiro (1993); as Table A6.1.1.
Notes:
1. Figures cover large corporations with annual sales of 1 billion baht in 1988.
2. Foreigner 100 per cent controlled and government partially owned companies have been excluded.
3. Subsidiaries of Siam Cement group and Suramahakhun group have been excluded.

APPENDIX 6.2: ENHANCEMENT OF CONTROL IN THE FAMILY-BASED (FBS) TYPE OF CORPORATE GOVERNANCE

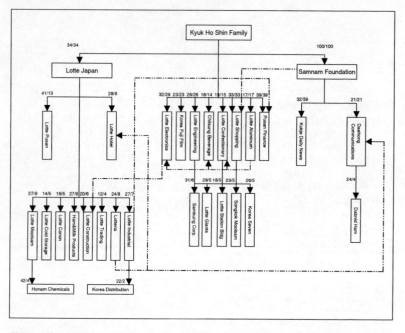

Figure A6.2.1 The Lotte Group (Immediate Control/Ultimate Cash-Flow Rights)
Source: Stijn Claessens, Simeon Djankov, Joseph P.H. Fan and Larry H.P. Lang (1999, p. 12).

APPENDIX 6.3:   ABOLITION OF REGULATIONS PROTECTING THE CHAEBOLS

External Shocks	Expected Changes	1998	1999	2000
Cross-shareholdings		Likely to be phased out to increase transparency	▲ 1998 Limited to 25% of net worth for top 30 chaebols		
Protection from M&A threats	"IMF crisis"	M&A market deregulation likely to result in hostile takeovers	▲ February 1998 Tender offer obligation abolished ▲ May 1998 Ceiling on foreign ownership abolished		
Lack of minority shareholder rights		Enhanced shareholder rights and monitoring system will provide disciplinary mechanisms	▲ 1998 Cumulative board voting expected	▲1999 Shareholder derivative lawsuits likely to be legalized	
Ability to grow via financial leveraging	Deregulation	Securing capital will become more difficult for chaebol Debt-to-equity ratio needs to conform to international standards	▲ 1998 No new cross-guarantees		2000 ▲ Cross-guarantees to be phased out
Strong coordination via chairman's office	Financial and political pressure	Dissolution of group chairman's office may lead to vacuum of control and coordination	▲1998 At least one outside board member ▲ 1998 Group chairman's office dissolved; each legal entity required to form its own board	▲1999 At least 25% of board to be outsiders	

Figure A6.3.1   Abolition of regulations protecting the chaebols
Source: Yuji Akaba, Florian Budde and Jungkiu Choi, 'Restructuring South Korea's Chaebol', *The McKinsey Quarterly*, 1998, number 4.

APPENDIX 6.4:   PERFORMANCE OF EAST ASIAN CORPORATE SYSTEMS: GROWTH, FINANCING AND LIABILITIES

In order to resolve what is the appropriate corporate governance system for East Asia in the wake of the crisis, we need to understand the performance of the corporates before the crisis. Generally, it appears that the high debt and leverage ratios were sources of potential problems. They became sources of actual problems with the capital account liberalization without adequate attention to the problems of short-term debt structures of the corporation.

One hypothesis about the recent financial crisis, as alluded to already, has been that it was caused – at least in part – by the weak performance and riskiness of corporate ventures. Before one can test the hypothesis in a rigorous way it is necessary to look at some basic indicators. In this appendix I will consider six salient indicators.
These are:

1. Real return on assets (RoA).
2. Sales.
3. Investment and capital.
4. Leverage.
5. Long-term debt.
6. Interest coverage.

Nominal rate of return on assets is measured as the ratio of EBIT (earnings before interest and taxes) at the firm level and total assets. Real rate of returns is the nominal return adjusted for rate of inflation.[15]

$$RoA = \frac{EBIT}{TA} - \pi \qquad (1)$$

where RoA = real rate of return on assets at the firm level
     TA = total assets at the firm level
     π = annual inflation rate

Table A6.4.1 shows the median RoA in percentage terms for eight Asian economies. It displays a fair degree of variation across these countries. For example, in Hong Kong, Korea and Singapore the RoA is, on average between 4 and 5 per cent. These rates are quite low compared with those of Thailand, the Philippines and Indonesia. For these countries RoAs vary between 8 and 10 per cent per year. Malaysia and Taipei, China occupy an intermediate position. These rates are measured after expressing all terms in the identity (1) in local currencies. Measuring

Table A6.4.1 Return on assets for eight Asian countries (assets measured by book value) *(%, medians, in real local currency)*

Country	1988	1989	1990	1991	1992	1993	1994	1995	1996	Average 1988–1996
Hong Kong	5.1	5.3	4.9	4.8	4.5	3.8	3.9	3.9	4.1	4.6
Indonesia	n.a	n.a	9.4	9.1	8.6	7.9	7.4	6.2	6.5	7.1
Korea	4.4	3.9	4.1	4.0	3.9	3.6	3.4	3.6	3.1	3.7
Malaysia	5.4	5.6	5.4	6.2	6.0	6.5	6.3	6.1	5.6	6.3
Philippines	N/A	N/A	N/A	7.1	6.4	8.1	8.5	6.8	8.4	7.9
Singapore	4.9	4.5	4.2	3.9	5.2	4.6	4.5	3.9	4.0	4.4
Taiwan	n.a	n.a	n.a	5.1	6.2	6.5	6.8	6.5	6.6	6.7
Thailand	10.8	11.0	11.7	11.2	10.2	9.8	9.3	7.8	7.4	9.8

Source: Claessens, Djankov and Lang (1998).

them in foreign currencies (for example, dollars) would simply show an upward adjustment for real exchange rate appreciation.

Table 6.4.2 gives the sales growth on a year-on-year basis for these eight countries. These figures also show some variation over time. On the average most of the corporations registered high sales growth. The MIT (Malaysia, Indonesia and Thailand) economies show very high average rates of growth, respectively; Taipei, China and Hong Kong are close behind with 9.3 and 9.2 per cent growth on average respectively. In 1996, however, Thailand, Indonesia, Taipei, China and Singapore showed a slower rate of growth. The export slowdown in 1996 is at least partly responsible for this.

Closely correlated with the high sales growth rate is the high volume of capital accumulation resulting from high rates of investment.

Table A6.4.2 Real sales growth (year-on-year) for eight Asian countries *(%, medians)*

Country	1989	1990	1991	1992	1993	1994	1995	1996	Average 1988–1996
Hong Kong	10.1	11.6	10.2	12.4	9.8	9.4	9.7	11.8	9.2
Indonesia	N/A	N/A	N/A	10.7	12.1	12.4	9.4	8.3	10.6
Korea	8.4	8.7	8.2	8.3	7.6	7.3	7.2	8.6	8.2
Malaysia	9.7	12.3	11.8	12.7	13.1	12.6	11.7	11.9	11.9
Philippines	n.a	n.a	n.a	8.4	6.7	7.6	10.6	12.2	8.2
Singapore	8.4	8.6	8.1	9.4	11.6	11.8	10.2	7.7	8.7
Taiwan	n.a	n.a	n.a	7.1	11.3	10.3	9.7	8.4	9.3
Thailand	11.6	10.3	10.8	9.6	8.3	10.1	10.7	5.7	9.7

Source: Claessens, Djankov and Lang (1998).

Table A6.4.3   Capital investment by the corporations in the World Scope
sample for eight Asian countries, 1988–96 *(%, medians)*

Country	1988	1989	1990	1991	1992	1993	1994	1995	1996	Average 1988–1996
Hong Kong	14.3	16.6	8.3	7.6	7.2	19.8	7.6	5.8	9.3	8.3
Indonesia	N/A	N/A	N/A	12.4	13.4	8.6	15.8	13.8	11.8	12.7
Korea	15.6	13.8	13.2	19.2	11.6	11.2	12.2	12.4	13.7	13.6
Malaysia	8.6	7.6	8.9	9.6	11.3	13.4	15.2	14.6	16.1	10.7
Philippines	N/A	N/A	N/A	9.1	8.9	7.8	13.5	14.1	14.5	10.8
Singapore	7.8	7.6	7.4	8.8	9.6	11.3	13.4	12.5	13.5	10.4
Taiwan	n.a	n.a	n.a	14.3	8.2	8.4	8.7	11.2	8.6	8.7
Thailand	10.4	12.9	12.3	15.0	14.9	15.0	14.7	14.5	5.8	13.8

Source: Claessens, Djankov and Lang (1998).

Table 6.4.3 demonstrates this proposition. Investment growth is measured as the ratio of new investments to existing fixed assets from 1988
to 1996. Indonesia, Korea and Thailand maintained remarkably high
rates of investment. Malaysia, Philippines and Singapore also registered
investment growth rates of over 10 per cent. In retrospect, questions
have been raised about the quality, rather than the quantity, of some of
these investments in the crisis countries.

In retrospect the data also show the degree of riskiness inherent in the
liabilities incurred by the corporations, especially in those crisis countries
with relatively low RoAs. Some of these countries (for example, Korea)
turned abroad for financing. Surprisingly even countries with high RoA
such as Indonesia and Thailand also borrowed heavily abroad. Domestic
bank lending, which has also become a characteristic of the East Asian
Miracle, has naturally been high also. Table A6.4.4 gives the leverage ratio
(i.e. debt over equity) for the eight countries. Interestingly, the ratios are not
the same in all countries. Korea's average of about 3.5 is about 4.5 times as
high as that of 0.82 for Taipei,China. Indonesia, Thailand and Hong Kong
also show high leverage. However, the case of Hong Kong shows that high
leverage may not necessarily result in systemic financial crisis, although the
aftermath of crisis in Asia has certainly weakened its economy.

It is also noteworthy that long-term debt has been low during the
period under consideration. This is illustrated in Table A6.4.5. With the
exception of the Philippines, the share is less than 50 per cent for all other
countries; Malaysia, Thailand and Taipei, China have the lowest shares
(29.2, 30.9 and 35.9 per cent respectively). In most cases there has been a
decline in the share of long-term debt beginning with the early 1990s.

Table A6.4.4 Leverage (debt/equity) for eight Asian countries (%, *means*)

Country	1988	1989	1990	1991	1992	1993	1994	1995	1996	Average 1988–1996
Hong Kong	1.832	2.311	1.783	2.047	1.835	1.758	2.273	1.980	1.559	1.902
Indonesia	n.a	n.a	n.a	1.943	2.097	2.054	1.661	2.115	1.878	1.951
Korea	2.820	2.644	3.105	3.221	3.373	3.636	3.530	3.776	3.545	3.467
Malaysia	0.727	0.810	1.010	0.610	0.627	0.704	0.991	1.103	1.176	0.908
Philippines	n.a	n.a	n.a	0.830	1.186	1.175	1.148	1.150	1.285	1.129
Singapore	0.765	0.922	0.939	0.887	0.856	1.102	0.862	1.037	1.049	0.936
Taiwan	n.a	n.a	n.a	0.679	0.883	0.866	0.894	0.796	0.802	0.820
Thailand	1.602	1.905	2.159	2.010	1.837	1.914	2.126	2.224	2.361	2.008

Source: Claessens, Djankov and Lang (1998).

Table A6.4.5 Long-term debt share for eight Asian countries (%, *medians*)

Country	1988	1989	1990	1991	1992	1993	1994	1995	1996	Average 1988–1996
Hong Kong	59.7	59.5	53.8	56.5	44.7	44.7	40.7	37.3	36.4	44.9
Indonesia	n.a	n.a	n.a	52.4	40.8	39.6	41.6	41.8	43.3	43.1
Korea	55.7	47.2	49.8	49.8	44.2	43.7	41.4	40.4	41.5	43.7
Malaysia	35.8	35.5	32.5	27.1	26.9	26.6	27.2	27.8	29.9	29.2
Philippines	n.a	n.a	n.a	57.2	53.1	50.3	50.2	49.8	51.4	52.2
Singapore	57.2	55.4	54.1	33.8	33.8	33.9	40.2	38.6	41.1	43.3
Taiwan	n.a	n.a	n.a	53.9	44.4	32.8	34.6	34.3	38.9	35.9
Thailand	58.1	49.8	38.8	34.3	25.2	26.4	27.6	32.9	32.8	30.9

Source: Claessens, Djankov and Lang (1998).

By itself debt, even short-term debt, does not imply that anything is seriously wrong as long as the ability to pay is not questioned by the creditors. It is useful to consider measures such as interest payment coverage (IPC) to see if there were indications of problems in this regard in the corporate sectors of some of the Asian economies. Interest payment coverage is defined as follows:

$$IPC = \frac{EBITDA}{Interest\ Expenses} \qquad (2)$$

where EBITDA = earnings before interest and taxes but adding back depreciation.

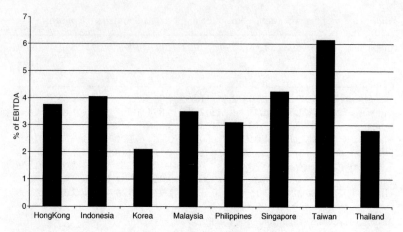

Figure A6.4.1   Interest coverage in eight Asian countries
Source: Claessens, Djankov and Lang (1998) (Interest payment coverage is equal to EBITDA/interest payment obligations).

IPC is a measure of how adequate operational cash flows (given by the size of EBITDA) are as compared with interest payment obligations (see Figure A6.4.1). The fact that the Thai and Korean corporations had very low IPCs (2.7 and 2.1 respectively) should have signaled (and probably had signaled in 1997) to the creditors that the corporate financing system was getting fragile. In Taipei, China, on the other hand an IPC of 6.1 looked quite secure.

However, the fragility of corporate finance depends not only on leverage ratios or IPCs, but also on the actual performance of corporations. The performance, as measured by sales and (to some extent) RoAs, did not seem problematic until the crisis. Since then, the link between corporate *performance* and corporate *governance* has become a major issue.

APPENDIX 6.5:   POLICY AND INSTITUTIONAL QUESTIONS

Once we have the typology offered in section 2 of this chapter it becomes possible to raise questions related to corporate governance structures for East Asia in a serious way. This is the task of this appendix. In particular, a set of policy and institutional issues can be raised clearly.

Within the general framework presented in section 2 the most important question is: what corporate governance structure is the most appropriate for particular Asian countries, given the present stage of development and the present institutional structure in that country? In order to address this question properly a number of fairly concrete questions will need to be answered. The following list of institutional questions tries to do this without being exhaustive. This is done in three steps. First, a series of concrete questions related to the possible transition from a FBS to a BLS governance is listed. Second, some specific questions related to a possible transition from a FBS to an EMS governance structure are listed. Finally, a two-part question addresses the general policy issues for institutional restructuring. It is hoped that these questions will give specificity to the reform agenda, force one to think more clearly about concrete resource requirements, and, most importantly, underline the problems of institutional change in the real world. As emphasized at the beginning, the purpose of the current chapter is not to answer all these questions, but to use these to ascertain in a tentative and preliminary way what the significant problems are for the transition to a better form of corporate governance in East Asia.

A. Questions related to the family-based system (FBS) and the bank-led system (BLS)

1. What circumstances may lead to the overexposure of banks and non-bank financial institutions (NBFI) under the FBS to risky sectors (e.g. real estate) and risky projects?

2. What conditions can ensure that the transition from FBS to BLS and to a system of financial restraint (as Stiglitz and others have described it) will *not* lead to overlending to the risky sectors and projects?

3. Are there problems that arise when the monitoring of corporations is primarily the responsibility of banks without being complemented by other financial institutions (Indonesia, South Korea)?

4. However, weak NBFIs also can cause problems (e.g. Thailand). What kind of policies and institutional reform can ensure that a transition from FBS to BLS in a country like Thailand will not cause the system to become vulnerable? Are there 'cultural' factors (e.g. with respect to how laws are interpreted or applied) that may also be important here?

5. It has been claimed that *unbalanced* financial systems led to a lack of risk diversification in Asian economies. How will transitions to a BLS from a FBS solve this problem?

6. Will allowing more foreign banks entry into the financial system make the governance of BLS better? How?

7. What should be the optimal capital-adequacy ratios for banks over the relevant time horizons (e.g. during the crisis period, medium term, long run)?

8. How can legal lending limits be designed to be more adequate than they are now?

9. How can the enforcement of the legal lending limits be strengthened?

10. How can asset classification systems be improved?

11. How can provisioning rules for possible losses be better designed and enforced?

12. How can the now universally acknowledged poor disclosure and transparency of bank operations be improved?

13. a. How can the lack of provisions for an exit policy for troubled financial institutions be addressed?

   b. More specifically, is there a need for completely specifying an orderly workout procedure? If so, how to do it? (There may be issues related to legal institutions of specific countries that are relevant here. So institutional studies by legal experts will be necessary for answering this question.)

14. How can we improve bank supervision, and the compliance with prudential regulations in general?

15. It has been shown that much of the lending was done on a collateral basis, rather than on a cash-flow basis. This obscured the need for analysing the profitability and riskiness of underlying projects. How can this lending practice be changed?

16. In the recent past, credit tended to flow to borrowers with relationships to government or private bank owners and to favoured sectors of the economy. How much of this was productive? What would be the best way to ensure that finances go to productive sectors and efficient firms after moving from FBS to BLS in these countries?

17. How can banking practices be moved towards proper evaluation of illiquid vs insolvent firms, lending based on projected cash flows, realistic sensitivity analysis and recoverable collateral values?

18. What should be the optimal liquidity requirements (one presumes that in most cases it should be higher) for the banks in the affected countries?

19. How to address the problems of special categories of weak financial institutions, e.g.
   (a) state banks in Indonesia
   (b) merchant banks in Korea
   (c) many other commercial banks in East Asia
   (d) finance companies in Thailand.

20. If the relationship between leverage and profitability is negative in East Asia, as some studies claim to have found, does this mean that

BLS may not be the proper corporate governance structure in East Asia after all?

21. How best can the problems of non-performing loans and bank-recapitalization be handled so that a move from FBS to BLS is a realistic option in the economies affected by the crisis?

B. Questions related to the possible transition from FBS to an equity market-led system (EMS)

1. The World Bank (1998) states: 'The main lesson from the South East Asian crisis is that it is important to take an integrated approach to the issues of corporate governance and financing.' Will transition to an EMS under the existing conditions lead to this type of integrated approach and consequent 'market disciplining' of corporate governance?

2. In particular, given the ownership concentration in business groups and control by a few families, how can credible reform be carried out rapidly?

3. Claessens, Djankov, Fan and Lang (1998) have shown that interlocking structures of share ownership and pyramidal share ownership lead to greater effective block ownership and control in East Asian firms. How can this be changed?[16]

4. Given the thinness of bond markets, what is the realistic time-frame in order for the countries of the region to be able to develop such markets with diverse type of bonds and sufficient market depth?[17]

5. What kind of regulatory reforms are necessary for reducing the agency costs and protecting the minority shareholders (and creating 'shareholder value' in general) in an 'institutionally-feasible' EMS structure of governance in East Asia?

6. Will increasing foreign presence in the equity market – especially the institutional investors – improve market discipline? Are there conditions such as 'bailing in' that may be important here? (Simply abolishing some laws, such as Thailand's Alien Business Law, may not be enough.)

7. a. How helpful will the inclusion of outside directors (now being tried in South Korea, perhaps following the Cadbury and Hampel reports in the UK) be in improving governance of the financial sectors and in turn the monitoring of the non-financial firms?

   b. How will it improve the governance and performance of non-financial firms directly?

8. Are the Takeover Codes adequate? If not (most likely they are not adequate) then how can these be improved? How long will it take?

9. a. How long will it take to review Securities Law adequately and to suggest real changes (not just a hasty, window-dressing job)?
   b. How long will it take to clarify and enforce ownership rights in equity markets and creditor rights in the bond market?
10. How to ensure that creditor rights are protected and management is appropriately disciplined in case of failure?
11. How can bank shareholders be forced to bear the risk of bank failure and be encouraged to monitor the banks?
12. Are proposals such as the one put forward by SET in Thailand for self-governance and monitoring put forth in 1997 credible? Can we compare with the Chilean reforms in corporate governance to get some clarity? How to evaluate the role of proposed rules (by outside experts) such as supermajority?
13. How can we carry out reforms such as de-leveraging through divestiture or sale of assets, streamlining of business units, operational restructuring and new equity infusion efficiency?
14. Will reviewing the process of appointment of commissioners to the SEC and similar administrative reforms help? How to make these credible and feasible?
15. Some institutional aspects (such as the slow speed of foreclosure as a result of slow court procedures and the lack of registries in Thailand) make rapid reform difficult. How to speed up the pace of desirable reforms, esp. in areas such as bankruptcy procedures, DIP type of arrangements etc.?

Overall questions

1. Ultimately, given the current political and economic situation and the existing institutional structures in the affected countries, what system of corporate governance will be the most efficient? Will the firm become a stakeholder firm (with managers, employees and shareholders all playing a role) or an Anglo-Saxon-style firm? Or will some kind of hybrid governance structure be the best?
2. Once we determine the answer to the above question, what specific policy measures will strategically be the most significant in helping the financial system navigate its way towards the optimal system?

APPENDIX 6.6:   SOME THEORETICAL ISSUES: INCOMPLETE CONTRACTS AND TRANSACTIONS COSTS

While during the last two decades the term corporate governance – often associated with phenomena such as takeovers, financial restructuring and institutional investors' activism – has entered the business and economics vocabulary, it is curious to note that the standard classical textbook theory of the firm has no place for the term. This is because in this theory the firm is an entity that maximizes profit (by duality theorem, minimizes costs) subject to technological constraints given by the production function. The firm itself is really a 'black box' that connects inputs to outputs efficiently. No assumptions are made with regards to the ownership of the firm beyond that of a general private ownership economy (Debreu, 1959). Therefore, possible conflicts between ownership and management identified by Berle and Means (1932) do not arise. Furthermore, under competitive conditions there is no economic rent to be divided among various parties ex post. Therefore, the issue of governance system – defined by Williamson (1985) as the set of constraints shaping the ex post bargaining over the quasi-rents generated in an enterprise – also does not arise.

Do things change if the firm is defined in a more realistic manner? Curiously, in a perfectly functioning contractual capitalism the answer is also no. Consider the definition of firm as a nexus of contracts. This is certainly a move towards greater realism. So the definition looks quite plausible, especially in the way that Alchian and Demsetz (1972) develop it. Yet, if all contracts could be specified completely then there would be nothing unique left to the concept of corporate governance. A complex set of contracts, written ex ante, would specify how to deal with every contingency, including the distribution of quasi-rents.

Faced with this difficulty some economists have defined the firm as a collection of physical assets that are jointly owned. This definition, introduced by Grossman and Hart (1986) and Hart and Moore (1988, 1998), starts from the position that not all contingencies can be covered by the initial set of contracts. Therefore, some way has to be found to confer rights of making decisions under exactly those contingencies that are unspecified in the initial contract as these contingencies are realized later. Therefore, ownership may matter precisely because it legally entitles the owners to make such decisions. Owners are thus the residual rights holders (hence the approach has been also called the property rights view of the firm) and can appropriate the quasi-rents. It leads to a non-trivial definition of corporate governance, since the non-contractual element (i.e. the allocation of ownership) differentiates corporate governance from contractual governance, which cannot be done within the complete contracts framework. Only in a world where contracts are incomplete – perhaps because some of them are contingent on future observable variables and either costly or impossible to write in advance – can there be some scope for governance ex post. In the world of incomplete contracts there are quasi-rents that must be divided ex post. This will involve real decisions to be made in the future. This contrasts sharply with the Arrow–Debreu world where all decisions (production, consumption and distribution) are made ex ante and no contracts can be renegotiated.

Notice that in the Arrow–Debreu context a very relevant real world question such as 'in whose interest should the corporate directors act?' cannot even be asked. The initial grand contract specifies completely how the board of directors should act under all contingencies. In the real world, as shown dramatically by the Asian crisis, this question has to be asked all the time. This makes the incomplete contracts and other related theoretical approaches relevant and appealing. In the Grossman–Hart–Moore view the residual rights of control are crucial because they allow ex post bargaining that can affect efficiency as well.

There are three principal ways in which corporate governance systems can affect efficiency. These can be called:

1. Ex ante incentive effects
2. Bargaining efficiency effects
3. Risk aversion aspects

Ex ante incentive effects

A classic example in business history discussed by Chandler and others is the Fisher Body case. In the 1920s this auto body manufacturer was asked by GM to locate its plants in close proximity to GM plants. The cost saving from lowered transportation costs and on-time delivery was quite obvious. However, locating close to GM would have meant that Fisher Body could not supply the other car manufacturers quite as easily and hence would have been in danger of becoming a 'captive' of GM. Possibly, its weakened bargaining power under these circumstances would have led to a lower share of quasi-rents generated by its relationship with GM (Klein et al., 1978). The dilemma was ultimately resolved when GM acquired Fisher Body. This acquisition, which changed the governance structure, led to more efficient plant location. Without a proper governance system, individually rational agents will not devote the right amount of resources to value-enhancing activities because they will not see their efforts as being properly rewarded. The phenomenon of managerial shirking can also be explained the same way.

Even more important perhaps is the fact that under an inappropriate governance system, rational agents will utilize resources in wasteful activities. Shleifer and Vishny (1989) point out that a manager may inefficiently force the firm to specialize in activities that he is best at running because this will increase his share of ex post rents. Milgrom (1988) draws attention to the fact that even subordinates without decision-making power will waste resources trying to curry favours with their superiors. Empire building by managers and their subordinates can at least partly be explained this way. Chandler's (1977) description of capital allocation under Durand at GM as 'a sort of horse trading' hints at this kind of problem. The move to the M-form, or multidivisional, structure increased the responsibility and autonomy of the divisional managers. Their pay-offs from inefficient rent-seeking were reduced considerably.

Milgrom and Roberts (1990) discuss the presence of 'influence costs' in many complex organizations. Organizational governance rules must be devised to minimize these influence costs. In a similar way Rajan and Zingales (1996, 1998) discuss the problems of inefficient 'power-seeking'. They argue that the more a firm's divisions have diverse investment opportunities, the more severe is the problem of 'inefficient power-seeking'. Not surprisingly, one of their findings is that the value of a diversified firm is negatively correlated with the diversity of the investment profile of its divisions. This type of analysis may be directly relevant to an understanding of the East Asian conglomerates.

Bargaining efficiency effects

Here we need to consider the problems of free-riding and of coordination costs, problems of information asymmetry between the different parties and liquidity constraints.

Consider a large and dispersed set of owners. Free-rider problems and the resulting failure to arrive at a collective decision may leave the managers free to appropriate the rent giving rise to 'agency and free cash flow problem' (Jensen and Meckling, 1976; Grossman and Hart, 1986). One can also think of allocations of control rights under which no compensating transfers à la Coase theorem can be made because one of the parties is facing a liquidity constraint (Aghion and Bolton, 1992). Rajan and Zingales (1996) also consider the possibility when there is no binding liquidity constraint but some agents have the alternative opportunity to invest in power-seeking activities. It is, therefore, quite possible that unless the governance structure generates the right incentives ex post bargaining could be inefficient. I will show later that this is a real possibility in the prevalent form of corporate governance in East Asia, under some circumstances.

Risk aversion aspects

A governance system may affect both the level and allocation of risk in the economy. Any contract (for example, an insurance contract) written in nominal terms generates some risk with respect to the future rate of inflation. If diversification of the portfolio is impossible the expected value of surplus generated by the contractual arrangements will decrease.

Fama and Jensen (1983a, b) offer an interesting perspective on the generation and allocation of risk under different forms of organizational arrangements and corporate governance. According to their analysis, the efficiency of a governance system can be measured by how well it allocates risk to the party most willing to bear the risk.

The upshot of the above discussion is that a corporate governance system could be judged to be efficient from several points of view. Optimally, in order to enhance the total value creation by the corporate organizational form, the governance structure must create incentives for maximizing productive investments. Incidentally, this will also involve minimizing inefficient power seeking, and inefficiency in ex post bargaining. A good governance system should also generate a minimal amount of risk and allocate this to those parties that are most willing and able to bear it.

The incomplete contracts framework of corporate governance is illuminating in underlining the value of governance. However, strictly speaking it applies only to entrepreneurial firms that are governed through shareholder activism. In order to understand the role of alternative governance structures we need to turn to alternatives that build on the insights of the incomplete contracts approach. In particular, relationship-based forms of corporate governance need to be understood in the context of their being embedded in a larger non-contractual institutional matrix of social relations. To concretize matters we need here an expanded typology and conceptual framework. The idea of a family-based corporate governance system in the East Asian context discussed in section 3 of this chapter is a preliminary step in this direction. In order to proceed more logically in this direction, however, some further distinctions must be made to begin with the difference between reforming exclusively the rules of corporate governance in a formal way and actually changing the institutional arrangements in practice must be recognized. In particular, the critical role of transactions costs in effecting institutional changes must be understood clearly.

A transactions cost perspective

It is important to realize fully the strategic nature of the transactions costs during the transition period. As Williamson (1995) has pointed out, the choice during the transition period is not between two sets of idealized institutions, but rather between an existing set and different strategies to change the systems to a better one. Khan and Lippit (1993a, b) also emphasized the role of uncertainty and bounded rationality of agents in defining any kind of after reform steady-state institutional set up.[18]

As the text points out (section 4), the enabling environment of either a transparent and effective legal system or a workable relationship between the government and business is necessary in order for corporations to perform efficiently. When legal institutions are not well developed transaction costs involved in dealing with market situations are high. It may be necessary to have relatively large family groups with their particular modus operandi in order to function in this environment. For example, through their intra-group network and their relationships with the government bureaucracy the family groups may be able to economize on transaction costs.

A similar argument applies with respect to the 'diversification discount' issue. In the literature on diversification in the developed economies the empirical findings show that on average a loss of value of about 5 per cent is recorded by companies that diversify beyond two segments. This loss, which has been called the 'diversification discount', is attributable to the loss of efficiency when a firm goes beyond its core competencies. However, in the Asian context, at an earlier stage of development transactions costs may be minimized by internalization through diversification. In other words the boundary between the firm and the market are extended from the firm which grows 'inclusively' by acquiring other firms.

Beyond this specific hypothesis, theoretically, transactions costs economics (TCE) regards transaction as the basic unit of analysis (Williamson, 1988). The incomplete contracts approach discussed earlier, and agency theory (AT) in general, takes the individual agent as 'the elementary unit of analysis'. Both offer micro-foundations of economic behaviour; however, TCE 'leads naturally to an examination of the principal dimensions with respect to which transactions differ' (Williamson, 1988, p. 571). This is crucial in analysing institutions with different enabling (or disabling) environments. Thus adaptation (or maladaptation) to a specific environment becomes a key institutional issue, as does governance with respect to specific structure of firms, their asset specificities, and the interrelation of the various stakeholders. All of these must be thought of in the real world policy context of concrete institutional analysis and the various transactions costs.[19] Given the costs of failed (or even successful) reforms it is important to pay attention to these costs. As Williamson (1995, p. 194) reminds us:

> All over the world, we're launching projects that have great potential for doing irreversible *economic* and *political* damage... We can't afford the experiment of developing five countries in five different ways and seeing which four countries get ruined. Instead, it will cost us much less in the long run if we hire *institutional economists* to find out what happened the last time.

7
Asian Banks: Can They Learn to Assess Risks Better? (with C.-S. Lin)

Hamlet: *What a piece of work is a man! how noble in reason! how infinite in faculties!* (*Hamlet*, II.2.319)

Puck: *Lord, what fools these mortals be!*
(*Midsummer Night's Dream*, III.3.116)

1 Introduction

After the discussion of corporate governance in the previous chapter, it would appear that Asian banking and financial sectors could be the source of further instability if no remedial actions are taken to improve their technical capacities. This is, unfortunately, true – almost a truism. The really important question to be considered is: can something be done to improve the banks' capacity to assess risks? The answer, happily, is yes. In this chapter, I discuss the case of Taiwan, where both central bank guidelines and technical improvements are helping to mitigate risk assessment problems. It has been suggested that the basic problem was lack of competition and openness. Foreign ownership has been suggested as a remedy, and many affected Asian economies, including Thailand and Korea, have implemented it. However, without proper technical capacities for risk evaluation and pricing risks, banks will not be able to carry out their capital allocation roles properly.

According to the above line of thinking we must now consider: can a bank learn to be more rational than it actually is, at any particular time in its historical trajectory? In this chapter, the question is answered affirmatively in the concrete context of banks managing their default risks.[1] The problem in this specific context is how to manage the default risk of commercial loans effectively. This has been one of the key questions posed in recent accounting and finance literature. The question is significant for both academic and practical purposes. Looking at the practical aspects, the evaluation process for commercial loans can be divided roughly into two stages. The first is the screening part before the loan is approved. This can be called 'the credit scoring model'. Each applicant is assigned a credit score after being evaluated according to some prespecified criteria. Whether a case is accepted or not is based on the score received when such criteria are applied. The second stage is the continuous monitoring after the loan has been approved. This can be termed 'the bankruptcy prediction problem'. After the commercial loan has been approved, one of the most important questions for the bank to answer is whether or not the debtor company will go bankrupt. Therefore, a warning system to predict the chances of bankruptcy is needed. These two successive stages raise prediction questions that can be viewed as problems of dichotomous choices: either accepting or rejecting a loan application; and, if it is accepted, then further continuing or stopping the commercial loan. This chapter focuses on the screening of the new commercial loan applicants as a specific context for learning to be (more) rational. This naturally leads to a focus on the problem of the predictability of the default loan before the loan is approved.

In section 2 below, I review the past literature related to the credit scoring model in the context of recursive learning in an imprecise environment. Section 3 describes the existing screening process in Taiwan's commercial banks, and shows how a neuro fuzzy model can be constructed for enhancing learning to be (relatively more) rational. In terms of the central theoretical question (namely, can banks learn to be rational?), the answer lies precisely in the ability to construct an appropriate knowledge base, and learning in a recursive way to predict the default loans better than other competing models of predicting default loans. The relative success in constructing and using the knowledge base in an imprecise, fuzzy world shows that our economic rationality is both bounded and capable of expansion. This is consistent with a realist epistemology, and lends support for economic learning under a realist ontology[2] of firms and their environments. The empirical results are shown in section 4. Finally, the chapter ends with a summary and the implications of the research efforts in section 5.

2 Some received views: a critical review

The past literature related to commercial loans can be classified according to the tools of analysis that are used. Some researchers use discriminant functions and logit type regression to construct the predictive model by using the financial ratios (Zavgren, 1985; Blum, 1974; Collins and Green, 1982; Dietrich and Kaplan, 1982; West, 1985; Srinivasan and Kim, 1987). The problem is that the relationship among the variables can be more complicated than the postulated simple linear relationship.

Some researchers have proposed the expert system in order to construct the predictive model (Chorafas, 1987; Duchessi, Shawky, and Seagle, 1988; Romaniuk and Hall, 1992; Yang et al., 2001). However, the knowledge base of the expert system is hard to derive. Some researchers have used neural networks to model the bankruptcy prediction problem (Quinlan, 1993; Altman, Marco, and Varetto, 1994; Boritz and Kennedy, 1995; Boritz, Kennedy, and Albuquerque, 1995; Atiya, 2001; Coats and Fant, 1993; Lenard, Alam, and Madey, 1995; Lacher et al., 1995; Sharda and Wilson, 1996; Tam and Kiang, 1992; Wilson and Sharda, 1994; Yang, 1999). While empirical studies show that neural networks produce better results for many classification or prediction problems, they are not always uniformly superior (Quinlan, 1993; Altman, Marco, and Varetto, 1994; Boritz and Kennedy, 1995; Boritz, Kennedy, and Albuquerque, 1995). Besides, the mapping process is too complicated to explain the relationships among the variables. It could only be seen as a black box. The learning processes need to be specified better in line with the recent advances in cognitive psychology, artificial intelligence and related fields.[3]

Furthermore, a sharp classification or unnatural approximating values during the evaluating process may result in unreasonable or incorrect outcomes. In other words, replacing an inherently fuzzy classification and measurement system with a non-fuzzy one actually leads to a loss of predictive precision. Given the inherent fuzziness in credit rating for commercial loans, the fuzzy approach is, therefore, a more reliable technique than the apparently more precise non-fuzzy ones. This line of thinking has led some researchers to develop a more reasonable credit-rating procedure through the use of fuzzy techniques. Zimmermann and Zysno (1983) used fuzzy operators to aggregate evaluation results from a four-level hierarchy of criteria. Levy et al. (1991) developed a computer-based system to evaluate a company's financial position based on fuzzy logic in determining whether to grant or deny the loan application. Furthermore, several studies (see, for example, Sugeno, Nishiwaki, Kawai, and Harima, 1986; Tahani and Keller, 1990; De Neyer, Gorez, and Barreto, 1993; Leszczynski, Penczek, and Grochulskki, 1985; Chen and Chiou, 1999) employ the fuzzy integral as a tool of information fusion to aggregate the credit information of loan applicants.

In addition to the literature related to the different techniques used, Edmister (1988) argued that numerical financial ratios and human credit analysis could be combined to produce more accurate evaluation results. Neglecting the information provided by these qualitative factors may result in undesirable consequences. Marais, Patell, and Wolfson

(1984) suggest that market information such as commercial paper ratings or stock price variability can be an effective substitute for extensive financial statement analysis.

In sum, it is possible to draw the following critical conclusions based on the above literature review.

1. The discriminant function and the logistic regression mainly deal with the linear relationships among the independent and dependent variables. If the true relationships among the variables are nonlinear, then these two methods are not appropriate.
2. The discriminant function and the logit type regression ignore the interaction between the variables in general. Therefore, a more detailed modelling of the relationship – particularly, the reasoning relationships – among the variables cannot be obtained through these two traditional statistical tools.
3. The expert system is a good approach to construct a warning system. However, it is, in practice, very difficult to get the correct 'knowledge base', and decide the relative importance of each rule. Even the expert cannot tell the relative importance of each rule.
4. Neural network is a good tool to get the mapping function between the independent and dependent variables. However, it is not sufficient by itself to explain the causal relationship among the variables. Further causal specification and testing are necessary conditions for a deeper non-Humean causal analysis.
5. In addition to the financial ratios, some qualitative variables such as the general management and some other perspectives and characteristics of the company are also helpful in evaluating each case. A tool capable of dealing with the qualitative variables and their interrelations is needed.

In order to solve the problems outlined above, I propose the use of neuro fuzzy technique combined with a fuzzy set theoretic approach. At the same time, I offer a somewhat novel interpretation of learning (in a neuro fuzzy setting) to be (more) rational in a world where rationality is bounded, but can also be improved through learning. The qualitative variables in the real world can be dealt with through the membership function of fuzzy logic. The functionality of fuzzy logic can be used to describe the vague[4] ordinary language definitions and relationships among the variables. The learning ability of the neural network can be used to adjust the relative importance of each decision rule. Finally, the knowledge base obtained from this technique can be used as a diagnostic system to see the heuristic reasoning process behind the screening result. This advances the project of understanding how banks can be conceptualized as members of an economic species in a competitive market setting with capacity to learn – but banks do not learn at the same time nor do they learn at an equal rate.

The concrete purpose of this chapter is to propose a screening model for commercial loans as an illustrative example of the more 'general learning to be rational' class of models and theories. The model presented here cannot only predict the default loan successfully, but it can also explain at least partially how the decision is made. The model can be used by bank regulatory agencies for loan examination and by bank loan officers for loan review after some practical modifications.

3 Methodology

3.1 The credit-rating system

Bank loan officers need to evaluate the loan risk before approving a particular loan. Presumably, this evaluation should be based on some relevant criteria. In Taiwan, the evaluation process is based on the 'Credit-Rating Table for Commercial Loan' compiled by Taiwan Bank in 1987. The evaluation items in this model consist of three main categories: financial conditions, general management, and character and perspective. Basically, the criteria listed under 'financial conditions' can be measured quantitatively. However, the other two categories are evaluated according to the loan officers' subjective judgements.

Each category contains several indicators. Each of these indicators in turn contains some evaluation criteria with various points based on the different satisfaction levels of these criteria. The basic structure of the evaluation variables is listed in Table 7.1.

The scores of quick ratio (FC11) and current ratio (FC12) add up to the liquidity ratios (FC1). Similarly the sum of the debt ratio (FC21) and the long-term asset efficiency ratio (FC22) give the financial structure ratios (FC2). Finally, liquidity ratios (FC1), financial structure ratios (FC2), profitability ratios (FC3), and efficiency ratios (FC4) add up to the financial conditions (FC).[5] For each company, the total score for the financial condition (FC), general management (GM), and characters and perspectives (CP) can be obtained by simply adding up all the scores.

Loan officers perform a credit-rating process, using quantitative methods to examine a company's financial position based on the previously determined evaluation criteria in assessing a company's credit level in

Table 7.1 Explanatory variables

Financial conditions (FC):
  Liquidity ratios (FC1):
    quick ratio (FC11)
    current ratio (FC12)
  Financial structure ratios (FC2)
    debt ratio (FC21)
    long-term asset efficiency ratio (FC22)
  Profitability ratios (FC3)
    net sales ratio (FC31)
    profit margin before tax (FC32)
    return on net worth before tax (FC33)
  Efficiency ratios (FC4)
    inventory turnover (FC41)
    receivables turnover (FC42)
    total assets turnover (FC43)
General management (GM)
  administrator's personal credit (GM1)
  administrator's management experiences (GM2)
  stockholders' structure type (GM3)
  average sale growth rate during the last three years (GM4)
  conditions of capital increment during the last three years (GM5)
  outstanding check records in banks (GM6)
Characters and perspectives (CP)
  equipment and technologies (CP1)
  product marketability (CP2)
  collateral (CP3)
  economic conditions of the industry in the next year (CP4)

---

toto. The problem is how to make the decision based on these three scores both more scientific and more effective. A neuro fuzzy (NF) approach is proposed in order to model the decision process. The NF approach is then compared with discriminant analysis and logit type regression. In the next two sections, a fuzzy logic system and then a neuro fuzzy model will be introduced.

3.2 Fuzzy logic system

Fuzzy logic deals primarily with the extent to which an object belongs to a (fuzzy) set. Usually the functional $\mu_A(x)$ is used to denote the extent to which object x belongs to fuzzy set A. A fuzzy logic system is constructed syntactically by introducing the logical relation of implication or the 'IF–THEN' rules to describe the relationship among independent and dependent variables. There are two main families of logical inferences covered under the names *modus ponens* and *modus tollens* in classical logic. In terms of modern logic the two forms can be described as follows:

If p and q are two *well-formed formulas (wff)* connected by the logical connective 'if...then', as 'if p then q', then *modus ponens* is simply the form of argument: p, therefore q. *Modus tollens* is: not q, therefore not p. In fuzzy logic, p and q can refer to 'vague' linguistic terms in a precise, *possibilistic* way.[6] The only difference between fuzzy logic and the traditional expert system is that the variables used in fuzzy logic are linguistic terms rather than numeric values as in the traditional expert system. Let FC, GM, CP and SCORE denote, respectively, the financial conditions, general management, character and perspectives, and the credit score of an applicant. A typical rule in a traditional expert system, for example, is stated as follows:

$$\text{If } FC > 30, \; GM > 20, \text{ and } CP > 16, \text{ then SCORE is } 10. \qquad (1)$$

A fuzzy logic rule is stated instead as follows:

If FC is **high**, GM is **low**, and CP is **high**, then SCORE is **medium**. (2)

where FC, GM, CP, and SCORE are called *linguistic variables* and high, medium, and low are called *linguistic terms*. Basically there are three main steps in building a fuzzy logic system: fuzzification, construction of the knowledge base, and defuzzification.

3.2.1 Fuzzification

Fuzzy logic uses linguistic terms to describe the characteristics of an object. For example, we use low, medium, and high to describe the extent of financial condition (FC), general management (GM), and character and perspective (CP) of an applicant. Each linguistic term is defined by a membership function. Figures 7.1a, 7.1b, 7.1c, and 7.1d are the membership functions for FC, GM, CP, and SCORE respectively. If the measurements of an applicant are $\{FC, GM, CP\} = \{30, 20, 16\}$, for example, then the corresponding values of each term can be seen from Figures 7.1a, 7.1b, and 7.1c as follows.

$$\text{FC: } \mu_{low}\,(30) = 0; \mu_{medium}\,(30) = 0.5; \mu_{high}\,(30) = 0.5$$

$$\text{GM: } \mu_{low}\,(20) = 0.28; \mu_{medium}\,(20) = 0.72; \mu_{high}\,(20) = 0$$

$$\text{CP: } \mu_{low}\,(16) = 0; \mu_{medium}\,(16) = 0.32; \mu_{high}\,(16) = 0.68$$

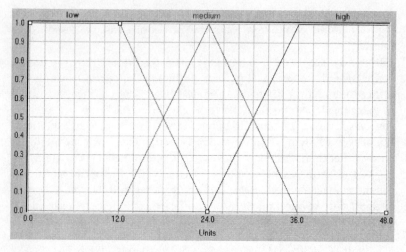

Figure 7.1a Membership function for linguistic variable FC

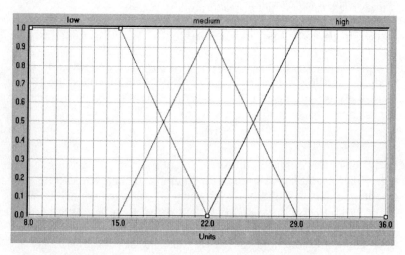

Figure 7.1b Membership function for linguistic variable GM

In other words, the corresponding values can be written as follows.

FC : {low, medium, high} = {0.00, 0.50, 0.50}.

GM : {low, medium, high} = {0.28, 0.72, 0.00}.

CP : {low, medium, high} = {0.00, 0.32, 0.68}.

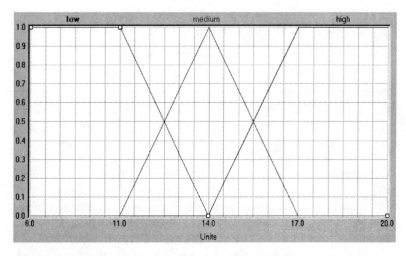

Figure 7.1c Membership function for linguistic variable CP

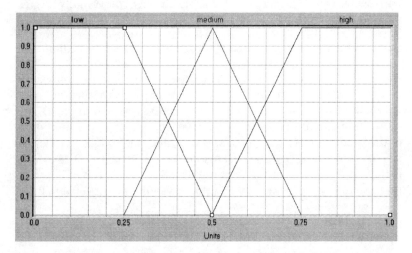

Figure 7.1d Membership function for linguistic variable credit score

An applicant with FC equal to 30 has membership function values for low, medium, and high equal to 0.00, 0.50, and 0.50 respectively. Since each linguistic variable after mapping can have different membership function values for different linguistic terms, it breaks the traditional binary logic that a case can only belong to or not belong to a category. This process is what we call *fuzzification*. The most commonly used membership functions are linear and spline functions.[7] Table 7.2 lists all the linguistic variables, their linguistic terms, and the variable types used in this chapter.

3.2.2 *Towards a model of bounded, but expanding rationality: the construction of the knowledge base*

The knowledge base is constructed by the 'IF–THEN' rules. Each rule has two parts, 'IF' and 'THEN' parts. The 'IF' part measures the extent to which the object satisfies the logical antecedent condition, the 'THEN' part is the response of the system. Of course, in the implication relation of any symbolic or mathematical logical system, say that of a first order predicate calculus, the 'THEN' part is the 'consequent'. It is supposed to logically follow from the sufficient logical conditions subsumed under the antecedent. Empirically, and in fuzzy logic the validity degree of the response depends on the satisfaction extent of the 'IF' part. Thus, in terms of symbolic logic, under fuzzification the sharp or strict sufficiency of the antecedent in a well-formed formula (wff) is lost, but partial consequences are still deducible through the validity degree relation. Take equation (2) for example,

IF FC is high, GM is low, and CP is high, then SCORE is medium, (2)

the validity degree of the then part depends on the *minimum* extent of each linguistic term in the if part according to the definition of Zimmerman and Thole (1978). In other words, $\mu_{A \cap B} = \min\{\mu_A; \mu_B\}$ The satisfaction extent of the 'IF' part of the above rule is the minimum of the validity of 'FC is high', 'GM is low', and 'CP is high'. That is the validity extent of 'IF' part is equal to min $\{0.50, 0.28, 0.68\} = 0.28$, which is the validity extent of the response. In other words, the response of this system is 'the SCORE is medium' with validity extent equal to 0.28.

Table 7.2 Linguistic variables, linguistic terms, and variable types

Linguistic variable	Linguistic terms	Type
FC	Low, medium, high	Input
GM	Low, medium, high	Input
CP	Low, medium, high	Input
SCORE	Low, medium, high	Output

3.2.3 Defuzzification

After fuzzification and inference procedure, each applicant will have a corresponding value for each linguistic term of the output variable. For example, the corresponding value of the linguistic term 'the SCORE is medium' is 0.28 for equation (2) for the above example. Assume that the corresponding values for the other linguistic terms are 'SCORE is low' is 0.1, and 'SCORE is high' is 0.2. The procedure to transform these linguistic values into the numeric output is called defuzzification. Basically it consists of two main steps. The first step is to find out the representative value for each linguistic term. Usually it is the value with membership function equal to 1. The second step is to summarize these linguistic outputs. For the second step, we do the weighted sum of the representative values and its corresponding extent values. For example, assume the representative values for each linguistic term of the output variable is {0.25,0.5,0.75} as depicted in Figure 7.1d, then with the corresponding validity extent of each linguistic term {0.10,0.28,0.20}, the final output value is equal to $0.10^*(0.25) + 0.28^*(0.5) + 0.20^q st(0.75) = 0.315$. In other words, the final credit score for this case is 0.315. This defuzzification method is called the method of gravity, which is one of the most commonly used defuzzification methods.[8]

Although fuzzy logic has been applied to many fields successfully, there are still two main shortcomings associated with this method. The first is how to decide the membership function for each linguistic term. The second is how to decide the relative importance of each rule. Therefore, some effective approach is needed to improve this method. One of the possible ways is to use the learning ability of the neural network to carry out the modification of the membership function and determine the relative importance of each rule. The technique to combine the knowledge base of fuzzy logic and the learning ability of neural network is called the neuro fuzzy technique.

3.3 Neuro fuzzy technique

In essence, the neuro fuzzy technique (from here on simply neuro fuzzy) is a fuzzy logic system with the learning ability of the neural network to modify its parameters, including the parameters of the membership function and the relative importance of each rule. There are different ways to combine these two techniques (Buckley and Hayashi, 1994; Nauck and Kruse, 1996; Lin and Lee, 1996). In practice, these methods turn out to be fairly similar. This chapter adopts the fuzzy associative memory (FAM) proposed by Kosko (1992). In this model, each rule is viewed as a neuron, and the weight of each rule is represented as the weight of each edge in the neural network. For each data point there is a predicted value generated by the system associated with a realized value. The training process will continue until the error between the predicted value and realized value is less than a certain threshold value.

The general neural network model used is:

$$\text{Output } Trend_{t+1} = F_2(w_2 F_1(w_1 x))$$

where F_1 and F_2 are the transfer functions for hidden node and output node, respectively. The most popular choice for F_1 and F_2 are the sigmoid function, $F(x) = 1/(1 + e^{-\alpha x})$, representing the activation function adopted in the calculation process, w_1 and w_2 are the matrices of linking weights from input to hidden layer and from hidden to output layer, respectively, x is the vector of input variables.

3.4   Research model

Based on the scores derived from the table compiled by Taiwan Bank, the research model of neuro fuzzy techniques is depicted as Figure 7.2. In addition to the FC, the qualitative variables, GM and CP, are included in the evaluation process. We use the fuzzy logic to construct the knowledge base to describe the relationship among the independent and dependent variables. The crucial step here is to fine-tune the knowledge base through the learning ability of the neural network based on the training data set. Finally we use the testing data set to validate the obtained model.

Since discriminant function and logistic analysis are now well documented, for example, see Pindyck and Rubinfeld (1998) and Sharma (1996), a detailed description will not be given here.

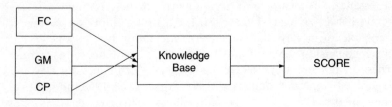

Figure 7.2   Research model

4 Empirical results

4.1 Data sample

This data set comes from one of the commercial banks in Taiwan. From a list of all of the borrowers who were still in contract with this bank on 30 September 2000, we select out all borrowers who have defaulted on their loan at some point. 'Default' is defined as those borrowers who failed to pay the interest within one week of the due date. There are a total of 76 such cases. In addition, we randomly choose other 195 normal counterparts.

The data set is divided into two parts – the training data set for model construction and the testing data set for validity testing of the model. Three different combinations of normal cases and default cases are formed for the training data set. Table 7.3 lists the composition of each sample for the training data set and the testing data set. For sample 1, the proportion of normal cases to default cases is 1:1. There are 50 normal cases and default cases for the training data set, and 145 normal cases and 26 default cases for the testing data set for sample 1. Sample 3 has 150 normal cases and 50 default cases for the training data set and 45 normal cases and 26 default cases for the testing data set.

4.2 Empirical results

Instead of setting the credit score as the dependent variable, we set the probability of default as the dependent variable. The value of the dependent variable is set to 1 for default cases and 0 for normal cases. The predicted value represents the probability that the case will be a default case. The higher the value predicted, the more probable it is that the event 'loan default' will happen. In this chapter, three different criteria are tested to decide the threshold values to determine whether a case is normal or not. These are: maximizing the total classification accuracy;

Table 7.3 The composition of different testing samples

Sample	Training data set		Testing data set		Total
	No. of normal cases	No. of default cases	No. of normal cases	No. of default cases	No. of cases
Sample 1 (1:1)	50	50	145	26	271
Sample 2 (2:1)	100	50	95	26	271
Sample 3 (3:1)	150	50	45	26	271

maximizing the testing power; and minimizing the misclassification cost. In the following, MDA, Logit, and NF are used to denote the multivariate discriminant analysis, logit type regression, and neuro fuzzy respectively.

4.2.1   *Maximizing total classification accuracy*

The model maximizing the total classification accuracy for the training data set is used to test the testing data set. The simulation results for the training data set and the testing data set are shown in Tables 7.4 and 7.5 respectively. The values in Tables 7.4 and 7.5 represent the total classification accuracy of each method for different samples.

It can be seen that NF can reach 99 per cent precision for the training data set for sample 1. Although NF can reach only 70 per cent for sample 1 of the testing data, it is still the best of the three methods considered here.

4.2.2   *Maximizing the testing power*

Maximizing the testing power means detecting the default cases as best as possible. Usually it goes with increasing the probability of misclassifying the normal cases into the default cases while decreasing the threshold value to increase the testing power. Tables 7.6 and 7.7 show the simulation results based on the criterion to maximize the testing power.

The values in Tables 7.6 and 7.7 represent the testing power of each method for different samples. It can be seen that NF can always detect the default cases for the training data set, as depicted in Table 7.6. For the testing data set, NF can also detect all the default cases for sample 1 and sample 2 as shown in Table 7.7. Still NF is the best of these three methods in terms of testing power.

4.2.3   *Minimizing the misclassification cost*

Since the misclassification cost is different for classifying a normal case into a default case and classifying a default case into a normal case, it is

Table 7.4   Total classification rate for the training set (%)

	Sample 1	Sample 2	Sample 3
MDA	64	62	61
Logit	63	67	75
NF	99	72	78

Table 7.5   Total classification rate for for the
testing set (%)

	Sample 1	Sample 2	Sample 3
MDA	64	60	62
Logit	64	78	61
NF	70	79	65

Table 7.6   Testing power for the training set
(%)

	Sample 1	Sample 2	Sample 3
MDA	56	58	62
Logit	98	78	28
NF	100	100	100

Table 7.7   Testing power for the testing set

	Sample 1	Sample 2	Sample 3
MDA	50	58	58
Logit	100	73	19
NF	100	100	85

not appropriate to view them as equal. The criteria to maximize the total
classification accuracy or maximize the testing power is not quite appropriate from a practical point of view. What the loan manager cares about
is finding out which decision has the least cost. Assume that the misclassification cost for classifying the normal case into default one is A,
and the misclassification cost for classifying the default case into a
normal one is 30A. The simulation results are listed in Tables 7.8 and
7.9 respectively for the training data set and the testing data set. The
values represent the cost associated with each method for different
samples. It can be seen that NF can find the decision with least cost
among these three methods either for the training data set or for the
testing data set.

4.3   Sensitivity analysis

Since the ratio of the misclassification cost is difficult to determine from
a practical point of view, eight different ratios are tested. Let the

Table 7.8   Total costs for the training set

Ratio	Sample 1	Sample 2	Sample 3
MDA	740A	400A	686A
Logit	82A	414A	1217A
NF	38A	69A	112A

Table 7.9   Total costs for the testing set

	Sample 1	Sample 2	Sample 3
MDA	477A	400A	379A
Logit	141A	278A	702A
NF	113A	198A	103A

misclassification cost for classifying the default case into a normal one be 5A, 10A, 15A, 20A, 30A, 40A, and 50A. The simulation results are listed in Tables 7.10, 7.11, and 7.12 for the training data set. Tables 7.13, 7.14, and 7.15 list the simulation results for the testing data set.

It can be seen that the difference among these three methods can become more obvious as the cost proportion increases. NF is the best one among these three methods except for the testing data with cost proportion 1:5. On the other hand, the performance of MDA and Logit is inconclusive.

Table 7.10   The sensitivity analysis results for the training data set with sample 1

	1:1	1:5	1:10	1:15	1:20	1:30	1:40	1:50
MDA	36A	124A	234A	344A	454A	674A	894A	1114A
Logit	37A	54A	59A	64A	69A	79A	89A	99A
NF	28A	38A	38A	38A	38A	38A	38A	38A

Table 7.11   The sensitivity analysis results for the training data set with sample 2

	1:1	1:5	1:10	1:15	1:20	1:30	1:40	1:50
MDA	57A	141A	246A	351A	456A	666A	876A	1086A
Logit	49A	106A	161A	216A	271A	381A	491A	601A
NF	42A	69A	69A	69A	69A	69A	69A	69A

Table 7.12   The sensitivity analysis results for the training data set with sample 3

	1:1	1:5	1:10	1:15	1:20	1:30	1:40	1:50
MDA	78A	154A	249A	344A	439A	629A	819A	1009A
Logit	50A	209A	389A	569A	749A	1109A	1469A	1829A
NF	45A	112A	112A	112A	112A	112A	112A	112A

Table 7.13   The sensitivity analysis results for the testing data set with sample 1

	1:1	1:5	1:10	1:15	1:20	1:30	1:40	1:50
MDA	61A	113A	178A	243A	308A	438A	568A	698A
Logit	63A	141A	141A	141A	141A	141A	141A	141A
NF	51A	113A	113A	113A	113A	113A	113A	113A

Table 7.14   The sensitivity analysis results for the testing data set with sample 2

	1:1	1:5	1:10	1:15	1:20	1:30	1:40	1:50
MDA	48A	92A	147A	202A	257A	367A	477A	587A
Logit	27A	82A	117A	152A	187A	257A	327A	397A
NF	25A	86A	106A	126A	146A	186A	226A	266A

Table 7.15   The sensitivity analysis results for the testing data set with sample 3

	1:1	1:5	1:10	1:15	1:20	1:30	1:40	1:50
MDA	48A	71A	126A	181A	236A	346A	456A	566A
Logit	28A	114A	219A	324A	429A	639A	849A	1059A
NF	25A	47A	57A	67A	77A	97A	117A	137A

4.4   Discussion

The Logit functions obtained from three different training data sets are as follows.

Sample 1:

$$\text{Ln } (p/1\text{-}p) = 3.0793 + 0.0071 \text{ FC} - 0.0539 \text{ GM} - 0.1497 \text{ CP} \qquad (3)$$

s	1.6689	0.0229	0.0426	0.0920
p-value	0.0650	0.1036	0.2061	0.7565

Sample 2

$$\text{Ln } (p/1\text{-}p) = 2.1980 + 0.0116 \text{ FC} - 0.0436 \text{ GM} - 0.1599 \text{ CP} \qquad (4)$$

s	1.3733	0.0205	0.0378	0.0725
p-value	0.1095	0.5699	0.2483	0.0275

Sample 3
$$\text{Ln}(p/1-p) = 1.3861 + 0.0141 \, FC - 0.0336 \, GM - 0.1506 \, CP \qquad (5)$$
s   1.2321   0.0190   0.0346   0.0672

p-value   0.2606 0.4582   0.3316   0.0251

An applicant is classified as being in default if the probability is greater than the threshold value. Equations 3, 4, and 5 indicate that the higher the value of GM and CP, the less is the probability of the applicant being in default. It is in the same direction as we would have expected. However, the FC factor has a sign that is different from what we expected. The reason can be the window dressing of the financial ratios, which makes this ratio no more effective in predicting the default case.

Fisher's linear classification functions obtained from these three different training data sets are obtained as follows.

Sample 1:
$$\text{SCORE} = -32.650 + 0.217^* FC + 0.847^* GM + 2.817^* CP \text{ (for normal case)}$$
(6)
$$\text{SCORE} = -29.646 + 0.224^* FC + 0.794^* GM + 2.671^* CP \text{ (for default case)}$$
(7)

Sample 2:
$$\text{SCORE} = -32.623 + 0.228^* FC + 0.964^* GM + 2.604^* CP \text{ (for normal case)}$$
(8)
$$\text{SCORE} = -29.687 + 0.239^* FC + 0.921^* GM + 2.443^* CP \text{ (for default case)}$$
(9)

Sample 3:
$$\text{SCORE} = -30.469 + 0.212^* FC + 0.853^* GM + 2.521^* CP \text{ (for normal case)}$$
(10)
$$\text{SCORE} = -27.923 + 0.225^* FC + 0.819^* GM + 2.368^* CP \text{ (for default case)}$$
(11)

A case is classified as default if the value calculated from the default equation is greater than the value calculated from the normal equation. It can be seen from these equations that the effect of variable FC is the least among these three variables in determining the credit score. And CP has the most influence. In other words, FC is the least significant among these three variables in predicting the likelihood of default.

Finally, we can consider the knowledge base obtained from the neuro fuzzy technique. Table 7.16 lists the rules with relative importance (DoS) greater than 0.9.

It can be seen that these rules do make sense. For rule 1, IF CP is low, FC is low, and GM is medium, THEN SCORE is high, which means that the reasoning process follows what we expect. Similarly, for rule 4, IF CP is high, FC is high, and GM is high, THEN SCORE is low, which is also in accordance with our intuition. As for the other situations, the rules can show the interactions among the variables.

Basically, MDA and Logit should perform equally well if the independent variables have multi-normal distribution/density functions and the relationships among the variables are linear. The difference between the Logit and NF implies the existence of the nonlinear relationship among the variables. The empirical results show that the NF can really provide the loan manager with the 'true' explanations behind the screening result in addition to the good prediction result in screening the applicants. Three different criteria to decide the threshold values show the robustness of the proposed NF model. Although the different compositions of the training data set will lead to different performance, however, NF still performs the best for different data samples.

5 Chapter summary

This chapter has attempted to advance towards a new conception of rationality by departing from the assumption of neoclassical maximizing behaviour under the usual preference relations. Concretely, I have proposed a screening model for the commercial loan credit rating based on the variables derived from the credit-rating table by using the neuro fuzzy technique, which combines the functionality of fuzzy logic and the learning ability of the neural network. The empirical results show that in addition to the better prediction results than can be obtained

Table 7.16 Knowledge base with relative importance greater than 0.9

No.	IF				THEN
	CP	*FC*	*GM*	*DoS*	*SCORE*
1	Low	Low	Medium	1	High
2	Medium	Medium	Medium	1	Medium
3	Medium	High	High	1	Medium
4	High	High	High	0.91	Low

from discriminant analysis and logit type regressions, the proposed model can also show the complex relationship among the variables through the knowledge base. This model can also be applied to the problem of bankruptcy prediction after some modifications. Ultimately, the hope is to create a more general model of learning embedded in the neuro fuzzy structure that will contain the present model as a special case. Although that goal remains elusive, enough progress has been made in the present context to demonstrate that it is rational to pursue the task of building a general 'learning to be rational model' in a world where rationality is bounded but amenable to gradual improvement under favourable circumstances.

The crucial question now is to what extent the various Asian countries can adopt the Taiwanese model. In Taiwan itself, the quality of information – particularly quantitative financial information – needs to be improved. The technical improvements and the reform of the financial system to make it more transparent and accountable must go hand in hand. The political will to reform and to create and utilize the requisite technical capacities is also necessary. International efforts can help, but the crucial reforms must be endogenous. The domestic political economy must change in such a way that reasonable policy reforms can occur without destabilizing the entire economy. A democratization of economic governance with input from a wide range of people, including academic experts, must become the norm if further progress is to be made.

8
Towards a New Global Financial Architecture

> Political economy has...turned out to be the Idiot Boy of the
> Scientific Family; all the more pitiful, as having been so bright
> at first; put up on a chair to recite by Dr. Adam Smith and
> Mr. Ricardo – and then somehow went wrong.
>
> Stephen Leacock, *The Boy I Left Behind Me*

1 Introduction

One underlying theme of this book has been that the Asian crisis holds
more general lessons than simply pinpointing the specific problems of
those Asian countries that were directly affected. In fact, this crisis
showed how the twenty-first century may become a dangerously
unstable epoch unless a new global financial architecture can be
created in the near future. The task may seem enormous and hopeless.
In a sense, this is rightly so. As long as we are trapped in a mode of
thinking that sees the only choice as being between the status quo
and the prohibitively expensive and politically impossible task of
creating a whole new structure of international and domestic institutions and organizations, this will be so. We need to somehow break
this impasse. In this chapter, I propose that we use a generally valid
evolutionary principle which I have termed the 'extended panda's
thumb'[1] principle to reform the IMF and create some regional institutions to move forward.

Ever since the Asian financial crisis (AFC), there have been criticisms
(and, lately, self-criticisms) of the IMF's response.[2] One consequence of
this has been a large number of proposals calling for the construction of
a new international financial architecture. Of course, this idea is not
new. The world had the discipline of the gold standard at an earlier
point in time. The demise of this finally came in the 1930s, and even
during the Second World War both Keynes from the British side and
White from the US side proposed alternative (but, in some respects,
closely related) plans for a postwar international financial architecture.

The Bretton Woods system that came into being preserved little of Keynes's proposals; but, flawed as it was, it survived for several decades, during which the global economy recovered and prospered. The demise of the Bretton Woods in the 1970s created various types of floating exchange rate mechanisms, and was accompanied by increased capital flows across borders. Then came the crises, particularly the Mexican crisis and finally the AFC, Brazilian, Russian and Argentine crises. It became increasingly difficult to support the old classical adjustment programmes with expenditure-adjusting policies – sometimes also accompanied by expenditure-switching policies. As the new-fangled capital account crises with real and persistent economic effects came to be better recognized for what they were – a new type of financial crisis – the old remedies came into question.

The purpose of this chapter, as already alluded to, is to look at the problem of finding or designing a proper global financial architecture (GFA from here on) from an evolutionary perspective. It is an important institutional issue to discover what type of GFA will be appropriate during the current period and in the foreseeable future. In this chapter, I will discuss the problems of national macroeconomic policies and governance within a framework of overall global and regional financial architectures. Whether state capacities exist for the formulation and implementation of national economic policies may depend in large measure on the kind of global and regional financial architecture in existence. Having adopted the methodological approach of evolutionary economics,[3] the institutions I discuss and the alternatives I propose can be seen as path-dependent evolutionary alternatives. They all also depend on a supporting structure of complementary institutional network (CIN). Global financial architecture (GFA) and regional financial architecture (RFA) both depend on their respective CIN within a global system of nation-states. Given the real interdependence within the system, all actors have some stake in sustained growth and stability with equity. Thus the central substantive argument of this chapter is that sustainable policies at the national level require a supporting network of GFA and RFA. Such national policies in their turn can contribute to the sustainability of the GFA and RFA. It can be shown that, following an evolutionary theory of international financial institutions, two broad types of possible global financial architectures can be identified. In this chapter, the first is called an *overarching type*, exemplified by the classical gold standard and the defunct Bretton Woods system. The second is called a *hybrid form* that allows for the existence and coevolution of some regional financial architectures as well. The changing roles of the

IMF and national economic policies can be examined within these two possible financial architectures under globalization.

Another potentially fruitful aspect of this approach is the adoption of a specific argument that relies on a fascinating evolutionary strategy first discussed popularly by Stephen Jay Gould (1980: ch. 1). This can be called *'the panda's thumb'* argument following the title of Gould's essay. According to Gould, whose argument David (1993) adapts for studying the evolutionary history of intellectual property rights institutions, the panda's 'thumb' is an ingenious trick of nature to utilize whatever anatomical material is available in order to serve further evolutionary ends. Although it functions as a thumb, the celebrated panda's thumb is, in reality, not a thumb at all, but a structure built from the enlargement of a bone that would really have been a part of the panda's wrist. But the panda can make do with this evolutionary contraption quite well. It can strip leaves from the bamboo plants and feed itself. The continued existence of the species shows the evolutionary value of such makeshift devices. As Gould puts it, the panda's thumb is 'a contraption, not a lovely contrivance.'

The same type of ingenuity can be seen to be at work in the evolution of human social institutions. Using this insight, David (1993) has offered a fascinating analysis of the evolution of the intellectual property rights institutions in the West. One of the most striking conclusions of his study is that in this case (and probably in general) we do not see institutions evolve along an optimal path. They are closer to the makeshift nature of the panda's thumb than to a careful solution to optimal design problems – a 'fact' that is usually the product of the economic historian's hindsight.

Implicit in David's analysis is also the idea that human institutions are subject to evolutionary change through various ingenious human manoeuvres. Although he does not discuss this explicitly, it is consistent with this line of thinking to emphasize the role of economic theory in the design of economic institutions. By a slight extension of the original 'panda's thumb' argument we can think of the role of an approximately accurate economic theory in a relevant area of institutional design as an enabling one. Contrariwise, an inaccurate or wrong theory – or worse, a wrong ideology – could lead to ill-fated moves that inflict considerable damage.

Incorporating a cautious role for economic theories and their institutional prescriptions in the history of the path-dependent evolution of institutions can be viewed as an 'extended panda's thumb' argument. This is the methodological approach of the present endeavour. Along with the caveats regarding choosing the inappropriate theory, I want to emphasize the role of uncertainty and the partial nature of our scientific knowledge. Furthermore, rationality is bounded and learning is costly. Therefore, the 'extended panda's thumb' argument places a great emphasis on the comparison and testing of various theoretical alternatives with different institutional and policy implications.

In this chapter, I want to argue that the design of a GFA will in all likelihood have to follow a 'panda's-thumb-like' development. Instead of jettisoning the IMF and other seemingly inefficient regional arrangements, I argue for serious institutional reform under the existing framework. Ironically, in a world of bounded rationality and uncertainty, such an approach will be relatively more efficient than the search for the 'optimal' institution under the assumptions of maximizing agents who face no computational or other costs of learning to be (more) rational.

There is another aspect of this particular extension of the 'panda's thumb' argument that also requires some emphasis. The role of structural unevenness in the global economy is particularly important to recognize within the proposed framework of analysis. The range of economies, the types of polities, the institutional capacities and resource endowments – including technological progress and capacities for innovation – all vary widely. A simple system based around the gold standard or adjustable peg or free and flexible exchange rate together with free multilateral trade under, say, the WTO arrangement may therefore be considered to be simplistic. It may serve the needs of one group of actors – for example, the advanced economies with well-developed financial services sectors – rather better than some others. How best to achieve a synchronized growth and development regime that is perceived to be fair by all is indeed a considerable challenge. The GFA is defined here as a system of global financial arrangements for international payments with specific rules and procedures for the member nations to follow. If there exists a similar institutional arrangement at the supranational but regional level only then I call it an RFA. It will be seen that one attractive solution to the problem of global unevenness is to design a GFA which also includes a number of RFAs as an integral part of the global financial system. It also turns out that such an institutional structure is also an evolutionary possibility if one takes 'the panda's thumb' argument seriously and adds to it an element of imperfect human design in a cooperative framework.

One caveat is warranted before we proceed any further. The 'extended panda's thumb' argument is not a deterministic one. Under any given set of circumstances, there is almost always more than one possible set of reforms guided by different theories. It is also possible to do nothing. All that the 'extended panda's thumb' argument says is: under situations where we cannot immediately develop new institutions, we can be guided by some approximately true economic theories to alter the functionalities of some of the existing institutions and organizations.[4] This may not work for all existing institutions. One cannot make a domestic commercial bank perform the functions that a reformed IMF may have to (and, in principle, can) perform. The necessary theoretical conditions for this 'transformed functionality' are: (i) the scope of the institution must in principle be extensible; and (ii) a mechanism must exist or can be created in order to find the resources and capabilities to carry out the new functions after institutional reform.

2 Financial evolution: debt contracts and equity in global capital markets

It is important to realize that both debt and equity markets are different from ordinary commodity markets. For example, unlike most market transactions, which are usually summarized in terms of prices and quantities, the debt contract is highly complex. The main reason for this is that the contract really is a promise. A debt contract simply entails a promise to repay principal and interest on an advance. The repayment is in the future; hence it is uncertain. Key features of this contract are:

1. quantity advanced;
2. specifying a given/variable rate of interest;
3. specifying when the loan will mature;
4. collateral that the borrower will provide as security for the lender;
5. specifying the conditions that determine if the loan is in default;
6. specifying the law under which the default must be adjudicated;
7. specification of the seniority of claim;
8. pledges in relation to further borrowing;
9. any further commitments by the lender;
10. provisions for transferability;
11. whether or not the contract is standardized in terms of provisions or denominations;
12. relevant tax features, such as tax-exemption features;
13. call provisions for early repayment.

Many of these features can be interpreted as means of overcoming uncertainty, transactions costs, and incomplete contracts. Recent developments in theory of corporate finance illuminate many of these aspects. However, 'globalization' has also internationalized risk, uncertainty and incompleteness. Some of these features are discussed later in this section.

For the moment we can observe that the key difficulty in the economics and the political economy of debt is the uncertainty surrounding the probability of default. Given bankruptcy costs, asymmetric information and incomplete contracts, default is an ever-present but uncertain factor. Using fuzzy set theory and neural network learning models, it can be shown that banks and other lenders can reduce this risk, but they can never eliminate it completely.[5] Much of the problem of domestic and international financial stability originates from this simple observation. But it can also be shown theoretically that despite its complexity, costs of default, lack of risk-sharing, and various market failures related to information problems debt is still the most efficient instrument for many, if not all financial transactions. Thus evolution of institutions of intermediation and a supporting CIN through legal and other institutional evolution makes sense from this perspective. However, because of the complex nature of these institutions, uniform progress towards optimality in an intertemporal sense cannot be guaranteed in advance. Furthermore, marketization in the real world is a complex activity involving both cooperation and conflict.

We owe to the classic work of Karl Polanyi (1944) the realist approach to institutional history. Polanyi shows, through his study of the British and West European capitalism under the gold standard, how the system broke down because of systemic counterpressures. Together with the classical liberal approach to international money, the attempt to commodify labour completely also met with resistance. Polanyi called such resistance and the initial policies of marketization, 'a double movement'. This type of double movement is also occurring – to at least some extent – under the present regime of globalization which, in its extreme forms, also tries to extend marketization globally within a neoliberal framework of optimality of the market system approach. However, both parts of such a double movement, in contrast to the powerful labour movements of the past, are still in their infancy. Even so, substantial instability is manifest in the global financial markets. As resistance to further marketization without regulation grows, the instabilities are likely to spread and result also in political and social instabilities as well. For this reason alone, it may be wise to adopt a new and more pragmatic approach to GFA that can help policy making for greater well-being in the nations of the world. As mentioned before, this will help prevent a third type of crisis: a political and social crisis. The developments in Indonesia during the AFC illustrate how suddenly such crises can break out. The evolutionary theory developed here actually suggests a pragmatic path-dependent institution-building approach to a hybrid GFA. But the process is likely to be quite complex.

It is because of such complexities that the term 'globalization', which is so much in vogue today, has to be used with caution. When viewed historically, it appears that globalization is a contradictory process of international economic integration that was severely interrupted by the First World War, the interwar depression, and the Second World War. The emergence of the Bretton Woods framework can be seen as a way to integrate the world with respect to trade while controlling the flow of private capital. The demise of Bretton Woods has set in motion forces of capital account liberalization that are often the most visible aspects of 'globalization'. However, even this process is fraught with new instabilities as evidenced by the Mexican and – more recently and even more dramatically – by the Asian financial crisis. At the same time integration of trade even within the standard neoclassical Heckscher–Ohlin–Samuelson model would imply a fall in the wages of unskilled workers of the north thus increasing inequality there (Krugman, 1996; Wood, 1994). The south is supposed to experience a more equalizing effect through trade; but there is very little empirical evidence of this. Therefore, it is necessary to treat the rhetoric of globalization with caution. At best, we are experiencing a 'fractured' globalization. Integration of financial markets, for example, can lead to great benefits for all in a truly liberal world of equal actors. However, in a world of unevenness the evolutionary paths may lead to crisis unless institutions are designed properly. Leaving everything to the markets may produce the supreme irony of ultimately leading to crises which prevent some very important capital and commodity markets from functioning.

For all of these reasons, it is best to ask what roles the global capital markets are supposed to perform in a world of free capital mobility. The functions are variously described, but mainly emphasize the global transfer of resources from savers to investors. In addition, the agglomeration of capital, selection of projects, monitoring, contract enforcement, risk-sharing and pooling of risks are also mentioned. All these are legitimate functions of capital markets. However, despite much talk the crucial problem of handling various kinds of risks and the inability of simple free markets with international capital mobility to contain these risks completely or even adequately, are nearly always elided. What are some of the most important categories of these risks?

Exchange rate risk refers to the possibility that a country's currency may experience a precipitous decline in value. This risk is present in any type of exchange rate regime, with full or even partial currency convertibility. Both floating exchange rates and pegging a currency to another single currency – or even a basket of currencies – present such exchange rate risks to various degrees. Complete elimination of this risk is possible only with one world currency, or a completely fixed exchange rate regime. For obvious reasons these are not current evolutionary options.

Capital flight risk refers to the possibility that both domestic and foreign holders of financial assets will sell their holdings whenever there is an expectation of a capital loss. Exchange rate risk is one possible avenue through which such expectations may be formed. As with many types of expectations formation mechanisms, in a world of nonlinearity, bounded rationality and uncertainty, a Keynesian type of short termism[6] takes over. Investors head for the hills simply on the basis of short-term calculations of possible loss, and herd behaviour is a likely outcome. Financial distress follows for the hapless country from which capital thus exits in a hurry. In the extreme situation of large short-term liabilities, the affected economy may land in a full-blown financial, or even economic crisis.

There is thus a systemic risk of financial fragility associated with the above risks. The risk of financial fragility also raises the question of the stability of a country's financial and political institutions. In some cases, an increase in this type of systemic risk raises the possibility of a financial meltdown. In the case of AFC, the risk of financial fragility increased over the 1990s through maturity mismatch of loans. The fact that many of the short-term loans were in foreign currencies without risk-sharing mechanisms such as currency swaps in place, created further exchange rate risk which also increased the potential systemic risk. This is consistent with the view of Knight (1998) who affirms that although globalization has brought about a spectacular increase in the flow of capital to emerging markets, the Asian financial crisis demonstrates that it can also create financial instability and contagion. Under fairly realistic conditions the banking system of emerging economies can respond in ways that intensify the impact of adverse shocks, causing severe macroeconomic repercussions and exacerbating systemic financial and economic fragility.

In this context, one could also mention the *illiquidity risk* faced by holders of long-term bonds as opposed to those who hold cash. This is what Keynes referred to, among other things, when he argued that there is a minimum below which the long-term rate of interest cannot fall. In a fragile financial system this type of risk increases, forcing those who can do so to rush to liquidate their positions. This, too, can result in herd behaviour and a vicious cycle. For business enterprises, with fragility *the insolvency risk* also increases in a causally reciprocal way.

In the case of AFC, we also witnessed another kind of cross-national risk for vulnerable economies that Knight (1998) and others have also recognized – the risk of contagion.[7] Some countries were unnecessarily victimized simply because expectations moved against their economic prospects as their neighbours experienced financial fragility and capital flight. This has important implications for both global and regional financial architecture. Both GFA and RFAs should try to minimize the contagion risk. Contagion can happen even without much financial and trade openness. However, the more integrated with the rest of the world, or even a region, an economy is, the more is the risk of contagion. There is some theoretical support for this last proposition in specific markets that are being globalized. For example, Calvo and Mendoza (1999) argue that the globalization of securities markets can promote contagion among investors by weakening incentives of gathering costly country-specific information because the marginal benefit of gathering information may be decreasing as securities markets become more global in scope.

The key problem which underlies the above risk scenarios, recognized by the practitioners long before theorists started to study it, is that given informational problems and the cost of building enforcing institutions, capital markets are almost always incomplete. Thus classical theorems of welfare economics no longer apply – even within a closed economy. In a world of open economies these problems become more severe, and are directly related to the lack of global institutions of governance. The recognition of this point underlies the various proposals advanced so far. As Eichengreen (1999a) documents, there are already many proposals for GFAs on the table. Even a partial cataloguing will have to include the many national proposals (e.g., US, UK, French and Canadian proposals), private proposals such as Soros' credit insurance agency, Edward's specialized agencies, Bergsten's target zones and so on and other international proposals. Among the international proposals could be included the IMF proposals, G-7 and G-22 proposals. Although they vary in scope and degrees of political realism, they have one common feature. All of them fall into the *overarching type* of GFA category.

Although many of the proposals for GFA are possible theoretical solutions the evolutionary approach looks at path dependence and sequential selection processes as crucial. We need to recognize that the actual evolution of such institutions of financial governance will depend crucially on the coordination among the actors, in particular among some key actors in the global system. This leads us to the consideration of an evolutionary structural theory of GFA and RFAs.

3   Extending the panda's thumb: an evolutionary theory of GFA and RFAs

The 'panda's thumb' argument can be extended to construct a theory of GFAs and RFAs. In order to motivate the discussion we can return to some aspects of AFC. In distinguishing among the countries that managed to survive the AFC and those that did not, John Williamson (1999, 2000), one of the main proponents of the 'Washington consensus', admitted that: 'The one dimension in which there is systematic difference between the two groups is with respect to whether or not they had liberalized their capital accounts.'

All Asian crisis countries had accepted the IMF's Article VIII obligations, as evident from the historical documents. But, as Bhagwati (1998) and others have pointed out, liberalizing trade and liberalizing the financial sector have different policy implications. In line with the discussion in the previous section, theoretically, one should carefully distinguish the welfare impacts of financial market liberalization in an uneven world from such impact in a smooth world of equals with information symmetry. Indeed, next to unevenness, the most critical element is the role and the presence of *asymmetric information*. In a financial market, gathering, selecting, using and providing information are central to its proper functioning, yet it is precisely here that market failures from asymmetric information can arise (Stiglitz, 1994).

But the evolutionary structural theory goes further than simply cataloguing moral hazard and adverse selection problems. On the *explanans* side are also *the asymmetries in the size, structure and capabilities of the economies and polities*. These asymmetries constrain some polities, particularly the economically disadvantaged ones, from developing as quickly as possible in an equitable manner. The recent UNCTAD report on the poorest underdeveloped countries points this out empirically.[8] The theoretical significance of these features of the real world is that no uniform set of rules can work for all of the economies and polities throughout the world. *A fortiori*, it follows that for GFA and RFAs to serve both poor countries and rich countries equally well, special provisions should be put in place.

It may appear that the least developed countries are only a special case. But that is not the case. The NIEs, the European social democracies,

Japan and so on each in its own way is also different. This poses a real theoretical challenge: how can we even attempt to theorize in the face of such diversity? The solution is through a consideration of the basic needs of the system and a consideration of whether these can be satisfied better under arrangements that are different from the IMF and the 'Washington Consensus'.

The work of Barry Eichengreen (1999a), and others[9] show that it is possible to move beyond the post-Bretton Woods situation. In contrast with the conservative Meltzer report, all of these authors emphasize the need to strengthen certain aspects of the IMF. However, not all of them recognize the crucial need also for the RFAs and the role they can play in creating an enabling environment for the state to implement beneficial economic policies. A completely evolutionary theory of GFA recognizes the need for RFAs from both an *evolutionary* and a *structural* perspective. Given the lack of political resolve – a point made forcefully by Eichengreen among others – there is little chance of creating *institutional structures* in the manner of the 1944 Bretton Woods agreement. The recent path of the world economy does not lead to this immediately. At the same time, neither does the recent path lead only to neoliberalism. It is possible both to reform the IMF, as Eichengreen suggests, and simultaneously to create new RFAs to complement such reforms. Thus this theory leads to the question of identifying a spectrum of GFAs. Most important among these are those that combine the GFAs like a reformed IMF with appropriate RFAs.

Formally, the heuristic argument presented above can be established via a careful consideration of *path dependence* during the evolutionary history of the GFA. In order to do this in a conceptually rigorous manner, the concept of *path dependence* itself has to be refined and formalized in a specific way. I have developed this idea elsewhere, and will only sketch the conceptual path to be followed briefly. As Figures 8.1, 8.2 and 8.3 show respectively there can be completely deterministic

Various types of path dependence

Event set at Time Period 0   leads to   event set in Period 1   leads to event

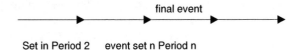

final event

Set in Period 2   event set n Period n

Figure 8.1   CD-type path dependence

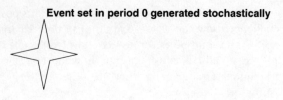

Event set in period 0 generated stochastically

Event set in period n is also generated stochastically

Figure 8.2   CS-type path dependence

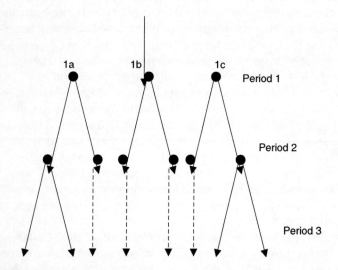

Figure 8.3   PD-type path dependence

(CD), completely stochastic (CS), and partially deterministic (PD) characterizations to path dependence. Eschewing the formal apparatus of graph theory and neural network dynamics which can be used to describe these rigorously, we can simply say that in deterministic path dependence there is only one choice of path. Everything is as it should be, since there are no bifurcations at any point in history. In fact, we can make a stronger statement. At *no* point in history is there even a *possibility* of even a bifurcation. Most people will see this as an extreme and, in the case of human institutional design, perhaps as an unrealistic case.

The purely stochastic case is all *random mutation*. Again, there is no way that conscious choice can play a role here either. Blind chance determines the outcome. The difference between type D path dependence and type CS path dependence is simply that in the former case the future can be predicted with probability 1, but in the latter case, at best a distribution of future states may be known. In some complex way, the conditional probabilities, if known in advance, may determine a stochastic path structure. But the very stochasticity makes the notion of path dependence of limited relevance in this case. We could define a further, *completely uncertain* 'path dependence' where not even a distribution of such states be known. But all three cases discussed so far theoretically foreclose the possibility of conscious choice and at least partial institutional design.

The last type of path dependence, i.e., the PD variety, leaves some room for evolution to be a result of at least some kind of boundedly rational human activities. As shown in Figure 8.3, given an array of possible paths at each point in history, there is some likelihood of being able to choose a particular path. The neural-network-type 'learning from history' modelling approach actually allows the process of (boundedly rational) learning to influence these likelihoods in the future. Thus a complex set of human activities including learning and improving policy making capabilities can influence which network of paths are followed over time. While the number of available paths at any point in history may be large, they are never infinite. Therefore, in most cases combinatorial mathematics will show the existence of the most likely evolutionary outcome. However, the caveat that large, seemingly random fluctuations (e.g., a war) can throw these calculations off is always a (rare) possibility.

Fortunately, barring events such as wars, revolutions, and complete meltdowns of financial systems, there are not at present an unmanageably large number of outcomes that are possible for the GFA. In fact, if we are willing to assume a continuum with nothing but an overarching *global* architecture for international finance with regional impurities added as another type we have just two types of possible evolutionary outcomes for the institutional history of GFAs from a theoretical point of view.

A further point regarding evolutionary mechanisms needs to be made before further consideration of the two types of GFAs. As noted before, the original 'panda's thumb' argument of Stephen Jay Gould see this adaptation as an ingenious if inelegant trick of nature to work with available material that can serve further evolutionary ends. Panda's thumb is, in reality, not a thumb at all, but a structure built from the enlargement of a bone that would originally have been a part of the panda's wrist. But the panda can make do with this evolutionary contraption quite well. It can strip leaves from the bamboo plants and feed itself. The continued existence of the species shows the evolutionary value of such makeshift arrangements. How can this metaphor fit the theory that we have developed so far?

Paul David makes the important observation that institutions may evolve in a similar fashion: 'Evolutionary processes in biology work largely with the materials that are readily available. So does institutional evolution...'[10] While this may not be the only way in which institutions evolve, there is a great deal of plausibility to the argument that in specific instances such as that of the evolution of intellectual property rights institutions 'the cunning of panda's thumb' may have a significant role to play. I would like to suggest that the same argument can also apply to a large extent in the evolution of complex institutional structures such as the GFA. However, a further modification is also necessary. This has to do with the role of evolutionary theory in institutional design.

We begin with the assumption that human design is not perfect. Our rationality is bounded, the social reality is complex and uncertainty is endemic. Therefore our theories are only approximations to a complex and fundamentally only partially knowable reality. However, to the extent that the theory offered gives a better approximation to reality than its rivals, such a theory can, to some extent, guide institution-building. The precise reach of the theory will determine the extent to which this is possible. At a minimum, the theory can offer some guidelines, as illustrated below. Such a theory combines the somewhat blind evolutionary forces at work with some cautious human design. Hence this approach to studying institutional design can be called 'the extended panda's thumb' approach.

4   What kind of thumb? Two broad types of GFAs following from the evolutionary theory

Consistent with the above discussion there are two main types of GFAs. The first type, which can be created at special evolutionary moments, can be called *overarching GFAs*. The gold standard under UK hegemony and Bretton Woods under the threats of a postwar depression are two examples of this phenomenon. Recent history does not support the hope that such events are about to happen again. Therefore, a second type of evolutionary path resulting in a hybrid form should be recognized. This is the hybrid coexistence of a GFA together with one or many RFAs. We can call this type a *hybrid GFA*. Once again, Asia after the AFC is a good place to begin our analysis.

In the Asian case, as many have observed, the financial sector liberalization followed the pre-AFC GFA by default. There were some short-term gains of the policy, but ultimately it brought about severe instability. More generally, as Kaminsky and Reinhart (1999a, b, c) show, based on an analysis of 76 currency crises, of which 26 are also characterized by banking crises, financial sector liberalization can result in a boom–bust cycle by providing easy access to short-term financing. Proponents of liberalization suggest some sort of micro sequencing in order to prevent such adverse consequences. With some variations, the most commonly suggested sequence is: improve the quality of regulation, make sure they are enforced, and then improve the supervisory mechanisms. Once the markets are liberalized, the level of bank's minimum capital requirements can be brought closer to what the Basel Accord requires.

As one author (Azis, 2002c) who, of course, does not use the same terminology as developed here, nevertheless points out, there is a contradiction in this type of GFA arrangement. Rushing to liberalize without thinking further about the consequences in the precise institutional contexts of these countries spelled disaster.[11]

IMF recommendations during this period led to the increase in interest rates. Because of the common prescription under the GFA this occurred in all Asian crisis countries. These high rates created more moral hazard and adverse selection problems, thus showing that the incentive system has indeed been altered, and led to the undertaking of bad risks by the banking sector (Hellman, Murdock and Stiglitz, 2000). As Azis (2002c) correctly observes:

> Under these circumstances, the amount of investment credits going to risky sector rose (adverse selection), the incidence of bail out in the absence of free-exit scheme also increased (moral hazard), and the subsequent banks' franchise values (expected returns) declined. All these are precisely what the "pre-conditions prior to liberalization" are expected *to avoid*. Thus, the implicit logic is inherently self-conflicting, i.e., expecting bank's prudent behavior while allowing 'franchise value' to fall. The suggested preconditions, although seemingly logical, simply do not match with the prevailing institutional conditions.[12]

The existing conditions were not correctly interpreted by the IMF observers because they approached it with an inappropriate theoretical orientation. As Azis further points out:

> The IMF persistently argued for liberalizing the sector and meeting the pre-conditions simultaneously. A study by the Fund on the

sequencing of capital account liberalization using the case of Chile, Korea, Indonesia and Thailand, for example, stresses the importance of proper sequencing if benefits from the liberalization are to be achieved and the risks to be minimized. The study also argues that financial sector liberalization, especially capital account liberalization, should be a part of a coordinated and comprehensive approach, in which the sequencing of regulatory and institutional reforms is critical. The design of macroeconomic and exchange rate policies should also play a vital role (Johnston, Darbar, and Echeverria, 1997). While intuitively making sense, such conclusions are too broad, far from being practical. No one would argue against the importance of making liberalization policy (or any policy for that matter) consistent with the prevailing macroeconomic policy. But how do you do it, remains unanswered. The information contained in such a study is of limited value to policy makers. Yet, while many countries still had problems to meet the stated preconditions, they were pushed to accelerate the liberalization policy by recommending one or two new measures to safeguard. *More often than not, these measures are based on the practice of developed countries that have different institutional conditions.* (emphasis mine)[13]

Here the author correctly pinpoints the failure to recognize unevenness as a key feature of the failure of the IMF to prescribe the correct medicine. In fact, the IMF did much worse – it prescribed the wrong medicine, a set of measures that worsened the impact of the AFC. This situation illustrates the danger of being in the grip of a (pseudo-)universalistic theory that simply cannot be applied to the real world of unevenness without serious distortions that may cause great harm. An alternative is to work with our type two hybrid combination of GFA and RFAs. Again, Asia can be used as an illustration. There are many aspects one could focus on; here I shall consider the debt and capital flows situation prior to the crisis in specific countries.

As both Tables 8.1 and 8.2 show, the borrowing in short-term markets and the increased flow of foreign capital occurred almost simultaneously in these countries. As the real exchange rate appreciated, competitiveness suffered, and the vulnerability to sudden reversals of capital flows increased. It must be emphasized that these were systemic features that went largely unnoticed by the IMF or the private sector. As is well known, in a nonlinear system the vulnerability to sudden shocks is a logical possibility. In the case of Asia, this became an empirical reality of nightmare proportions.

Table 8.1   External debt outstanding (US$ billion)

	1990	1991	1992	1993	1994	1995	1996
ASEAN-4							
External debt	144.3	166.1	180.9	194.1	221.8	257.0	274.5
Short-term debt	25.7	33.8	41.7	49.6	58.2	69.8	80.4
(% of total debt)	17.8	20.3	23.0	25.6	26.2	27.2	29.3
Long-term debt	118.6	132.3	139.2	144.5	163.6	187.2	194.1
(% of total debt)	82.2	79.7	77.0	74.4	73.8	72.8	70.7
Indonesia							
External debt	69.8	79.9	88.3	89.6	96.6	116.3	118.1
(% of GDP)	65.9	68.4	69.0	56.6	54.6	53.3	52.0
Short-term debt	11.1	14.3	18.1	18.0	17.1	24.3	29.3
(% of total debt)	15.9	17.9	20.5	20.1	17.7	20.9	24.8
Long-term debt	58.7	65.6	70.2	71.6	79.5	92.0	88.8
(% of total debt)	84.1	82.1	79.5	79.9	82.3	79.1	75.2
Debt-service ratio	30.9	32.0	31.6	33.8	30.0	33.7	33.0
Malaysia							
External debt	16.0	18.1	19.8	23.2	24.8	33.2	31.6
(% of GDP)	37.6	37.9	34.6	37.1	37.5	40.3	38.1
Short-term debt	1.9	2.1	3.6	6.9	6.2	7.3	7.5
(% of total debt)	11.9	11.6	18.2	29.8	25.0	22.0	23.7
Long-term debt	14.1	16.0	16.2	16.3	18.6	25.9	24.1
(% of total debt)	88.1	88.4	81.8	70.2	75.0	78.0	76.3
Debt-service ratio	10.3	7.7	6.6	7.7	7.7	6.1	6.0
Philippines							
External debt	30.3	32.2	33.3	35.7	39.3	39.5	45.7
(% of GDP)	69.1	71.5	62.3	66.1	61.3	53.2	56.0
Short-term debt	4.4	4.9	5.3	5.0	5.7	6.0	6.3
(% of total debt)	14.5	15.2	15.9	14.0	14.5	15.2	13.8
Long-term debt	25.9	27.3	28.0	30.7	33.6	33.5	39.4
(% of total debt)	85.5	84.8	84.1	86.0	85.5	84.8	86.2
Debt-service ratio	27.0	23.0	24.4	25.5	18.5	15.1	15.4
Thailand							
External debt	28.1	35.9	39.5	45.7	61.1	68.1	79.0
(% of GDP)	32.9	36.4	35.5	41.7	45.3	47.0	49.9
Short-term debt	8.3	12.5	14.7	19.7	29.2	32.2	37.3
(% of total debt)	29.5	34.8	37.2	43.1	47.8	47.3	47.2
Long-term debt	19.8	23.4	24.8	26.0	31.9	35.9	41.7
(% of total debt)	70.5	65.2	62.8	56.9	52.2	52.7	52.8
Debt-service ratio	16.9	13.0	13.7	18.5	15.6	11.7	14.5

Sources: International Financial Statistics, 1997; World Debt Tables, 1996.

Table 8.2   Net capital flows (% of GDP)

	1983–88	1989–95	1991	1992	1993	1994	1995	1996	1997
China									
Net private capital flows	1.2	2.5	1.7	−0.9	4.5	5.6	5.2	4.7	3.7
Net direct investment	0.4	2.9	0.9	1.7	5.3	5.9	4.8	4.6	4.3
Net portfolio investment	0.2	0.2	0.1	—	0.7	0.7	0.1	0.3	0.2
Other net investment	0.5	−0.6	0.7	−2.6	−1.5	−0.9	0.2	−0.3	−0.8
Net official flows	0.3	0.5	0.3	0.8	0.9	0.4	0.3	0.2	−0.1
Change in reserves	−0.4	−2.2	−3.7	0.5	−0.4	−5.6	−3.2	−4.0	−4.5
Indonesia									
Net private capital flows	1.5	4.2	4.6	2.5	3.1	3.9	6.2	6.3	1.6
Net direct investment	0.4	1.3	1.2	1.2	1.2	1.4	2.3	2.8	2.0
Net portfolio investment	0.1	0.4	—	—	1.1	0.6	0.7	0.8	−0.4
Other net investment	1.0	2.6	3.5	1.4	0.7	1.9	3.1	2.7	0.1
Net official flows	2.4	0.8	1.1	1.1	0.9	0.1	−0.2	−0.7	1.0
Change in reserves	—	−1.4	−2.4	−3.0	−1.3	0.4	−0.7	−2.3	1.8
Malaysia									
Net private capital flows	3.1	8.8	11.2	15.1	17.4	1.5	8.8	9.6	4.7
Net direct investment	2.3	6.5	8.3	8.9	7.8	5.7	4.8	5.1	5.3
Net portfolio investment	n.a.	n.a.	n.a.	n.a.	n.a.	n.a.	n.a.	n.a.	n.a.
Other net investment	0.8	2.3	2.9	6.2	9.7	−4.2	4.1	4.5	−0.6
Net official flows	0.3	—	0.4	−0.1	−0.6	0.2	−0.1	−0.1	−0.1
Change in reserves	−1.8	−4.7	−2.6	−11.3	−17.7	4.3	2.0	−2.5	3.6
Philippines									
Net private capital flows	−2.0	2.7	1.6	2.0	2.6	5.0	4.6	9.8	0.5
Net direct investment	0.7	1.6	1.2	1.3	1.6	2.0	1.8	1.6	1.4
Net portfolio investment	—	0.2	0.3	0.1	−0.1	0.4	0.3	−0.2	−5.3
Other net investment	−2.7	0.9	0.2	0.6	1.1	2.5	2.4	8.5	4.5
Net official flows	2.4	2.0	3.3	1.9	2.3	0.8	1.4	0.2	0.8
Change in reserves	0.5	−1.1	−2.3	−1.5	−1.1	−1.9	−0.9	−4.8	2.1
Thailand									
Net private capital flows	3.1	10.2	10.7	8.7	8.4	8.6	12.7	9.3	−10.9
Net direct investment	0.8	1.5	1.5	1.4	1.1	0.7	0.7	0.9	1.3
Net portfolio investment	0.7	1.3	—	0.5	3.2	0.9	1.9	0.6	0.4
Other net investment	1.5	7.4	9.2	6.8	4.1	7.0	10.0	7.7	−12.6
Net official flows	0.7	—	1.1	0.1	0.2	0.1	0.7	0.7	4.9
Change in reserves	−1.4	−4.1	−4.3	−2.8	−3.2	−3.0	−4.4	−1.2	9.7

Source: IMF, *World Economic Outlook*, December 1997.

With most debtors being in the corporate sector during the AFC, the capacity to invest became severely constrained. The debt-deflation scenario became the reality because the price effects of depreciated exchange rates did not occur until much later, if at all. Hence, the initial currency crisis became first a more general financial crisis and then a full-blown economic crisis. In Indonesia it also became a social and political crisis present in the region.

The Asian crisis showed that the composition of capital flows matters. The fact that there were sudden reversals of capital flows during 1997 and 1998 led many to believe that most capital flows in the region were of a portfolio investment type. Reversals of such capital can strain the region's financial system sufficiently to cause or exacerbate its collapse (Rodrik and Velasco, 1999). However, while it is true that portfolio investment was on the rise, data indicate that foreign direct investment (FDI) remained the largest in all Asian crisis countries. As shown in Table 8.1, in all Asian crisis countries foreign debts increased persistently up to the onset of the crisis. These are debts of the private sector from foreign private lenders. Regional monitoring with the help of a theory such as the one proposed here could have caught the problem and a regionally, ultimately globally, coordinated solution could be attempted. But this was never a possibility under the then existing circumstances. We now know that financial and balance of payments crises became interlinked precisely because of the existence of foreign-currency-denominated liabilities (foreign debt) in the domestic financial system (Krueger, 2000). This hindsight can be used to develop RFAs in Asia, Latin America and a few other regions.

5   The role of an RFA: a counterfactual experiment with the Asian case

The previous discussion raises the logical question: if an RFA for Asia had been in place during the AFC, would it have responded any differently to the crisis? In order to answer this question it is useful to start with a review of the actual policy prescriptions advanced by the IMF.

A 'Washington Consensus' policy mix of monetary tightening and fiscal restraints was imposed as part of the IMF conditionalities. The experience during the Mexican crisis in 1995 had convinced the Fund that such a policy mix was appropriate for Asia as well, despite the fact that the pre-crisis conditions in Asia were substantially different.[14] Another element emerged in Asia that was indeed new. The IMF suggested a rather radical and fundamental change in the countries' institutional structure.[15] In the event, neither set turned out to have been well-conceived.

As already observed, the Fund's insistence on tightening the monetary policy severely by raising interest rates turned out to be both incorrect and counterproductive. Its arguments for remaking many institutions in Asia did not make evolutionary sense, although everyone would agree that ending corruption, curtailing special business privileges, and imposing the practice of good governance, including good corporate governance, were worthy goals.[16] But quite apart from the well-known fact that this falls outside the Fund's mandate, such adjustments at the time could result in further instability. In the words of Morris Goldstein, an ex-IMF staff member: *'both the scope and the depth of the Fund's conditions were excessive . . . They clearly strayed outside their area of expertise . . . If a nation is so plagued with problems that it needs to make 140 changes before it can borrow, then maybe the fund should not lend'* (New York Times, 21 October 2000). Although not a conscious advocate of the evolutionary theory advanced here, Goldstein's long experience and firm grasp of institutional matters led him to the right conclusions in this matter.

In contrast with the behaviour of the IMF, a regional financial architecture, had it been in place, could have done at least the following on the basis of applying an evolutionary theory of financial instabilities under globalization:

1. Through constant regional monitoring it would have sensed the danger ahead of time. Even a regional monitoring unit alone would have been able to do better than the IMF team in Asia.
2. Through constant formal and informal contact with the officials in member governments and the private sector, it would have sized up the possible extent of the problem earlier and better than did the IMF.
3. Through prompt and early action it would have provided liquidity to the system, and punished bad management in coordinated measures with the national governments.
4. It would have been able to start regional discussions about bankruptcy and work out procedures by keeping in close touch with the history and legal issues facing particular countries.
5. It would have been in a position to use both moral suasion and toughness to keep both regional creditors and debtors in line.

The fundamental requirement for this, however, was an actually existing RFA with enough liquidity and technical expertise. The Asian

Development Bank provided quite a bit of liquidity to Korea in particular, but did not even have a monitoring unit when the crisis broke out. Furthermore, the autonomy and integrity of any future RFA, in Asia and elsewhere, are issues that need discussion. The relationship between the RFAs and the IMF also needs to be further specified. These are matters that are of necessity evolutionary by nature. In this chapter, I have tried to specify some principles that may help in selecting the more beneficial evolutionary path.

One such principle has been 'the extended panda's thumb' during evolution. In the case of GFA, this strengthens the case for the hybrid variety. Using both the existing global institutions such as the IMF, and building upon existing regional initiatives, may offer a better chance of creating a beneficial 'makeshift' hybrid GFA than the textbook-type 'pie-in-the-sky' schemes correctly dismissed by Eichengreen. However, Eichengreen does not consider the role of RFAs in his otherwise excellent analysis. One way to read the present chapter is to see it as filling this gap by using 'the extended panda's thumb' principle in conjunction with some other arguments.

6   Towards a workable hybrid GFA: RFAs, the IMF and national policy management during transition

6.1   RFA as part of a hybrid form of GFA

If the argument presented so far is valid, then several propositions can now be accepted. First, there may be more than one evolutionary possibility; so there may not be a unique, global optimum set of institutions. Second, the goal of achieving stability and sustainable growth in a world of scarce resources leads to exercising prudence as a principle, particularly when costs are distributed unevenly over space and time. Third, a combination of global institutions with regional- and national-level institutions may provide more public good than focusing simply at the global level. The case for RFAs has so far rested implicitly on the third proposition. I now wish to elaborate more on this point and link it to the formulation of national economic policies and institution-building at the national level as well. It is best to focus again on a concrete case such as the post-crisis Asia to give substance to the formal argument.

Since the crisis, the IMF, the World Bank and national policy making bodies have been in intense consultation. The individual East Asian economies have taken numerous measures, such as improving bank supervision, and allowing greater exchange rate flexibility, to inoculate themselves against future capital account shocks. However, most of them are still vulnerable to large negative capital account shocks. The national strategy of having a very large stock of foreign reserves to deal with large capital flight may work, but it is an extremely expensive strategy. No one can foretell how frequent such crises may be, or how expensive; but if the past is any guide, even infrequent crises can be quite expensive to manage in this manner. This is not to say that such measures should not be taken. On the contrary, these measures are and should be a part of the transitional national management strategy. However, more is clearly needed. It seems that, following this logic, an increasing number of East Asian policy makers are realizing that although they may not have the capacity to change the international financial architecture immediately, creating a regional financial architecture may be an attainable goal. There can be a whole range of regional financial cooperation policies leading to more permanent institution-building. These could begin with a peer review process such as the G-7 process. Using this as the reference point, a move to mutual liquidity provision and some form of enforcement mechanism could be adopted. These could be enhanced through exchange rate coordination and enhanced surveillance process. Ultimately, such a process could evolve into an RFA that could have its own institutional and organizational structure.

In the Asian case, such an evolutionary process has already started. The most important steps taken so far are: the Manila Framework Group Meeting, the ASEAN Surveillance Process, the ASEAN+3 Surveillance Process, and the Chiangmai Initiative-related Surveillance Process.

It can be said that the performance of the Manila Framework Group as a mechanism for regional financial cooperation and regional financial surveillance has not yet reached its full potential. The reasons are related to institutional incapacity which has prevented the parties from clearly specifying the objectives of information exchange and surveillance. Consequently, no priorities, targets, and rules have been set for the process of information exchange and surveillance. Most importantly, there is no actual peer review process – the surveillance process seems to involve simply a general discussion of the global and regional economic outlook. Finally, there appears to be no attempt to formulate any country-specific or region-wide recommendations for policy actions – a point to which I will return at the end.

The other processes also have much room for improvement and actual prospects for improvement, as shown by the Chiangmai Initiative-related

Surveillance Process. In addition to an expanded ASEAN Swap Arrangement (ASA) that includes all ASEAN members and a network of bilateral swap agreements among ASEAN countries plus China, Japan and South Korea, this initiative has opened the door for further discussion about concrete policy coordination and institution-building. In so far as the swap arrangements are concerned, currently 10 per cent of the swap arrangements can be disbursed without IMF involvement.

Even with this modest beginning, there is now a need for the swap-providing countries to formulate their own assessments about the swap-requesting country. The costs of such information gathering can be reduced through regional cooperation. Such a move will also make it possible to pre-qualify members for assistance if and when the need for such assistance arises. This will also help to fight contagion and prevent capital flight when actions are taken promptly before a crisis point is reached because of avoidable delays. Acting in accordance with the principles of prudent management stated earlier, there could be a regular policy dialogue at the deputy minister level.

Finally, at the organizational level, the evolutionary approach could lead to the establishment of an independent surveillance unit to serve as the core of an RFA, and to lead the policy dialogue. The proposed policy dialogue process should pay particular attention to the root problems in East Asia's weak financial systems (for example, prudential supervision, risk management, and corporate governance), and actively promote the development and integration of long-term capital markets. At this point, it is not essential to pinpoint any further the precise organizational blueprint for such an RFA; but the point that the process underway can result in an appropriate institutional structure with proper organizational design is important to grasp. Evolutionary economic theory suggests that an open architecture will be better able to absorb future shocks, learn from them, and modify itself. Once again, such practice is closer to an 'extended panda's thumb' type of evolution than the striving for a global optimum.

There are two key aspects of such an interrelated architecture that will crucially affect the workability of a possible RFA in Asia or in any other region. First, the willingness of a reformed IMF to permit the RFAs to have a certain degree of regional autonomy. For this the complementarity and burden-sharing aspects of the GFA with RFAs need to be recognized. This is a special case of complementary institutional network (CIN). Second, and another instance of CIN, is the viability and cooperation at the national level. A slogan accompanying globalization is that the nation-state can no longer act on its own. This may be true in certain areas of macroeconomic policy, but across a wide range of issues from tax policies to environmental policies the national governments can – within limits – formulate and implement policies. In the area of finance, even under WTO rules, there are possibilities of not only policy man-oeuvring but also of institutional reform and new institution-building. In addition to addressing such matters as prudential supervision, risk management, and corporate governance the need for building other institutions for risk-sharing, human development and policy dialogues within the nation loom large as tasks during the transitional manage-ment at the national level.

6.2   The changing role of the IMF within a hybrid GFA

I have already alluded to some of the ways in which the IMF will need to reform if the hybrid form of GFA I am suggesting here is to become a viable option for institution-building. It should also be noted in support of this argument that the IMF has already gone through a long phase of an 'extended-panda's-thumb'-like transformation in the post-Bretton Woods era. Monitoring the performance of developing countries and suggesting frequent adjustment programmes, and finally during the AFC, suggesting sweeping institutional reforms in the affected countries were not part of the Bretton Woods IMF's modus operandi. Here I offer a more systematic approach for a further 'extended-panda's-thumb'-like development of the IMF guided by two underlying principles:

1. *The principle of symmetry*, i.e., the surplus and deficit countries should be treated equally. This was, of course, recognized by Keynes quite early on, but it did not find a place in the ultimate design of the Bretton Woods institutions.
2. *The principle of burden-sharing*, i.e., during episodes of crisis manage-ment the IMF will share the management burden with the RFAs and through them also with the affected countries and their neighbors.

Both of these principles recognize the practical impossibility of the IMF being transformed into a global central bank in the near future. What the IMF cannot do now and will not be able to do in the foreseeable future is to follow Bagehot's dictum to lend freely against good collateral at a high interest rate in times of crisis. Unless SDRs become the com-monly accepted and easily expandable means of settlement, this role will remain foreclosed.[17] It is unlikely that the principal shareholders of the IMF will allow such a change to occur. Also, compared to a national central bank dealing with a problematic domestic financial institution, the IMF has a limited ability to force corrective action. Yet, there will clearly be a role for IMF lending, and the consequent moral hazard will need to be recognized. But just as the moral hazard from having fire-fighters ready to fight fires does not compel thoughtful communities to abolish fire stations, the global community also cannot abolish the IMF, or reduce its resources simply because there is a moral hazard problem associated with such institutions. The second principle above – the principle of burden-sharing with the RFAs, national governments and the private sector – should go some distance towards both increasing the overall resources available, and mitigating the moral hazard.

In addition, the Fund can make a concerted effort to manage private creditors. Most important from the point of view of managing crises will be the incorporation of new provisions on loan contracts so that orderly workout procedures become feasible. The Fund can also lend into arrears as a means of providing debtor-in-possession financing. Such a provision, along with more direct measures vis-à-vis the creditors, can help to bring the creditors to the bargaining table during a crisis.

Such measures to manage the creditors should also be complemented by increased surveillance of the financial markets. Strengthening supervision is one aspect. Arriving at independent assessments of financial risk is another, related aspect of moving in this direction. However, it is important to realize that even after adopting this stance, the risk of crises will still remain. Not all crises can be foreseen, much less prevented. The best that can be done is to draw the countries, the private sector and the RFAs together in an effort to strengthen the financial structures, including information gathering and processing capabilities. A cooperative structure in which the Fund recognizes the need for hybridity will also help to reduce the reaction time.

Reducing the reaction time can only help if the policies undertaken are not positively harmful – even if they are not successful in achieving their aims. The IMF has been correctly criticized for suggesting a 'one-size-fits-all' policy package. Here again, a changed institutional structure with a more flexible IMF will mean a case-by-case approach in which the RFAs will play a significant role. National economic policies such as requiring borrowers to unwind positions in increasingly risky situations, curbing excessive foreign borrowing, limiting portfolio investment, and adopting cautionary policies towards derivatives and off-balance sheet items may need to be examined as serious policy options. Tobin tax, or individual country taxes of the Chilean variety, should also be given serious consideration. The mantra of free capital movements together with the refrain that there is no alternative needs to be revised appropriately to incorporate the available tools that the Fund can help countries use to mitigate the risks arising from such capital movements.

It is not clear that the Fund will be able to do much to institute a more stable exchange rate regime. The pegged rate system, advocated among others, surprisingly, by *The Wall Street Journal*, will create one-way bets for speculators. Free floating, on the other hand, can lead to disasters when exchange rates collapse suddenly instead of finding a new stable equilibrium. Such perverse dynamics were observed during the AFC, particularly in the case of Indonesia. Neither currency boards nor perfect flexibility can prevent vulnerable currencies from collapsing. Rather a managed float before any signs of crisis appear together with a prudent management of the financial and real sectors would seem to be both pragmatic and feasible at this point. Strengthening the capacities of central banks will reap greater rewards than urging the IMF to twist the arms of the countries through conditionalities.

7   Summary and conclusions

This chapter has taken an evolutionary approach in studying the prospects for a global financial architecture. The theory of institutional change that is the outcome of this effort has been called 'an extended panda's thumb' (EPT) approach. The EPT approach to institutional change involves the incorporation of a cautious role for economic theories and their institutional prescriptions in the history of the path-dependent evolution of institutions. This methodological and theoretical approach comes with some caveats. Along with the caveats regarding the real possibility of choosing the scientifically inappropriate theory, there is also an emphasis on the role of uncertainty and the partial nature of our scientific knowledge. Furthermore, the EPT approach assumes that rationality is bounded and learning is costly. Therefore, the 'extended panda's hand' argument places a great emphasis on the comparison and testing of various theoretical alternatives with different institutional and policy implications.

In this chapter, I have argued that the design of a GFA would in all likelihood have to follow an extended 'panda's-thumb-like' development. Instead of jettisoning the IMF and other seemingly inefficient regional arrangements, I argue for serious institutional reform within the existing framework using appropriate theoretical and empirical guidelines. Ironically, in a world of bounded rationality and uncertainty, such an approach will be relatively more efficient than the search for the 'optimal' institution under the assumptions of maximizing agents who seemingly face no computational or other costs of learning to be (more) rational.

In times of crisis, there are well-meaning suggestions of radical institutional restructuring that fade away when the immediate crisis is over. Only a few farsighted or worrying types may still voice lingering concerns. The AFC, and the proposals for an *overarching type* of GFA – to use the terminology developed here – and the subsequent fate of these proposals is a case in point. However, the history of crises shows that they cannot be prevented once and for all in a monetary economy with unpredictable ebbs and flows in capital movements. This history also shows that financial markets have short memories and limited long-term learning capacities.

Given these features of the real economic world, an evolutionary approach admits of multiple evolutionary equilibria, and a need for realistic institutional design that recognizes path dependence without the disabling – and in most cases incorrect – slogan that there is no alternative. Such an approach applied to recent economic history leads to the identification of two broad categories of global financial architectures. The *hybrid* variety advocated here on the basis of both realism and systemic efficacy will nevertheless involve much institution-building that is always fraught with the danger of 'politics-gone-awry'. Thus the political problems of coalition-building and ensuring the least cost cooperative outcome need attention. The limited achievements and remaining problems that can be seen from the Asian example discussed here should provide concrete motivation to think further about the problems of designing institutions in the real world.

Given the evidence presented here, the 'panda's thumb' argument, complemented by a role for appropriate theories of institutional mix and design, can be used to start some fruitful discussion about the role a reformed IMF can play in creating a new GFC. Equally important, from the evolutionary theoretical perspective, is the possible usefulness of the RFAs. In these regards, the hybrid GFA can be a really ingenious way to use the complementarity of global and regional institutions effectively.

APPENDIX 8.1: EVOLUTIONARY GROWTH DYNAMICS – SOME USEFUL EVOLUTIONARY ECONOMICS THEOREMS

Theorem A1: Given the dynamical evolutionary system $f'(v,t)$ defined on the real Euclidean space and weak monotonicity as a selection mechanism, any

asymptotically stable point is the Nash equilibrium of an appropriately defined bimatrix evolutionary game.
Proof: (Nachbar, 1990, modification in Khan, 2002c).

Theorem A2: Every equilibrium of a gradient-monotonic evolutionary system can be sustained as a Nash equilibrium of an appropriately defined bimatrix evolutionary game.
Proof: (Khan, 2002c).

9
General Conclusions: From Crisis to a Global Political Economy of Freedom

> Future:
> That period of time in which our affairs prosper, our friends are true, and our happiness is assured.
>
> Ambrose Bierce, *The Cynic's Word Book*

> Human blunders usually do more to shape history than human wickedness.
>
> A.J.P. Taylor, *The Origins of the Second World War*

Writing in 1926, in a biographical essay on Edgeworth, Keynes underlined some of the problems of complex human systems:

> We are faced at every turn with problems of organic unity, of discreteness, of discontinuity – the whole is not equal to the sum of the parts, comparisons of quantity fail us, small changes produce large effects, the assumptions of a uniform and homogeneous continuum are not satisfied.[1]

If anything, the world economy at the start of the twenty-first century – even more so than during the interwar period – shows the kind of complexity captured in Keynes's words above. Fortunately, complex systems theory and international economics theory have both made some progress since those dark days. Although we are still far from having a genuinely complete theory of complex economic systems, efforts are underway that have already borne some interesting fruit in several, albeit limited areas. The present endeavour can be seen as a modest step towards understanding some facets of complex open economies with financial systems. I have tried to orient my study methodologically in such a way that both the possibilities of inductive logic and deductions from principles can be fully utilized. It is important to stress the 'realist' methodology implicit in this effort. The concrete 'facts' are understood to be theory-laden. However, correct theoretical terms are taken to be precisely those that approximate to the real structure and dynamics of the global economy. In causal terms, complex causal structures can be inferred to the best of our ability by using the conceptual, modelling and econometric techniques available to us at present. Given advances in theory and techniques in the future, our knowledge of the underlying causal relations is likely to improve.

Thus, the results obtained in this book can only be viewed as tentative and subject to future revisions and updating. Yet, it must be said that by using a number of approaches – historical and political economic, statistical, conceptual and formal nonlinear modelling approaches among them – an attempt has been made to advance our knowledge of the dynamics of economies with complex financial systems as much as possible. In this final chapter I wish to sum up the most important aspects of my findings from two complementary points of view – one positive and the other normative.

The first is the analysis of complex economic systems. Here, methods of nonlinear modelling both of decisions in a single financial entity such as a bank, and of decisions in an economy-wide framework have been used. For microanalysis, the neural network approach in particular would seem to hold much promise. Although not widely used in economic analysis to date, in the future, learning models that start from an assumption of bounded rationality would become more useful in analysing complex economies. Likewise, nonlinear modelling of financial economies in an economy-wide sense will also gain ground. These are hopeful predictions; but given the need to stabilize the global economy there is a strong case to be made for the further use and development of such models.

On the other hand, the global economy is also a *political economy*. Hence the problem of global financial architecture – to mention just one pressing global issue – cannot be simply a problem of technical economic and econometric modelling, no matter how sophisticated and 'realistic'. In fact, it can be argued that a 'realistic' model will have to include political economic elements – at least implicitly. At the same time it must be recognized that the state of the art of such political economic modelling is still rather primitive. Instead of simplifying radically to fit the needs of formalization, much can also be learned from a rigorous ordinary language political economic analysis. Each of the country chapters in this book contains such analysis, as the astute reader must have noticed already. The formal modelling and a rigorous ordinary language political economic analysis are in fact complementary.[2]

Instead of summarizing both of these approaches on a chapter-by-chapter basis, I want to raise a more fundamental question here: what are the characteristics of the global financial markets that lead to its repeated instabilities? Various theoretical answers to this question can be given, and many of them have been discussed in the preceding chapters. For the purpose of discussing the 'complexity' approach developed in this book, several features of global financial markets are worth emphasizing. First of all, global capital and financial markets – even more than purely domestic markets – are characterized by serious problems of asymmetric and incomplete information. Second, these problems are faced by agents who are rational only in a bounded rationality sense. Third, the risky nature of projects cannot always be completely priced even if there is no fundamental uncertainty; however, there could also be a Knightian type of uncertainty as opposed to just risk, or at least a Keynesian type of uncertainty where only qualitative comparisons of future states are possible. In either case, expected value maximization of portfolios is impossible, and much of the standard mean-variance or other techniques of statistical portfolio value analysis assuming a parametric distribution for formalizing the looking forward into the future becomes inapplicable.

Even without the radical characterization of the capital markets under the third point above, the increasing international exposure of both equity funds in the advanced countries and the financial systems in the newly industrializing and other developing countries has meant that in-depth information about the underlying values of the assets and liabilities is less than perfect. At the same time, the speed of shock transmission has increased because of technological advances and liberalization. This leads, among other effects, to a strong possibility of widespread contagion. Another way of putting it is that contagion risk increases with financial liberalization in a world that is simultaneously undergoing an information technology revolution.

In the discussion on corporate governance, both the seriousness of agency problems and the wider context in which we need to address these were emphasized. For bank lenders and portfolio investors, the agency problems are exacerbated because they can exercise little control over the assets and their market values. The only international safeguards that exist are implicit bailout prospects by the IFIs or governments creating moral hazard. If such bailouts come at some cost – thus mitigating the moral hazard problem to some extent – then the logical loss-minimizing strategy is to avoid assets which cannot be liquidated quickly if things go wrong suddenly. One logical outcome of this strategy is short-termism. The international portfolio investors and bank lenders use 'rapid exit' as a means for dealing with and containing downside risk. Therefore financial 'quick ratios' such as the ratio of a country's short-term foreign liabilities to central bank reserves become signals to watch. Whenever the signal indicates downside risk and someone acts to exit, a cascading downward rush towards lowering asset values and a financial crash may result.

Another consequence of the above characteristics of the liberalization of emerging markets is that fund managers do not see acquisition of control or even more information as a way of handling risk. Rather they seek portfolio diversification. This practice is justified by a theory that assumes a lack of covariance among the emerging market instruments so that different country risks can be played off against one another. However, this move can also lead to significant instabilities in the emerging markets, particularly when the fund managers act according to the herd instinct. It is also interesting to note that despite a large literature on equity market-based (EMS) corporate governance system, such behaviour does not always result in good corporate governance. In fact, the managers of firms have strong incentives to push for short-term upward movements in stock prices. Under lax regulatory and accounting practices, these objectives can often lead to distorted information and misleading financial statements. This makes the goal of achieving a transparent and accountable financial system harder, not easier as some simplistic theories would predict.

The main overall consequence for the financial and capital markets of the above observations is a complex kind of market failure. Asset prices and interest rates do not fully reflect risk. Lenders in the domestic markets usually – though not always – handle this type of failure through aggregate credit rationing. There are always potential borrowers – even borrowers willing to pay a higher than market rate of interest – who are refused loans. This is consistent with the particular portfolio allocation rules adopted by rational lenders in such markets. Internationally, adverse perceptions of risk by lenders that may not be connected with long-term underlying asset values can destabilize these markets. It can be shown theoretically that in the case of adverse news in a world where the shock travels in a cascading nonlinear fashion, the cumulative effect can be a complete loss of foreign capital and reserves. This is, in fact, embedded in our economy-wide model.

Add to this the fact that while the portfolio allocation rules in a developed country fund may be marginal adjustment overall, the emerging market part of this portfolio is far from marginal for the emerging market country. For this country – for example, Thailand in 1997 – the marginal adjustments by the developed country fund managers may lead to a huge outflow launching a full-blown financial crisis. Thus unevenness of the economies has a significant role to play in explaining the capital account crises we have observed.

The volatility of the short-term capital movements in turn can have concrete economic consequences. The actual impact depends upon the various linkages and the strength of the capital 'surges' – both in and outflows. But overall, the mean output may fall and the variances of major macroeconomic variables may increase. This makes the problem of creating more productive investment, more and better-paid jobs, and social safety nets for the vulnerable groups much more difficult. Given that the capacities of many states in developing countries are already quite weak in these respects, volatility weakens these still further. While we attempt to build the 'missing institutions' in developing countries, the urgent problems of the weakest open economies need to be discussed also.

Thus before going any further a detour to consider the problems of poverty alleviation in these countries may throw some light on how different sets of economies must be dealt with differently in an uneven world. Thus, for the poorer countries opening up should be accompanied by a flow of official and NGO aid with the condition that governance should be improved. New aid and investment policies must be connected to a new trade policy. Liberalizing the Generalized System of Preferences (GSP) under which the industrialized countries would exempt imports from these countries while maintaining tariffs on imports from other countries, is an urgent task. The United States can take a bold step by unilaterally liberalizing its GSP towards indebted poorer countries. This will generate not only the moral pressure for the other G-7 countries to follow but will in the meantime confer an advantage to US firms trading and investing in these countries. Even a gradual liberalizing would help enormously, although progress will be slower than in the case of immediate liberalization. The economic assistance policy needs also to be geared towards helping the small producers through providing funds and expertise. On the technological front, the G-7 countries and the multilateral aid agencies can help by financing and arranging for granting the poorer countries access to the global communications networks.

These problems are also faced by other developing countries, albeit to a lesser extent. What happened during the Asian and Argentine financial crises was that many middle-class people also faced the prospect of sudden poverty. Creation of a safety net for these people in such (relatively more affluent) economies is another urgent task. Since the private sector is not entrusted with this task, at least in the short to medium term, other actors have to step in. It should be recognized that poverty alleviation has been embraced as a major goal by the multilateral banks. Therefore, it is natural to expect them to play a leading role in this respect. To the extent that an increase in their capital base is necessary for this purpose, this should be accepted as a global responsibility.

The prospects of global financing bring us back to the problems of the unevenness and other failures of global capital markets. In the discussion of global financial architecture, I emphasized the role that can be played by a hybrid structure. I also emphasized the following two principles:

1. *The principle of symmetry*, i.e., the surplus and deficit countries should be treated equally. However, it was not realized in the past; nor is it likely to be realized in the near future. Nevertheless, there are various ways to pursue this as a goal even under the current set up of the IMF. If serious efforts are made to follow this principle by a reformed IMF, that will be an important step towards a new and better GFA.
2. *The principle of burden-sharing*, i.e., during episodes of crisis management the IMF will share the management burden with the RFAs and through them also with the affected countries and their neighbours.

It should be kept in mind that, in keeping with the 'extended panda's thumb' argument, both of these principles recognize the practical impossibility of the IMF being transformed into a global central bank in the near future. What the IMF cannot do now and will not be able to do in the foreseeable future is to follow Bagehot's dictum to lend freely against good collateral at a high interest rate in time of crisis. Unless SDRs become the commonly accepted and easily expandable means of settlement, this role will remain foreclosed. It is unlikely that the principal shareholders in the IMF will allow such a change to occur.[3] In addition, compared to a national central bank dealing with a problematic domestic financial institution the IMF has only limited capacities to force corrective action. Yet, there will clearly be a role for IMF lending, and the consequent moral hazard will need to be recognized. But just as the moral hazard from having fire-fighters ready to fight fires does not compel thoughtful communities to abolish fire stations, the global community cannot abolish the IMF, or reduce its resources simply because there is a moral hazard problem associated with such institutions. The second principle above – the principle of burden sharing with the RFAs, national governments and the private sectors – should go some way towards both increasing the overall resources available, and mitigating the moral hazard.

It has also been pointed out that while the Fund cannot now, or even in the near future, be expected to act as a global central banker, pressures for increasing the net supply and poor country allocations of SDRs could have beneficial effects. Even if the increases are not significant in the short run, the tendency will keep alive the eventual goal of forming a global central bank, as Keynes had envisioned. More practically, putting pressure on the IMF to grant new SDRs in order to finance the stabilization of primary (and perhaps other) commodity prices will lead to benefits for both the developing and the developed countries in the intermediate run. The stabilization of these prices will help many developing countries to avert balance of payments (BoP), disasters. Furthermore, to the extent that the unusual price increases, such as the oil price increase in the 1970s, create general inflationary pressures such pressures can also be averted. A smooth international transactions pattern will thus be consistent with domestic price stabilization as well.

I also emphasized that the Fund could make a concerted effort to manage private creditors. Most important from the point of view of managing crises will be the incorporation of new provisions on loan contracts so that orderly workout procedures become feasible. The Fund can also lend into arrears as a means of providing debtor-in-possession financing. Such a provision, along with more direct measures vis-à-vis the creditors, can help to bring the creditors to the bargaining table during a crisis.

But the major emphasis in terms of the proposal for a hybrid GFA has been on the role that regional financial architectures (RFAs) – if they were to be created – could play in the future. Here it may be instructive to reconsider the Asian case. From the policy perspective, it is important to know if the existence of an Asian RFA would have helped in any way during the AFC. This is really a counterfactual question which asks: if an RFA for Asia had existed during the AFC, how would it have responded to the crisis that would have been different?

In contrast with the behaviour of the IMF, within the proposed hybrid GFA, a regional financial architecture, had it been present, could have done at least the following on the basis of applying an evolutionary theory of financial instabilities under globalization:

1. Through constant regional monitoring it would have sensed the danger ahead of time. Even a regional monitoring unit alone would have been able to do better than the IMF team in Asia.
2. Through constant formal and informal contact with the officials in member governments and the private sector, it would have assessed the possible extent of the problem earlier and better than did the IMF.
3. Through prompt and early action it would have provided liquidity to the system, and punished bad management in coordinated measures with the national governments.
4. It would have been able to start regional discussions about bankruptcy and work out procedures by keeping in close touch with the history and legal issues facing particular countries.
5. It would have been in a position to use both moral suasion and toughness to keep both regional creditors and debtors in line.

The fundamental requirement for this, however, was an actually existing RFA with enough liquidity and technical expertise. The Asian Development Bank provided a reasonable level of liquidity to Korea in particular, but did not even have a monitoring unit in place when the crisis broke out. Furthermore, the autonomy and integrity of any future RFA, in Asia and elsewhere, are issues that need discussion. The relationship between the RFAs and the IMF also needs to be further specified. These are matters that are, of necessity, evolutionary by nature.

It is important to realize that the root causes of crises were not prevented from being actualized by the 'Washington consensus' policies in effect. Accelerated financial liberalization, exchange rate anchoring, and encouraging private portfolio capital inflow did not lead to the desired growth and stability. To be sure, there may be short-term gains. But these gains can exacerbate herd behaviour and the problems that arise from such behaviour. Once the macroeconomic balances are obtained via structural adjustment and inflation is under control, market liberalization may bring in both financing for real sector projects and hot money. If all of the main short-term indicators turn positive for a while investors tend to ignore some fluctuations. For example, large current account deficits – the case of Thailand readily comes to mind – may be seen as being simply the algebraic counterpart to a positive capital account balance. Thus, an accounting identity, or at best a result of equilibrium in balance of payments, is taken as the causal evidence for success in attracting foreign investment. By the same token – as the chapter on corporate governance issues showed in detail – corporate debt and high leveraging may be construed as global financial diversification. In retrospect, we can see that it requires much close analysis to determine if the external deficit reflects a private savings–investment gap and rational decisions about intertemporal consumption smoothing. Private sector decisions have turned out to be much more myopic than assumed by the received doctrines. Our approach of boundedly rational agents teaches us to take myopic behaviour seriously, and asks: under what kind of environment can agents learn not to be myopic?

Another failure has been that of the private credit rating agencies. These agencies failed to predict the collapse in both Mexico and Asia. Apart from problems with techniques that are backward-looking, there are deeper issues at stake here. The use of information by the rating agencies seems to be deficient. The tendency is to interpret matters in such a way as not to destabilize the market in a good equilibrium. But in a bad equilibrium the rating agencies also engage in herd behaviour and rapid nonlinear downgrading can occur. There is also the question of how the ratings are used and the consequences that follow; but this is a systemic problem rather than that of the credit agencies.

Because credit rating and its use are systemic issues, competent international bodies can play a stabilizing role here. In the hybrid global financial architecture proposed in this book, such public–private hybridity can also be helpful. In addition to investigating what role the IMF, possible RFAs and other international public bodies can play, we can also explore the prospects of using bodies such as the International Association for Insurance Supervisors (IAIS) and the International Organization of Securities Commissions (IOSCO).[4]

Related to such hybrid structures are possible extensions of bank supervision capabilities outside of G-10. The publication of the Basel Committee's 'Core Principles for Effective Banking Supervision' establishing best practices represents a substantial step forward. Supervision of cross-border banking is another area of concern. The report on offshore banking and 'the Supervision of Cross-border Banking' received the endorsement of banking supervisors from 140 countries in the International Conference of Banking Supervisors in Stockholm. Although these are encouraging steps, much remains to be done. In addition, much depends upon the sharing of information and cooperation across borders among the supervisors. Regulatory forebearance is another problem that is relevant for both state-owned financial institutions and privately owned ones in many countries.

Whether all these add up to an adequate framework for financial stability is the crucial question. The BIS now has an expanded membership.

But the BIS itself has no regulatory functions as such, and seems reluctant to play a more active role. The US Treasury also does not seem particularly willing to cede authority of cross-border intervention to a body it does not control. In effect, the G-7 countries themselves may not be able to agree about the role of the BIS. Partly as a result of this, the United States seems more content with the IMF expanding its regular article IV consultations with the member countries to examine the quality of domestic banking supervision. In a way, the IMF's move towards pressuring for capital account liberalization can be seen as a tactic to enhance its capacity to control the financial policies of the less powerful member countries. Reforming the IMF constitution in this direction will create additional risks from capital flow surges globally. The argument in this book has been that a hybrid structure that respects the practical policy issues arising from unevenness will be more stable than a sudden move towards uniform capital account liberalization. This conclusion seems to have been borne out by the facts of global financial instability even from such moves for a subset of developing and newly industrializing economies.

While this book endorses the positive good that can come from the type of enhanced cooperation discussed above, and from enhanced 'mutual recognition agreements' there are problems that should not be overlooked. The US-supported mutual recognition agreements, in particular, can become a form of disguised protection for the US banks and financial services institutions. At the same time such extension of mutual recognition would surely increase the extraterritorial powers of US regulators such as the SEC and the Fed. Legally, it may also expose the US authorities to claims from US investors if there were to be crises in markets outside of the United States whose regulatory system has been certified by the United States through a mutual recognition system. But, as I have emphasized, used with care – keeping the above and other possible problems in mind – these types of bilateral arrangements can also be a part of the hybrid system.

There are other proposals such as the international credit insurance corporation that do not seem to be viable at the present time. Because of the risk of contagion, the pooling of risks necessary for any insurance scheme to work may be difficult if not impossible to achieve. Problems of moral hazard and adverse selection will arise more frequently and massively, requiring the payment of premiums that may indeed be prohibitive.

Once again, however, the idea of funding this with new issues of SDRs is not entirely lacking in merit. Availability of a fund like this could mean conditional lending of last resort. Such lending could also happen more quickly than in the past. Having a large amount of international liquidity would also lessen the risk of a major asset deflation during a period of crisis. After crisis, in order to mitigate any possible inflationary impact, the loans could be paid back quickly by the borrowing countries, or, in some cases, long-term bonds could be issued.

From the above discussion it should be clear that the creation of a new hybrid GFA is the supreme political task of creating a new global political economy amidst the ruins of financial and real economic crises. The Asian financial crisis and the Argentine crisis both identified specific institutional features. They also showed the failures of the so-called 'developmental states'. The truth about these crises is that these are largely private sector problems in a lax national and global regulatory environment. Excessive lending beyond the dictates of prudential regulations – had they existed internationally or enforced properly – by private banks and non-bank financial intermediaries in developed countries to private banks and corporations in developing countries was at the core of the crises. Since this was not a sovereign debt problem, the usual intergovernmental or IMF prescription was not likely to work and in fact did not work.[5] Another characteristic was the credit rationing in the global capital markets. It was the decisions of the lenders that dictated the capital flows. Hence, the so-called 'developmental state' had in fact little to do with the heydays of success, or the bleak days of failure that followed. The only difference was that the bleak post-crisis days showed up the real weaknesses of these states in the global political economy.

Finally, the studies of the political economy of capital flows should pay close attention to the problems related to the lenders since these really are the key actors. The key problem faced by the lenders is that of managing risk by whatever means. Sometimes this may be consistent with a stable and orderly market – the key goal of the national governments and the international authorities. But quite often – as shown both empirically and theoretically – the private sector actions can be destabilizing. A deeper look at the problem shows that a proper economic and political economy analysis both point to the problem of missing institutions. The foregoing analysis of crises largely underlined four types of missing institutions.

First, there is the lack of a global central bank. This missing institution means that the job of providing enough liquidity, particularly during times of crisis, cannot be carried out adequately. As a result, illiquid, but not insolvent banks and financial institutions, as well as other productive enterprises may go bankrupt. As pointed out, the IMF is not up to this task at present and may not be for some time. A hybrid structure with regional provision of liquidity is therefore an urgent reformist and new institution-building task.

Second, the need for international prudential regulation of financial services. As shown here, the Basel system is far from adequate. Again, a hybrid form with national and perhaps regional components may be the best realistic response that the global system can make at this time.

Third, many capital and financial markets – for example, long-term bond markets – are themselves missing. If not altogether missing, they are so thin that no real capital accumulation can occur through their marginal functionings. In developed countries this problem is addressed by the existence of market makers. In fact, these are considered so crucial that some theorists with in-depth knowledge of real financial institutions, make the study of market making the starting point of their analysis. This is the approach followed, for example, by Charles Goodhart in his path-breaking study of monetary economics. The crucial point to recognize is that such market makers do not exist in most global financial markets. We do not know if and when they will emerge. We also do not know how their activities might be coordinated once they do emerge. In the mean time, no international body seems to be ready or capable of discharging the task of market makers. Here is a palpable concrete example of how complex developed financial economies really are.

Fourth, as the chapter and particularly the section on corporate governance and legal structures showed, transaction costs are indeed high without a smoothly functioning adequate legal system. While no unique system may be optimal – the difference between the Common Law and the Continental Legal Systems shows this – a certain degree of integrity in dispute settlement mechanisms, including bankruptcy and orderly workout procedures, may be essential. Without these, the rule for both foreign investors and domestic companies may be quick returns and capital flight in times of trouble. In a hybrid system, some degree of capital control and building of domestic legal institutions may be a prelude to creating a more appropriate body of regional and international dispute settlement mechanisms.

Although we have not arrived at a complete theory of the new capital account type of financial crisis, the main outline is by now clear. Open capital accounts and weak banking and financial sectors are a combustible mix. In the presence of nonlinear, complex interrelations, discontinuities, uncertainty etc., the behaviour of boundedly rational agents may tend towards cascading herd behaviour. Likewise, governments may also panic. Thus, according to this 'complexity' view of capital account crises, there is no magic formula short of complete autarky to prevent capital account crises. However, even under conditions of autarky financial fragility could arise from purely domestic factors. Such fragility could also result in a financial crisis. Given the benefits of openness, autarky is really a counsel of despair. What it is important to realize is that there is a need to have a coupling of domestic policies and regulatory environment with the regional and global financial architecture. However, we must now, at the end of our endeavour, turn from issues of pure finance to the broader question of the implications of sound finance for well-being.

Sound finance and economic growth may go together under an appropriately designed global economic regime. However, the results of growth must still be evaluated from the point of view of human well-being. In the standard utilitarian approach this can be done by choosing an appropriate social welfare function (SWF) where both levels of income and the distribution of income are arguments. Given a preference for equality at a given level of income, only certain SWFs are technically admissible.[6]

A more elaborate evaluation of well-being has been proposed by various theorists drawing upon the insights of Adam Smith. Sen is the originator of this 'capabilities approach' in recent times. The theoretical criticisms of the utilitarian approach proposed by Sen, Nussbaum and others that this approach reduces all qualities into quanta of utilities is a serious one. Nussbaum gives a graphic example of this by quoting the exchange between Mr Gradgrind, economist and grief-stricken father, and his pupil Bitzer. Bitzer outdoes his mentor by adhering to a strict code of utilitarian rationality that cannot comprehend a father's grief. I have pursued a similar line of criticism in a number of recent papers, and in my book *Technology, Development and Democracy*. This approach makes the capabilities both increase steadily on average and tend to equalize them among diverse individuals. In effect, as the following discussion makes clear, we are asking: how can we increase and equalize real, positive freedom for individuals?

In discussing the well-being implications of sound global finance, therefore, I wish to adopt a version of the social capabilities approach. It is not my intention here to present detailed empirical indicators of well-being and to show how these are affected by the crisis and its aftermath. This is the subject of a future volume. Here I simply wish to pose clearly the conceptual problem of evaluating the consequences of reforms. The institutional reforms and changes proposed here, and by scholars who suggest alternative structures, must be proven to be capability-enhancing, or at least not to be capability-reducing. But first we still need to ask: what is meant by capabilities, both abstractly and concretely?

Capabilities can be construed as general powers of human body and mind that can acquired, maintained, nurtured and developed. They can also (under circumstances such as malnutrition or severe confinement) be diminished and even completely lost. I have emphasized elsewhere the irreducibly social (not merely biological) character of these human capabilities. Sen himself emphasizes 'a certain sort of possibility or opportunity for functioning'.

In order to assess financial reforms and structures from a capabilities perspective we need to go further and try to describe more concretely what some of the basic capabilities may be. David Crocker has given an admirable summary of both Nussbaum's and Sen's approaches to capabilities in a recent essay. Relying mainly on Nussbaum, but also drawing on other sources (shown below), he has compiled a list that is worth reproducing here:

Basic Human Functional Capabilities (N and S stand for 'Nussbaum' and 'Sen', respectively; the quoted items come from Nussbaum unless otherwise noted).

1. Capabilities in Relation to Mortality

   N and S: 'Being able to live to the end of a complete human life, so far as is possible'
   1.2.   N: Being able to be courageous

2. Bodily Capabilities

   N and S: 'Being able to have good health'
   2.2.   N and S: 'Being able to be adequately nourished'
   N and S: 'Being able to have adequate shelter'
   2.4.   N: 'Being able to have opportunities for sexual satisfaction'
   2.5.   N and S: 'Being able to move about from place to place'

3. Pleasure

   3.1.   N and S: 'Being able to avoid unnecessary and non-useful pain and to have pleasurable experiences'

4. Cognitive Virtues

    4.1. N: 'Being able to use the five senses'
    4.2. N: 'Being able to imagine'
    4.3. N: 'Being able to think and reason'
    4.4. N and S: 'Being acceptably well-informed'

5. Affiliation I (Compassion)

    5.1. N: 'Being able to have attachments to things and persons outside ourselves'
    5.2. N: 'Being able to love, grieve, to feel longing and gratitude'

6. Virtue of Practical Reason (Agency)

    6.1. N: 'Being able to form a conception of the good'
           S: 'Capability to choose'; 'ability to form goals, commitments, values'
    6.2. N and S: 'Being able to engage in critical reflection about the planning of one's own life'

7. Affiliation II (Friendship and Justice)

    7.1. N: 'Being able to live for and to others, to recognize and show concern for other human beings, to engage in various forms of familial and social interaction'
    7.1.1. N: Being capable of friendship
             S: Being able to visit and entertain friends
    7.1.2. S: Being able to participate in the community
    7.1.3. N: Being able to participate politically and being capable of justice

8. Ecological Virtue

    8.1. N: 'Being able to live with concern for and in relation to animals, plants and the world of nature'

9. Leisure

    9.1. N: 'Being able to laugh, to play, to enjoy recreational activities'

10. Separateness

    10.1. N: 'Being able to live one's own life and nobody else's'
    10.2. N: 'Being able to live in one's very own surroundings and context'

11. Self-respect

    11.1. S: 'Capability to have self-respect'
    11.2. S: 'Capability of appearing in public without shame'

12. Human Flourishing

    12.1. N: 'Capability to live a rich and fully human life, up to the limit permitted by natural possibilities'
    12.2. S: 'Ability to achieve valuable functionings'

To facilitate this ordering, it might be better for practical rationality and affiliation to 'infuse' but not 'organize' the other virtues. Crocker contrasts Nussbaum's approach with Sen's. Sen's and Nussbaum's lists differ at a few points. For Sen, the bodily capabilities and functionings (2) are intrinsically good and not, as they are in some dualistic theories of the good life, merely instrumental means to other (higher) goods. In interpreting Aristotle, Nussbaum distinguishes between bodily functionings that are chosen and intentional – for instance, 'chosen self-nutritive and reproductive activities that form part of a reason-guided life' – and those that are non-intentional – such as digestion and other 'functioning of the bodily system in sleep'. She may want to say that intentional bodily actions that lead to being well-nourished and healthy are intrinsically good, but that being healthy or having good digestion are not functionings (because not intentional) and are valuable only because of what they enable us to do. Another option open to her would be to adopt Sen's view of bodily states and processes, whether intentional or not, as both intrinsically and instrumentally good, but to still hold that they were less valuable than other inherently good capabilities/functionings.

Furthermore, Nussbaum has included items 5 and 8–10, for which Sen has no counterparts. These items are welcome features. Item 8, which I have called 'ecological virtue', is an especially important recent addition to Nussbaum's outlook. In a period when many are exploring ways of effecting a convergence between environmental ethics and development ethics, it is important that an essentially anthropocentric ethic 'makes room' for respect for other species and for ecological systems. Worth considering is whether Nussbaum's 'ecological virtue' is strong enough. Perhaps it should be formulated to read: 'Being able to live with concern for and in relation to animals, plants, and nature as intrinsically valuable.' Item 9 injects some appealing playfulness in a list otherwise marked by the 'spirit of seriousness'. What explains the presence of these items on Nussbaum's list, their absence on Sen's list, and, more generally, the more concrete texture often displayed in Nussbaum's descriptions? One hypothesis is that the differences are due to Nussbaum's greater attention, in her Level 1, to the limits, vulnerabilities, and needs of human existence. Further, it may be that Nussbaum's richer conception of human beings derives from making use of the storytelling imagination far more than the 'scientific intellect'. On the other hand, Sen helpfully includes the good of self-respect, a virtue that enables him to find common ground with Rawls and to establish links with the Kantian ethical tradition, in which moral agents have the obligation to respect all persons, including themselves, as ends-in-themselves.

Both Sen and Nussbaum agree, however, that these capabilities are distinct and of central importance. One cannot easily trade off one dimension of capability against another. At most, one can do so in a very limited way. They cannot be reduced to a common measure such as utility.

As Crocker points out, the 'capability ethic' has implications for freedom, rights and justice going far beyond simple distribution of income considerations. If one accepts the capability approach as a serious foundation for human development, then it follows that going beyond distributive justice is necessary for a complete evaluation of the impact of economic policies.

In evaluating international financial regimes and national economic policies from this perspective we wish to consider not only the question of efficiency but also the whole set of questions regarding human freedom – in particular, the positive human freedom to be or to do certain things. Thus, the creation of markets and efficient production by itself would mean very little if it led to a lopsided distribution of benefits. Worse yet, if markets and other institutions led to phenomena such as reduced life expectancy, increased unemployment, reduced consumption levels for many and deprivation for certain groups such as women and minorities then they will not even be weakly equitable global economic structures. On the contrary, under such circumstances, the global markets and other financial institutions will be strongly inequitable from the capability perspective.

It is because of this perspective that the earlier positive analysis of the problems of global financial markets and institutions needs to be put in a completely transparent 'social capabilities' framework. Such a framework is openly normative and makes a strong ethical case for helping the disadvantaged to increase their capabilities towards achieving equality of capabilities. Thus poorer nations and poor people in the global economy deserve a special ethical attention within any proposed global financial architecture. As Khan (1998) shows in the context of adopting innovation structures leading to increased productivities, ultimately the aim of any increase in productivity needs to be the increase of freedom. Such freedom, as Sen (1999) points out, has both an instrumental value and a 'constitutive' value. Instrumentally, freedom as social capabilities can lead to further increases in productivity. Thus even a hard-nosed, efficiency-driven analysis must address this aspect as an empirically relevant issue.

The thrust of the previous chapters has been to show how bad theories – regardless of their ideological leanings, left, right or centre – can lead to bad policies. Likewise, a refusal to face up to serious ethical issues of equity and well-being for all can also lead to a troubled society. As we move towards the creation of a global society, where individuality and rich diversity reflected in differences of cultures and social practices leading to well-being are equally respected, we can do no less than make a genuine attempt to approach the reforming of old financial structures and building new financial institutions with a clear ethical perspective of global citizenship. Efficiency and equity are both important and sometimes can be achieved together. At other times at least short-run trade offs must be considered carefully. Here, the advances in economic theory – both positive and normative – can play a modest but useful role. Therefore, in the realm of crisis prevention and crisis management, the minimization of costs and the maximization of the benefits from any financial system must be guided by advances in both positive economic theories and economic ethics.

If the main argument advanced in this book is correct, the global financial markets need monitoring and a proper global financial architecture needs to be erected for both efficiency and equity reasons. From the efficiency side the argument – in a world of undiversifiable systemic risks – has been quite clearly one of exercising prudence through appropriate national and international institutional arrangements that can formulate and implement policies better than in the past. On the equity side, the foregoing argument would lead towards creating institutions and policies that protect not just creditors, but also the ordinary citizens. In particular, careful attention must be paid to the problems of the disadvantaged and the vulnerable groups. Adequate social safety nets must be in place before the crisis, and a swift response after the crisis to meet their urgent needs must be ensured. A more democratic decision making before the crisis could better realize such administrative structures. Once again, good governance at all levels is essential. If the twenty-first century is to be safer, with a more civilized global society, then these democratic imperatives must be heeded along with the technical advice that economists can give from time to time. Thus the role of both economists and political economists – modest as they are in reality – can nevertheless play a constructive role in making this century a more civilized one than all the previous epochs. The choice of proper theories, their further development and correct application are, therefore, among the most urgent tasks faced by our profession. This book may be considered as one small step by a single individual towards fulfilling these tasks.

Notes and References

2 The Beginning of the Crisis: Thailand

1. It is interesting that in the euphoric 1990s many Asian capitals – from Taipei to Bangkok – aspired to become regional financial centres. In retrospect even the relatively more realistic APROC (Asia Pacific Regional Financial Center) plan of Taiwan seems to have been overly ambitious. One can only wonder about the financial hype that led the Thai authorities to grossly overestimate the potential of Bangkok as a regional financial centre.
2. Chaiyasoot Naris (1995) 'Industrialization, Financial Reform and Monetary Policy', in Medhi Krongkraew (ed.), *Thailand's Industrialization and Its Consequences* (London: Macmillan), pp. 177–8.
3. Two failing banks that did not submit acceptable recapitalization plans – the First Bangkok City Bank and the Siam City Bank – were nationalized on 9 February 1998. The capital losses at the Bangkok Bank of commerce and Bangkok Metropolitan Bank were simply written-off.
4. H.A. Khan (1998) 'A Quick Note on Financial Crisis with Some Estimates of the Social Cost for Thailand', unpublished paper, Asian Development Bank and University of Denver.

3 The Crisis Spreads: Indonesia (with Arry Basuseno)

1. See Franco Modigliani and M. Miller, 'The Cost of Capital, Corporate Finance, and the Theory of Investment', *American Economic Review*, June 1972.
2. See also Yung Chul Park, 'Concept and issues', in Patrick, T., Hugh, and Yung Chul Park, *The Financial Development of Japan, Korea, and Taiwan: Growth, Repression, and Liberalization*, New York, Oxford University Press, 1994, pp. 8–10.
3. Depending on the source of information, the inflation rates in the mid-1960s range from 500 per cent up to 1200 per cent. The 'official' Bank Indonesia rate was 650 per cent in 1965.
4. Binhadi, *Financial Sector Deregulation Banking Development and Monetary Policy the Indonesian Experience* (Jakarta: Institut Bankir Indonesia, 1995), p. 13.
5. In the BE (Bonus Export) system the foreign exchange was surrendered to the central bank. In exchange the exporter received BE certificates that could be sold to importers. Thus there was no direct market for the actual foreign exchange.
6. Binhadi, *Financial Sector Deregulation*, p. 20.

5 Finance in a Complex Capitalist Economy: Failures of Global Markets and Developmental States

1. There is a debate about whether total factor productivity increased or not. Khan (forthcoming, a and b) offers a review of the literature and an alternative approach applied to Korea and Taiwan.
2. Khan (1998 and 2002e) describes and offers mathematical models of such modern technology systems called POLIS (positive feedback loop innovation system) which are then applied to both South Korea and Taiwan.
3. Other export incentives include rebates of custom duties and commodity taxes on imported raw materials, tax exemptions, retention of foreign exchange earnings for the import of raw materials and machinery, etc.

6 Corporate Governance: a New Theory and Reform of the Family-Based Corporate Governance System in Asia

1. It should also be mentioned at this point that this chapter is only concerned with privately owned and controlled firms. Many of the conceptual issues discussed here are, of course, similar. But SOEs form a distinct category and their governance should be analysed separately. I am grateful to Sadrel Reza for helpful discussions with regards to SOEs.
2. As Suehiro (1993, 1997) correctly points out '[t]he body of research...confronting directly the phenomenon referred to as "family business" is surprisingly small in quantity and rather shallow in its theoretical consideration of the subject matter' (1993, p. 379). Within the scanty theoretical tradition, starting with Berle and Means (1932) and especially in Chandler (1977), the passing away of family enterprise and the rise of the 'managerial firm' has been accepted as an indisputable stylized fact. In reality, however, family-based enterprises and family control have been remarkably obdurate, especially in Asia. See also the interesting work by Okazaki (2001) on the role of *Zaibatsu* in prewar Japan.
3. Prof. Miwa at Tokyo University has argued, based on his empirical research, that in Japan equity markets, rather than banks, played a crucial role in financing (and perhaps governance also). This interesting and controversial research counters the traditional bank-based view of finance during early phases of economic development – at least in the case of Japan. See Miwa and Ramseyer (2000).
4. These terms are defined with greater precision in the next section. See also Rajan and Zingales (1998) and Zingales (1997) for a discussion of closely related conceptual issues. Kim and Rhee (1999) present some interesting empirical results.
5. It should be pointed out that in order for the BLS to be an effective system of governance at all the banks must have the incentives and capacity to monitor the firms to which they lend. This clearly depends on the location (in a functional sense) and political power of the banks in the overall financial system. As some researchers (for example, Suehiro for Thailand, Sato for Indonesia and Nam for South Korea) have pointed out, in many Asian

countries the banks themselves are family-based or are under the influence of government which may be more motivated by short-run political pressures rather than long-run economic interests. Clearly, under such circumstances banks are neither well governed themselves, nor can they govern their debtor firms. One crucial precondition for moving to BLS is, therefore, to have effective governance of the banks themselves so that their position as monitors become viable.

6. As mentioned earlier, even the family-based corporates are relatively little studied. Hence, it is not surprising that almost no attention has been devoted to a systematic study of their structure, conduct and performance until recently. Recent work by Khanna and Palepu (1996, 1999) on India and by Claessens, Djankov, Fan and Lang (1998, 1999) and Claessens, Djankov and Lang (1999) are important beginnings of serious research in this area.

7. It should be mentioned that other forms of classification are also possible. For example, Lehman (1997) offers a sixfold classification comprising of the Rheinal, Mediterranean, Japanese keiretsu. The Korean chaebol, the Chinese bamboo network and the Anglo-American systems. It can be seen that most of his categories are sub-species of FBS and BLS systems. Thus, his classification is consistent with the above threefold classification with the exception that his conceptualization minimizes the growth potential of what he quaintly calls 'the Chinese bamboo network'. It is, of course, entirely proper and desirable to look into the sub-categories of FBS if and when necessary. In this chapter chaebols are treated as one such special sub-category of FBS.

8. Claessens, Djankov and Lang (1999), 'Who Controls East Asian Corporations', p. 3.

9. As pointed out by Yuri Sato during a discussion at ADBI, this problem became quite acute in the case of Indonesia before the crisis when the domestic banks borrowed from foreign banks and lent to their business groups without being monitored by anyone.

10. Singapore also has some large family-controlled businesses. However, on the whole, the government-linked corporations, the relatively well-functioning banking system and the presence of multinationals are the major factors in corporate governance. See also Linda Lim (1983).

11. Testing such hypotheses would require micro, firm-level data. There are several data bases of this type, including the World Scope Database, which has more than 2,500 observations for East Asian firms.

12. Of course, there are alternative hypotheses as well. Two of these are the reduction of firm-specific risk and expropriation of wealth from minority shareholders.

13. This usage of 'market within the firm' is not literally true, of course, unless a market simulation via shadow pricing is attempted. I have conformed here with the standard literature (see, for example, Williamson, 1985; Khanna and Palepu, 1997; Claessens et al., 1999) rather than coin another, less metaphorical term.

14. See for example, A. Sen, *Development as Freedom*, and H.A. Khan, *Technology, Development and Democracy* for a discussion of this alternative normative approach.

15. There are, of course, other measures of RoA, for example operational margin. This measure shows less cross-country differences. But again, Singapore and

Korea turn out to be relatively lower margin producers. On this, see Claessens, Djankov and Lang (1998).

16. For some interesting evidence on shareholder activism in the Japanese context see Kim and Rhee (1999).

17. This, in fact, is one of the most important policy issues for Asia in the medium term. I am grateful to Hitoshi Nishida and Toshio Karigane for helpful discussions regarding the development of bond markets

18. Khan and Lippit (1993a, b) consider the specific problem of defining a steady state under environmental constraints. However, their treatment of bounded rationality and uncertainty can be carried over to other relevant contexts.

19. Williamson (1988) discusses four types of *ex post* costs: '[t]hese include (1) the maladaptation costs incurred when transactions drift out of alignment in relation to what Masahiko Aoki refers to as the 'shifting contract curve', (2) the haggling costs incurred if bilateral efforts are made to correct *ex post* misalignments, (3) the setup and running costs associated with the governance structures (often not the courts) to which disputes are referred, and (4) the bonding costs of effecting secure commitments...'.

7 Asian Banks: Can They Learn to Assess Risks Better? (with C.-S. Lin)

1. The empirical illustration presented later in the text draws heavily upon my joint work-in-progress with C.-S. Lin without implicating him in any of the substantive, epistemological or ontological interpretations that I have presented in this chapter.

2. This is indeed crucial, and sets the present work apart from both the 'as if...' variety without ontological commitments and the 'satisficing' school which is essentially empiricist in a phenomenological way. Usually, the theorists in both schools have not directly confronted the difficult philosophical issues.

3. This is in fact the ultimate aim of the project. In this chapter, the 'black box' problem is not solved except to show that neural networks with hidden layers can learn satisfactorily in some circumstances. The moving euilibria may not necessarily converge to the rational expectations equilibrium in the 'stationary state', however.

4. The classic discussion of vagueness beyond Wittgenstein's idea of 'family resemblances' is Max Black (1937). See also Birkhoff and von Neumann (1936). For more recent discussions, see Rescher (1969) and Kosko (1992).

5. For the detailed formulas for each item please refer to Chen and Chiou (1999).

6. However, there are still some unsolved logical problems – the most important being the Duhem-Quine problem of joint hypotheses. Roughly, neither inference form can work because both p and q (but particularly p) are very rarely, if ever, single hypotheses.

7. Please refer to Zimmermann (1991) for details.

8. Please refer to Tong and Bonissone (1984) and Zimmermann (1987) for the other defuzzification methods. And please refer to Klir and Yuan (1995) for the detailed discussion of fuzzy logic.

8   Towards a New Global Financial Architecture

1. See Khan (2002a, b, c, d).
2. See for example, Blustein (2001).
3. For a discussion and review of recent literature, please see Akram (2002).
4. In fact, the IMF has already done it (albeit somewhat unconscious of the underlying theoretical justification) once by focusing on the structural adjustments in indebted Third World countries. Since 1973, the traditional Bretton Woods era functions of IMF have practically almost ceased to exist.
5. See for example, Khan (2002a), 'Can Banks Learn to Be Rational?', Discussion Paper no. 2002 CF-151, Graduate School of Economics, University of Tokyo.
6. See Keynes (1936), in particular the discussion of long-term expectations in chapter 12.
7. Of course, the risk of contagion is always present whenever a financial crisis breaks out. Whether actual contagion is observed depends on a number of factors, including the domestic economy's ability to fight off speculative attacks.
8. See UNCTAD (2002), particularly sections 5 and 6.
9. See for example, Azis (1999), Khan (forthcoming a), Sachs, Tornell and Velasco (1996), Sachs and Woo (2000), Summers (2000), Tobin and Ranis (1998), and Yoshitomi and Ohno (1999).
10. See David (1993, p. 23).
11. But when the Asian crisis countries liberalized the financial sector in the 1980s, the aforementioned preconditions (assumptions) were not in place. Yet, they were rushed to liberalize by the IFI. Ironically, when at the early stage the policy showed favourable impacts, e.g., higher economic growth, greater access to financial services, the IFI applauded it. But when the crisis hit, the very same countries previously praised were swiftly placed into the category of those with misplaced development strategies. All of a sudden, nothing was right with these countries. When confronted with such an embarrassing contradiction, the international institutions are quick to claim that they actually *saw* the faults, and *already reminded* the governments about the existing flaws (e.g., weak banking system, unsustainable exchange rate system, and widespread corruption). Azis (2002c) p. 3.
12. Azis (2002c, p. 3).
13. Ibid., pp. 3–4.
14. James Tobin and Gustav Ranis were among those who believed that the IMF programmes in Asia were based on the Fund's experiences with Mexico in 1994: 'The IMF's Asian packages are based on its experiences with Latin America, in particular with Mexico in 1994' (Tobin and Ranis, 1998).
15. Azis (2002c, p. 7) suggests: 'The experience with policy adjustments of this kind in Eastern Europe and the former Soviet Union (from communism to market economy) had inspired the Fund to do the same thing in Asia'.
16. See Khan (1999a, b, and 2001) on Asian corporate governance reform, and the sketch of an evolutionary theory.
17. It is, however, still useful to urge the expansion of SDRs both as an ultimate 'global central banking' role for the IMF down the line and also as a source of financing for some global projects. For one such specific proposal for enhancing commodity price stabilization facilities, see Khan (2002d).

9 General Conclusions: From Crisis to a Global Political Economy of Freedom

1. Keynes (1971–9), vol. X, p. 261.
2. A more detailed methodological discussion is given in my 'On Paradigms, Theories and Models', June 2002. University of Tokyo, CIRJE Discussion paper no. 2002-CF-156.
3. However, this should not be ruled out completely. Pressures for increased supply of SDRs will be beneficial in specific ways, as argued below.
4. In fact the Bank for International Settlements (BIS) made a successful bid to host IAIS in 1996. If BIS – with cooperation from the US – can become more capable of helping in the supervision of non-bank financial institutions, that will be a significant step towards global stability.
5. Of course, questions can be raised as to whether the IMF recipe worked even in the sovereign debt case. For a review of the pro and contra literature on this, and some novel theoretical arguments and empirical results in the African context, see Khan (1997b).
6. For example, Schur-concave SWFs are examples of just such 'equality preferring' SWFs.

Bibliography

Aghion, P., P. Bolton and L. Felli, 'Some Issues on Contract Incompleteness', London School of Economics Working Paper (London, 1997).

Aghion, P., M. Dewatripont and P. Rey, 'Renegotiation Design with Unverifiable Information', *Econometrica*, 62 (1994) 257–82.

Agonsin, M., 'Capital Inflows and Investment Performance: Chile in the 1990s', in R. French-Davis and H. Reisen (eds), *Capital Flows and Investment Performance: Lessons from Latin America* (Paris: OECD, 1998).

Akaba, Yuji, Florain Budde and Jungkiu Choi, 'Restructuring South Korea's Chaebol', *The McKinsey Quarterly*, 4 (1998).

Akram, Tanweer, 'The Evolution of Globalization', *Working Paper*, Columbia University, 2002.

Akyuz, Y., 'Taming International Finance', in J. Michie and J. Grieve Smith (eds), *Managing the Global Economy* (Oxford: Oxford University Press, 1995).

Akyuz, Y., 'New Trends in Japanese Trade and FDI: Post-industrial Transformation and Policy Challenge', in R. Kozul-Wright and R. Rowthorn (eds), *Transnational Corporations in the Global Economy* (London: Macmillan, 1998).

Akyuz, Y. (ed.), *Reforming the Global Financial Architecture* (Geneva: UNCTAD, 2002).

Akyuz, Y., Change Ha-Joon and R. Kozul-Wright, 'New Perspectives on East Asian Development', *Journal of Development Studies*, 34(6) (1998) 4–36.

Akyuz, Y. and A. Cornford, 'International Capital Movements: Some Proposals for Reform' in J. Michie and J. Grieve Smith (eds), *Managing the Global Economy* (Oxford: Oxford University Press, 1995).

Alchian, A. and H. Demsetz, 'Production, Information Costs, and Economic Organization', *American Economic Review*, 65(5) (1972) 777–95.

Alesina, Alberto, 'Macroeconomics and Politics', *NBER Macroeconomic Annual* (Cambridge, MA: MIT Press, 1988), pp. 13–52.

Alesina, Alberto, and R. Gatti, 'Independent Central Banks: Low Inflation at Low Cost?', Papers and Proceedings of the 107th Annual Meeting of the American Economic Association, *American Economic Review*, May 1995.

Alesina, Alberto, and Larry Summers, 'Central Bank Independence and Macro-economic Performance', *Journal of Money, Credit and Banking*, 25 (1993) 151–62.

Alesina, Alberto, and Guido Tabellini, 'Rules and Discretion with Non-Coordinated Monetary and Fiscal Policies', *Economic Inquiry*, 25 (1987) 619–30.

Altman, E., G. Marco, and F. Varetto, 'Corporate Distress Diagnosis: Comparisons Using Linear Discriminant Analysis and Neural Networks', *Journal of Banking and Finance*, 18 (1994) 505–29.

Amsden Alice, *Asia's Next Giant: South Korea and hate Industrialization* (Oxford: Oxford University Press, 1989).

Aoki, Masahiko, *The Economic Analysis of the Japanese Firm* (Amsterdam: North-Holland, 1984).

Aoki, Masahiko and H.K. Kim (eds), *Corporate Governance in Transitional Economies: Insider Control and the Role of Banks* (Washington DC: The World Bank, 1995).

Aoki, Masahiko, H.K. Kim and Masahiro Okuno-Fujiwara, *The Role of Government in East Asian Economic Development: Comparative Institutional Analysis* (Oxford: Clarendon Press, 1996).

Arestis, P. and M. Sawyer, 'What Role for the Tobin Tax in World Economic Governance?', in J. Michie and J. Grieve Smith (eds), *Global Instability: the Political Economy of World Economic Governance* (London: Routledge, 1999).

Ariyoshi, A., K. Habermeier, B. Laurens, I. Otker-Robe, J. Canales-Kriljenko and A. Kirilenko, *Country Experiences with the Use and Liberalization of Capital Controls* (Washington, DC: IMF, 2000).

Asian Development Bank, 'ADB Regional Study on Capital Market Development', *RETA*, 5770, Manila, Philippines, 1999.

Atiya, A.F., 'Bankruptcy Prediction for Credit Risk using Neural Networks: a Survey and New Results', *IEEE Transactions on Neural Networks*, 12(4) (2001) 929–35.

Azis, Iwan J., 'Currency Crisis in Southeast Asia: the Bubble Finally Bursts', paper presented at the 45th Annual Conference on the Economic Outlook, organized by Research Seminar in Quantitative Economics (RSQE), University of Michigan, USA, 20–21 November 1997.

Azis, Iwan J., 'Do We Know the Real Causes of the Asian Crisis?', *Global Financial Turmoil and Reform: a United Nations Perspective* (Tokyo: The United Nations University Press, 1999).

Azis, Iwan J., 'Modeling the Transition From Financial Crisis to Social Crisis', *Asian Economic Journal*, 14(4) (2000) 357–87.

Azis, Iwan J., 'Modeling Crisis Evolution and Counterfactual Policy Simulations: a Country Case Study', *ADB Institute Working Paper*, 23 (Tokyo, 2001a).

Azis, Iwan J., 'Cautions Surrounding Financial Sector Liberalization: a Modeling Approach', *Asia Policy Forum on Sequencing Domestic and External Financial Liberalization* (Asian Development Bank Institute, Tokyo, 20–1, December 2001b).

Azis, Iwan J., 'What Would Have Happened in Indonesia if Different Economic Policies had been Implemented When the Crisis Started?', *The Asian Economic Papers* (Cambridge, MA: MIT Press, 2002a).

Azis, Iwan J., 'IMF Perspectives and Alternative Views On the Asian Crisis: an Application of Analytic Hierarchy Process and Game Theory Approach', in Partha Gangopadhyay and Manas Chatterji (eds), *Globalization and Economic Reform* (Cheltenham: Edward Elgar Publishing, 2002b).

Azis, Iwan J., 'Financial Sector Liberalization and the Asian Financial Crisis: The IFI Got it Wrong Twice', Working Paper, 2002c.

Azis, Iwan J. and Willem Thorbecke, *The Effects of Exchange Rate and Interest Rate Shock on Bank Lending*, mimeo, Cornell University, January 2002.

Baker, D., R. Pollin, and M. Schaberg, 'The Case for a Securities Transaction Tax', mimeo, Department of Economics, University of Massachusetts, 1995.

Bank of Indonesia, *Annual Reports*.

Banuri, T. (ed.), *Economic Liberalisation: No Panacea* (Oxford: Oxford University Press, 1991).

Barro, R., 'Inflation and Economic Growth', *Bank of England Quarterly Bulletin*, 35(2) (May 1995) 166–76.

Barro, Robert and David Gordon, 'Rules, Discretion, and Reputation in a Model of Monetary Policy', *Journal of Monetary Economics*, 12 (1983) 101–22.

Basel Committee on Banking Supervision, 'An Internal Model-Based Approach to Market Risk Capital Requirement', Basle, April 1995.

Bekaert, Geert, Campbell R. Harvey, and Christian Lundblad, 'Does Financial Liberalization Spur Growth?', *NBER Working Paper*, 8245, Cambridge, Massachusetts, 2001.

Bello, Walden, 'Government, Markets and Countryside Development in the Asian NICs: Myths, Realities and Lessons for the Phillipines', *Issues and Letters*, Quezon City: Phillipines Center for Policy Studies, November–December, 1995.

Bello, Walden, 'Addicted to Capital: the Ten-year High and Present-day Withdrawal Trauma of Southeast Asia's Economies', *Issues and Letters*, Philippine Center for Policy Studies, September–December, 1997.

Bello, Walden, 'The Rise and Fall of Southeast Asia's Economy', *The Ecologist*, 28(1), (January/February 1998) 9–17.

Berg, Janine, and Lance Taylor, 'External Liberalization, Economic Performance, and Social Policy', *Working Paper, No. 12*, Center for Economic Policy Analysis (CEPA), New York, 2000.

Berglöf, Erik, 'Reforming Corporate Governance: Redirecting the European Agenda ', *Economic Policy*, 24 (1997) 93–123.

Berle, A.A. and G.C. Means, *The Modern Corporation and Private Property* (New York: Macmillan, 1932).

Bernanke, Ben, Thomas Laubach, Frederic Mishkin, and Adam Posen, *Inflation Targeting* (Princeton: Princeton University Press, 1999).

Bernanke, Ben and Frederic Mishkin, 'Central Bank Behavior and the Strategy of Monetary Policy from Six Industrialized Countries', *NBER Macroeconomics Annual* (Cambridge, MA: MIT Press, 1992).

Benston, G., 'Safety Nets and Moral Hazards in Banking', in K. Sawamoto, Z. Nakajima, and H. Tagushi (eds), *Financial Stability in a Changing Environment* (London and New York: Macmillan and St Martin's Press, 1995).

Bhagwati, Jagdish, 'The Capital Myth', *Foreign Affairs*, (May/June 1998).

Binh, Tran-Nam and Mark McGillivray, 'Foreign Aid, Taxes and Public Investment: a Comment', *Journal of Development Economics*, 41 (1993) 173–6.

Birkhoff, G. and J. von Neumann, 'The Logic of quantum Mechanics', *Annals of Mathematics*, 37(4) (1936) 823–43.

Biro Pusat Statistik (BPS), Jakarta, *National Income Accounts*, various years; *Social Accounting Matrices*, various years.

Black, M., 'Vagueness: an Exercise in Logical Analysis', *Philosophy of Science*, 4 (1937) 427–55.

Blinder, Alan, *Central Banking in Theory & Practice* (Cambridge, MA: MIT Press, 1998).

Blum, M., 'Failing Company Discriminate Analysis', *Journal of Accounting Research*, 12 (1974) 1–25.

Blustein, Paul, *The Chastening: Inside the Crisis that Rocked the Global Financial System and Humbled the IMF* (New York: Public Affairs, 2001).

Booth, Anne, 'Survey of Recent Developments', *Bulletin of Indonesian Economic Studies*, 24(1) (1988) 1–26.

Bordo, Michael and Finn Kydland, 'The Gold Standard as a Rule', *National Bureau of Economic Research Working Paper*, 3367 (1990).

Boritz, J., and D. Kennedy 'Effectiveness of Neural Network Types for Prediction of Business Failure', *Expert Syst. Appl.*, 9 (1995) 504–12.

Boritz, J., D. Kennedy, and A. Albuquerque, 'Predicting Corporate Failure using a Neural Network Approach', *Intelligent Systems in Accounting, Finance, and Management*, 4 (1995) 95–111.

Bosworth, Barry P., Rudiger Dornbusch, and Raul Laban (eds), *The Chilean Economy: Policy Lessons and Challenges* (Washington, DC: The Brookings Institution, 1994).

Brent, Robert J., *Tobin Tax versus Reserve Requirements: Which Capital Control Works Better?*, mimeo, the Asian Development Bank Institute, 1999.

Briault, C., A. Haldane, and Mervyn King, 'Independence and Accountability', *Working Paper*, 49, Bank of England (1996).

Browne, Stephen, *Foreign Aid in Practice* (New York: New York University Press, 1990).

Bryan, L., *Breaking Up the Bank: Rethinking and Industry Under Siege* (Homewood, IL: Dow Jones-Irwin, 1988).

Buckheit, Lee C. and Ralph Reisner, 'Latin American Debt in the 1990s: a New Scenario for Creditors and Debtors', *Northwestern Journal of International Law and Business*, 16(1) (1995) 1–4.

Buckley, J.J. and Y. Hayashi, 'Fuzzy Neural Networks: a Survey', *Fuzzy Sets and Systems*, 66 (1994), 1–13.

Buiter, Willem H. and Anne C. Sibert, *UDROP: a Small Contribution to the New International Financial Architecture*, mimeo, University of Cambridge and Birkbeck College, University of London, 1999.

Bulletin of Indonesian Economic Studies, *Economic Surveys* (Canberra: Australia, various years).

Burch, P.H., *The Managerial Revolution Reassessed: Family Control in America's Large Corporations* (Lexington, MA: Lexington Books, 1972).

Burnside, Craig, Martin Eichenbaum and Sergio Rebelo, 'Prospective Deficits and the Asian Currency Crisis', *Working Paper Series*, Federal Reserve Bank of Chicago, WP-98-5 (1998).

Burton, John, 'Bruising Battle at Korea IMF Talks', *Financial Times* (3 December 1997).

Burton, John, 'Painful Prospect', *Financial Times* (8 December 1997).

Burton, John, 'Anger at IMF Terms May Boost Korean Opposition', *Financial Times* (11 December 1997).

Bush Task Force, *Blueprint for Reform: the Report of the Task Group on Regulation of Financial Services* (Washington DC, 1984).

Calomiris, Charles W., 'The IMF's Imprudent Role as Lender of Last Resort', *Cato Journal*, 17 (1998) 275–95.

Calomiris, Charles W., 'Is Deposit Insurance Necessary? A Historical Perspective', *Journal of Economic History*, 50(2) (1990) 283–95.

Calomiris, Charles W., *Reforming the Global Financial System*, mimeo, 1999.

Calvo, Guillermo A., 'Comment on Sachs, Tornell and Velasco', *Brookings Papers on Economic Activity*, 1 (1996).

Calvo, Guillermo A., 'The Simple Economics of Sudden Stops', *Journal of Applied Economics*, 1(1) (1998a) 35–54.

Calvo, Guillermo A., *Capital Markets Contagion and Recession: an Explanation of the Russian Virus*, mimeo, University of Maryland, 1998b.

Calvo, Guillermo A., and Enrique G. Mendoza, 'Regional Contagion and the Globalization of Securities Markets', *NBER Working Paper*, W7153 (June 1999).

Campillo, Marta, *Essays on Consumption and Inflation*, Boston University Dissertation Library, 2000.

Capie, Forrest, Charles Goodhart and Norbert Schnadt, *The Development of Central Banking* (Cambridge: Cambridge University Press, 1994).

Capie, F. and G. Wood, *Unregulated Banking: Chaos or Order?* (London: Macmillan, 1991).

Caplin, Andrew and John Leahy, 'Business as Usual, Market Crashes, and Wisdom After the Fact', *American Economic Review*, 84 (1994) 548–65.

Caramazza, Francesco and Jahangir Aiz, 'Fixed or Flexible? Getting the Exchange Rate Right in the 1990s', *Economic Issues*, 13, International Monetary Fund (1998).

Cashel-Cordo, Peter and Steven G. Craig, *Donor Preferences and Recipient Fiscal Behavior: a Simultaneous Analysis of Foreign Aid Fungibility and the Flypaper Effect* (Manuscript, Canisius College, Buffalo, NY, 14208, 1992).

Castello-Branco, M. and Swinburne, 1991, M., 'Central Bank Independence: Issues and Experience', *IMF Working Paper*, 91/58 (Washington, DC, International Monetary Fund, 1991).

Cecchetti, Stephen, 'Central Bank Accountability in Formulating Monetary Policy', Federal Reserve Bank of New York. Seminar on Current Legal Issues Affecting Central Banks, 1998.

Cerra, Valerie and Sweta Charman Saxena, *Contagion, Monsoons, and Domestic Turmoil in Indonesia: a Case Study in the Asian Currency Crisis*, mimeo, 1998.

Chandler, A.D., *The Visible Hand: the Managerial Revolution in American Business* (Cambridge, MA: Harvard University Press, 1977).

Chandler, L., *The Economics of Money and Banking*, 6th edn (New York: Harper & Row, 1973).

Chang, Ha-Joon, 'The Korean Crisis: a Dissenting View', *Third World Economics*, (16–31 January 1998) 1555–61.

Chang, H.-J., 'Korea: the Misunderstood Crisis', *World Development*, 26(8) (1998) 1555–62.

Chang, H.-J., H.-J. Park and C.G. Yoo, 'Interpreting the Korean Crisis: Financial Liberalization, Industrial Policy and Corporate Governance', *Cambridge Journal of Economics*, 22 (6) (November 1998) 735–46.

Chang, Min, *Central Bank Independence and Monetary Effects* (Michigan State University, 1997).

Chang, Roberto, and Andres Velasco, 'The Asian Liquidity Crisis', *NBER Working Paper*, W6796 (November 1998).

Chang, Robert, and Andres Velasco, 'Financial Fragility and the Exchange Rate Regime', *NBER Working Paper*, 6469 (1998).

Chen, L.H. and T.W., Chiou, 'A fuzzy Credit-Rating Approach for Commercial Loans: a Taiwan Case', *OMEGA, International Journal of Management Science*, 27 (1999) 407–19.

Chin, Kok Fay and K.S. Jomo, 'Financial Liberalisation and Intermediation in Malaysia', in K.S. Jomo and Jagaraj Shyamala (eds), *Globalisation and Development: Heterodox Perspectives* (Basingstoke: Palgrave – now Palgrave Macmillan).

Chinn, Menzie D., 'Before the Fall: Were East Asian Currencies Overvalued?', *NBER Working Paper*, W6491 (April 1998).

Chinn, Menzie D. and Michael P. Dooley, 'Money and Policy in Japan, Germany, and the United States: Does One Size Fit All?', *NBER Working Paper*, 6092 (1997).

Cholada, Ingsrisawan and Parista Yuthamanop, 'Troubling New Era Awaits Bang-kok Post Year-end Economic Review 1997' (1998).

Chorafas, D.N., 'Expert System at the Banker's Reach', *International Journal of Bank Marketing*, 5 (1987) 72–81.

Chossudovsky, Michel, 'The IMF Korea Bailout', *Third World Resurgence*, 89 (January 1998).

Claessens, Stijn, Simeon Djankov, and Giovanni Ferri, *Corporate Distress in East Asia: Assessing the Impact of Interest and Exchange Rate Shocks* (mimeo, The World Bank, 1998).

Claessens, Stijn, Simeon Djankov, Joseph P.H. Fan and Larry H.P. Lang, *Ownership Structure and Corporate Performance in East Asia* (The World Bank, Mimeo, 1998).

Claessens, Stijn, Simeon Djankov, Joseph P.H. Fan, and Larry H.P. Lang, 'Expro-priation of Minority Shareholders: Evidence from East Asia', The World Bank, *Working Paper* (1999).

Claessens, Stijn, Simeon Djankov and Larry H.P. Lang, 'East Asian Corporates: Growth, Financing and Risks over the Last Decade', World Bank, *Working Paper* (1998).

Claessens, Stijn, Asli Demirguc-Kunt, and Harry Huizinga, 'How Does Foreign Entry Affect the Domestic Banking Market?', *World Bank Policy Research Work-ing Paper*, 1918 (1998).

Claessens, Stijn, Simeon Djankov and Larry H.P. Lang, 'Who Controls East Asian Corporations', The World Bank, *Working Paper* (1999).

Clarke, George, Robert Cull, Laura D'Amato and Andrea Molinari, *On the Kindness of Strangers? The Impact of Foreign Entry on Domestic Banks in Argentina* (mimeo, The World Bank, 1999).

Coats, P., and L. Fant, 'Recognizing Financial Distress Patterns Using a Neural Network Tool', *Financial Management*, 22 (1993), 142–55.

Collins, R.A. and Green, R.D., 'Statistical Method for Bankruptcy Forecasting', *Journal of Economics and Business*, 34 (1982), 349–54.

Cooper, Richard N., 'Should Capital Account Convertibility be a World Objec-tive?' in S. Fischer (ed.), *Should the IMF Pursue Capital Account Convertibility?*, *Essays in International Finance* 207 (Princeton, NJ, 1998).

Cooper, Richard N., 'Exchange Rate Choices', in Jane S. Little and Giovanni P. Olivei (eds), *Rethinking the International Monetary System*, Conference Proceed-ings, Federal Reserve Bank of Boston (1999).

Corbo, Vittorio and Stanley Fischer, 'Lessons from the Chilean Stabilization and Recovery', in Barry P. Bosworth, Rudiger Dornbusch, and Raul Laban (eds), *The Chilean Economy: Policy Lessons and Challenges* (Washington, D.C: The Brook-ings Institution, 1994).

Council of Foreign Exchange and Other Transactions, 'Internationalization of the Yen for the 21st Century' (Japan: Ministry of Finance, 20 April 1999).

Courchene, Thomas, *Money, Inflation, and the Bank of Canada* (Toronto: C.D. Howe Research Institute, 1976).

Cowan, K. and Jose De Gregorio, 'Exchange Rate Policies and Capital Account Management: Chile in the 1990s', in R. Glick (ed.), *Managing Capital Flows and Exchange Rates: Perspectives from the Pacific Basin* (Cambridge University Press, 1998), pp. 465–88.

Cozier, Barry and Gordon Wilkinson, 'Some Evidence on Hysresis and the Costs of Disinflation in Canada', *Bank of Canada Technical Report*, 55 (1991).

Crow, John, 'What to do about the Bank of Canada', *Bank of Canada Review*, (June 1992) 3–10.

Cuddington, John, 'Capital Flight: Estimates, Issues, and Explanations', *Essays in International Finance*, 58 (1986).

Cukierman, A., *Central Bank Strategy, Credibility, and Independence: Theory and Evidence* (Cambridge, MA: MIT Press, 1992).

Cukierman, A., 'Central Bank Independence and Monetary Control', *Policy Forum of The Economic Journal*, 104 (November 1994) 1437–48.

Cukierman, A., S. Webb, and B. Nevapti, 'Measuring the Independence of Central Banks and its Effects on Policy Outcomes', *World Bank Economic Review*, 6(3) (September 1992) 353–98.

Cull, Robert, *The Effect of Deposit Insurance on Financial Depth: a Cross-Country Analysis* (mimeo, 1998).

David, Paul, 'Intellectual Property Institutions and the Parda's Thumb: Patents, Copyrights, and Trade Secrets in Economic theory and Policy, in M.B. Wallerstein, M.E. Mogee and R.A. Schoen (eds), *Global Dimensions of Intellectual Property Rights in Science and Technology* (Washington, DC: National Academy Press, 1993).

Dawe, S., 'Reserve Bank of New Zealand Act 1989', *Reserve Bank Bulletin*, 53(1) (1990) 29–36.

Dean, M., and Pringle, R., *The Central Banks* (London: Hamish Hamilton, 1994).

Debelle, Guy, *The End of Three Small Inflations* (Cambridge, MA: MIT Press, 1994).

Debelle, Guy, and Stanley Fischer, *How Independent Should a Central Bank Be?* (Center for Economic Policy Research (Stanford)-Federal Reserve Bank of San Francisco conference, San Francisco, 4 March 1994).

Debelle, Guy, Paul, Masson Miguel Savastano, and Sunil Sharma, *Inflation Targeting as a Framework for Monetary Policy* (IMF Publications, 1998).

Debreu, Gerard, *Theory of Value* (New Haven, CT: Cowles Foundation, 1959).

De Gregorio, J., Sebastian Edwards, and Rodrigo O. Valdes, 'Capital Controls in Chile: an Assessment', paper presented at the 11th IASE-NBER conference (1998).

De Gregorio, J., Sebastian Edwards, and Rodrigo O. Valdes, *Controls on Capital Inflows: Do They Work?* (mimeo, 2000).

Dekle, Robert, Cheng Hisao and Siyan Wang, *Interest Rate Stabilization of Exchange Rates and Contagion in the Asian Crisis Countries* (mimeo, August 1999).

De Kock, M.H., *Central Banking*, 4th edn (New York: St Martins Press, 1974).

Demirgüç-Kunt, Aslï and Enrica Detragiache, 'The Determinants of Banking Crises: Evidence from Industrial and Developing Countries', *Policy Research Working Paper*, 1929, The World Bank (1998).

Diamond, D., 'Debt Maturity Structure and Liquidity Risk', *Quarterly Journal of Economics*, 106 (1991) 709–37.

Demirgüç-Kunt, Aslï and Ross Levine, 'Stock Market Development and Financial Intermediaries: Stylized Facts', *World Bank Economic Review*, 10(2) (1996) 291–321.

Demirgüç-Kunt, Aslï, Ross Levine, and Hong-Ghi Min, 'Opening to Foregin Banks: Issues of Stability, Efficiency and Growth', in *The Implications of Globalization to World Financial Markets* (The Bank of Korea, 1998).

Demirgüç-Kunt, Aslï and Vojislav Maksimovic, 'Institutions, Financial Markets, and Firm Debt Maturity', *Journal of Financial Economics* (1998).

De Neyer, M., R. Gorez and J. Barreto, 'Fuzzy Integral Action in Model Based Control Systems', Second IEEE International Conference on Fuzzy Systems, 1, 172–7, 1993.

Dietrich, J.R. and R.S. Kaplan, 'Empirical Analysis of the Commercial Loan Classification Decision', *The Accounting Review*, 57(1) (1982), 18–38.

Ding, Wei, Ilker Domac and Giovanni Ferri, *Crisis, Adjustment, and Reform in Thai Industry* (mimeo, World Bank, 1998).

Dollar, David and Mary Hallward-Driemeier, *Crisis, Adjustment, and Reform in Thai Industry* (mimeo, World Bank, 1998).

Domac, Ilker and Giovanni Ferri, 'The Real Impact of Financial Shocks', *World Bank Policy Research Working Paper*, 2010 (1998).

Domac, Ilker and Giovanni Ferri, 'The Real Impact of Financial Shocks: Evidence from Korea', unpublished manuscript, East Asia Pacific Region, the World Bank, Washington DC (1998).

Doner, Richard F. and Daniel Unger, 'The Politics of Finance in Thai Economic Development', in Stephen Haggard, Chung H. Lee and Sylvia Maxfield (eds), *The Politics of Finance in Developing Countries* (Ithaca: Cornell University Press, 1993).

Doner, Richard F. and Anek Laothamatas, 'Thailand: Economic and Political Gradualism', in Stephan Haggard and Steven B. Webb (eds), *Democracy, Political Liberalization and Economic Adjustment* (New York: Oxford University Press, 1994).

Dooley, Michael, 'The IMF, Crisis Management and Bailing in the Private Sector', paper presented at the Carnegie-Rochester Conference Series, Financial Crisis and the Role of the IMF, 19–20 November 1999.

Dornbusch, Rudiger and Sebastian Edwards, 'Exchange Rate Policy and Trade Strategy', in Barry P. Bosworth, Rudiger Dornbusch and Raul Laban (eds), *The Chilean Economy: Policy Lessons and Challenges* (Washington, DC: The Brookings Institution, 1994).

Duchessi, P., H. Shawky and J.P. Seagle, 'A Knowledge-Engineered System for Commercial Loan Decision', *Financial Management*, 17 (1988) 57–65.

Dymski, G. and R. Pollin, *New Perspectives in Monetary Macroeconomics* (Ann Arbor, MI: Michigan University Press, 1994).

Eatwell, John, 'International Financial Liberalization: the Impact on World Development', Discussion Paper Series, Office of Development Studies, United Nations Development Programme, New York, May, 1997a.

Eatwell, John, selected extracts in John Eatwell, 'International Financial Liberalisation: the Impact on World Development', *International Journal of Technical Cooperation*, 3(2) (Winter 1997b) 157–2.

Edmister, R.O. 'Combining Human Credit Analysis and Numerical Credit scoring for Business Failure Prediction', *Akron Business Economic Review*, 19(3) (1988) 6–14.

Edwards, Sebastian, *Real Exchange Rates, Devaluation, and Adjustment: Exchange Rate Policies in Developing Countries* (Cambridge, MA: MIT Press, 1989).

Edwards, Sebastian, 'About the IMF', *Financial Times* (13 November 1998a).

Edwards, Sebastian, 'Capital Flows, Real Exchange Rates, and Capital Controls: Some Latin American Experiences', *NBER Working Paper*, 6800 (1998b).

Edwards, Sebastian, 'How Effective Are Capital Controls?', *NBER Working Paper*, 7413 (1999a).

Edwards, Sebastian, 'On Crisis Prevention: Lessons from Mexico and East Asia', *NBER Working Paper*, 7233 (1999b).

Edwards, Sebastian and Julio Santaella, 'Devaluation Controversies in the Developing Countries', in Michael Bordo and Barry Eichengreen (eds), *A Retrospective on the Bretton Woods System* (Chicago: University of Chicago Press, 1993).

Edwards, Sebastian and Miguel A. Savastano, 'Exchange Rates in Emerging Economies: What Do We Know? What Do We Need to Know?', *NBER Working Paper Series*, 7228 (1999).

Eichengreen, Barry, *Golden Fetters* (New York: Oxford University Press, 1992).

Eichengreen, Barry, *Globalizing Capital* (Princeton: Princeton University Press, 1996).

Eichengreen, Barry, *Capital Controls: Capital Ideas or Capital Folly?* (mimeo, November 1998).

Eichengreen, Barry, *Toward a New International Financial Architecture: a Practical Post-Asia Agenda* (Washington, DC: Institute for International Economics, 1999a).

Eichengreen, Barry, *Is Greater Private-Sector Burden Sharing Impossible?* (mimeo, 1999b).

Eichengreen, Barry and Ricardo Hausmann, 'Exchange Rates and Financial Fragility', *NBER Working Paper*, 7418 (1999).

Eichengreen, Barry and Donald Mathieson, 'Hedge Funds: What Do We Really Know?', *Economic Issues*, 19, International Monetary Fund (1999).

Eichengreen, Barry, Michael Mussa, Giovanni Dell'Ariccia, Enrica Detragiache, Gian Maria-Ferretti and Andrew Tweedie, 'Liberalizing Capital Movements: Some Analytical Issues', *Economic Issues*, 17, International Monetary Fund (1999).

Eichengreen, Barry, Andrew Rose, and Charles Wyplosz, 'Speculative Attacks on Pegged Exchange Rates: an Empirical Exploration with Special Reference to the European Monetary System', in Mathew Canzoneri, Paul Masson and Vittorio Grilli (eds), *The New Transatlantic Economy*, (Cambridge: Cambridge University Press, 1994).

Eichengreen, Barry, Andrew Rose, and Charles Wyplosz, 'Contagious Currency Crises', *NBER Working Paper*, 5681 (1996).

Eichengreen, Barry and Christof Ruehl, 'The Bail-in Problem: Systemic Goals, Ad Hoc Means', *NBER Working Paper*, 7653 (2000).

Eichengreen, Barry and Charles Wyplosz, 'The Unstable EMS', *Brookings Papers on Economic Activity* (1993) 51–143.

Eichengreen, Barry and Charles Wyplosz, 'Taxing International Financial Transactions to Enhance the Operation of the International Monetary System', in M. Haq, I. Kaul and I. Grunberg (eds), *The Tobin Tax: Coping with Financial Volatility* (Oxford: Oxford University Press, 1996).

Eichengreen, Barry, and R. Portes, *Crisis? What Crisis? Orderly Workouts for Sovereign Debtors'* (London: Center for Economic Policy Research, September 1995).

Eijffinger, Sylvester and Jacob De Haan, 'The Political Economy of Central Bank Independence' *Special Paper in International Economics*, 19, Princeton University (1998).

Europa World Yearbook (London: Europa Publications Ltd., various years).

Eyzaguirre, Nicolas and Fernando Lefort, 'Capital Markets in Chile, 1985–97', in Guillermo Perry and Danny M. Leipziger (eds), *Chile: Recent Policy Lessons and*

Emerging Challenges (WBI Development Studies, Washington, DC: World Bank, 1999).

Eyzaguirre, Nicolas and Klaus Schmidt Hebbel, *Encaje a la Entrada de Capitales y Ajuse Macroeconomico* (mimeo, Central Bank of Chile, 1997).

Fama, E., 'Banking in the Theory of Finance', *Journal of Monetary Economics*, 6(1) (January 1980) 39–57.

Fama, E. and M.C. Jensen, 'Separation of Ownership and Control', *Journal of Law and Economics*, 26 (1983a) 301–25.

Fama, E. and M.C. Jensen, 'Agency Problems and Residual Claims', *Journal of Law and Economics*, 26 (1983b) 327–49.

Faust, J. and Lars Svenson 'Transparency and Credibility: Monetary Policy With Unobservable Goals', *CEPR Working Paper* 1852 (1998).

Feldstein, Martin, 'The Political Economy of the European Economic and Monetary Union: Political Sources of an Economic Liability', *The Journal of Economic Perspectives*, 11(4) (Fall 1997) 23–42.

Feldstein, Martin, 'Refocusing the IMF', *Foreign Affairs* (March/April 1998).

Fernandez-Arias, E. and Ricardo Hausmann, 'What's Wrong with International Monetary Financial Markets?', paper presented at the Tenth International Forum on Latin American Perspectives, 25–6 November 1999.

Fetter, Frank, *Development of British Monetary Orthodoxy* (Cambridge, MA: Harvard University Press, 1965).

Financial Stability Forum, *Report of the Working Group on Highly Leveraged Institutions* (5 April, 2000a).

Financial Stability Forum, *Report of the Working Group on Offshore Centers* (5 April, 2000b).

Financial Stability Forum, *Report of the Working Group on Capital Flows* (5 April, 2000c).

Fischer, Stanley, 'Dynamic Inconsistency, Co-operation, and the Benevolent Dissembling Government', *Journal of Economic Dynamics and Control*, 2 (1980) 93–107.

Fischer, Stanley, *Indexing, Inflation, and Economic Policy* (Cambridge, MA: MIT Press, 1986).

Fischer, Stanley, 'Modern Central Banking', paper presented at the Bank of England's Tercentenary Celebration, London, June 1994.

Fischer, Stanley, 'Central Bank Independence Revisited', papers and proceedings of the Hundred and Seventh Annual Meeting of the American Economic Association, *American Economic Review* (May 1995).

Fischer, Stanley, 'Capital-Account Liberalization and the Role of the IMF', in *Should the IMF Pursue Capital Account Convertibility?: Essays in International Finance*, 207 (Princeton: Princeton University Press, 1998).

Fischer, Stanley, 'On the Need for an International Lender of Last Resort', paper presented for delivery at the Joint Luncheon of the American Economic Association and the American Finance Association, New York, January 1999.

Fischer, Stanley, 'Asia and the IMF', a speech delivered at the Institute for Policy Studies, Singapore, June 1, 2001.

Fisher, Irving, *The Purchasing Power of Money* (New York: Macmillan Co., 1912).

Flood, Robert, and Peter Garber, 'Collapsing Exchange-Rate Regimes: Some Linear Examples', *Journal of International Economics*, 17 (1984) 90–107.

Flood, Robert, and Nancy Marion, 'Perspectives on the Recent Currency Crisis Literature', *NBER Working Paper*, 6380 (January 1998).

Flood, Robert P., and Peter M. Garber, 'Gold Monetization and Gold Discipline', *Journal of Political Economy*, 92(1) (1984) 90–107.

Folkerts-Landau, David, Donald Mathieson, and Garry Schinasi, 'Capital Flow Sustainability and Speculative Currency Attacks', *Finance and Development* (International Monetary Fund, 1997).

Folkerts-Landau, D. and C. Lindgren, 'Toward a Framework for Financial Stability', *IMF World Economic and Financial Surveys*, January 1998.

Frankel, Jeffrey A., 'No Single Currency Regime is Right for All Countries or At All Times', *NBER Working Paper*, 7338 (1999).

Frankel Jeffrey A. and Andrew K. Rose, 'An Empirical Characterization of Nominal Exchange Rates', in Gene Grossman and Kenneth Rogoff (eds), *Handbook of International Economics 3* (Amsterdam: North-Holland, 1995), pp. 1689-1729.

Frey, Bruno and Friedrich Schneider, 'Competing Models of International Lending Activity', *Journal of Development Economics*, 20, (1986) 224–45.

Friedman, M., 'The Case of Flexible Exchange Rates', in *Essays in Positive Economics* (Chicago: University of Chicago Press, 1953).

Friedman, M., *A Program for Monetary Stability* (New York: Fordham University Press, 1960).

Friedman, M., 'Should There be an Independent Monetary Authority?', in L. Yeager (ed.), *In Search of a Monetary Constitution* (Cambridge, MA: Harvard University Press, 1962).

Friedman, M., 'The Role of Monetary Policy', *American Economic Review*, 58(1) (March 1968).

Friedman, M., 'Monetary Policy: Theory and Practice', *Journal of Money, Credit and Banking*, 1982; reprint in E. Toma and M. Toma (eds), *Central Bankers, Bureaucratic Incentives and Monetary Policy* (Dordrecht: Martinus Nijhoff, 1986).

Friedman, M., and Schwartz, A., *A Monetary History of the U.S., 1876–1960* (Princeton: Princeton University Press, 1963).

Furman, Jason and Joseph E. Stiglitz, 'Economic Crises: Evidence and Insights from East Asia', *Brookings Papers on Economic Activity*, 2 (1998) 1–136.

Gale, D. and M. Hellwig, 'Incentive-Compatible Debt Contracts: the One-Period Problem', *Review of Economic Studies*, 52 (1985) 647–63.

Gang, Ira N. and Haider Ali Khan, 'Modelling Foreign Aid and Development Expenditures', paper presented at AEA conference, Atlanta, 1989.

Gang, Ira N. and Haider Ali Khan, 'Some Determinants of Foreign Aid to India, 1960–1986', *World Development*, 18 (1990) 431–42.

Gang, Ira N. and Haider Ali Khan, 'Foreign Aid, Taxes and Public Investment', *Journal of Development Economics*, 34 (1991) 355–69.

Gang, Ira N. and Haider Ali Khan, 'Reply to Tran-Nam Binh and Mark McGilliray, Foreign Aid, Taxes and Public Investment: a Comment', *Journal of Development Economics*, 41 (1993) 177–8.

Gang, Ira N. and Haider Ali Khan, 'Foreign Aid and Development Expenditures: Does the Policymaker Make Any Difference?', unpublished paper, 1994.

Gang, Ira N. and Haider Ali Khan, 'Does the Policymaker Make Any Difference? Foreign Aid in a Bounded Rationality Model', *Empirical Economics* (September 1999).

Garcia, Gillian G.H., 'Deposit Insurance: a Survey of Actual and Best Practices', *IMF Working Paper*, WP/99/54 (1999).

Gavin, Michael and Ricardo Hausmann, 'The Roots of Banking Crises: the Macro-economic Context', in Hausmann and Rojas-Suarez (eds), *Banking Crises in Latin America* (Baltimore: Inter-American Development Bank and John Hopkins University Press, 1996), pp. 27–63.

Geographic Distribution of Financial Flows to Developing Countries (Paris: OECD, various years).

Gerlach, Stefan and Frank Smets, 'Contagious Speculative Attacks', *European Journal of Political Economy*, 11 (1995), 5–63.

Ghosh, Swati, R. and Artish R. Ghosh, 'East Asia in the Aftermath: Was There a Crunch?', *IMF Working Papers*, WP/99/38 (1999).

Ghosh, A. and S. Phillips, *Interest Rates, Stock Markets Prices, and Exchange Rates in East Asia* (mimeo, International Monetary Fund, 1998).

Ghosh, Atish R., Ann-Marie Gulde, Jonathan D. Ostry and Holger Wolf, 'Does the Exchange Rate Regime Matter for Inflation and Growth?', *Economic Issues*, 2, International Monetary Fund (1996).

Ghosh, Jayati, Abhijit Sen and C.P. Chandrasekhar, 'Southeast Asian Economics: Miracle or Meltdown?', *Economic and Political Weekly* (12–19 October 1996).

Gilpin, Robert, *Global Political Economy* (Princeton, NJ: Princeton University Press, 1999).

Goeltom, Miranda S., 'Indonesia's Financial Liberalisation: an Empirical Analysis of 1981–1988 Panel Data', Institute of Southeast Asian Studies, Singapore, 1995.

Goldberg, Linda, B. Gerard Dages, and Daniel Kinney, 'Foreign Domestic Bank Participation in Emerging Markets: Lessons from Mexico and Argentina', *NBER Working Paper Series*, 7714 (2000).

Goldfajn, Ilan and Taimur Baig, 'Monetary Policy in the Aftermath of Currency Crisis', *IMF Working Paper*, WP/98/170 (1998).

Goldfajn, Illan and Taimur Baig, 'Monetary Policy in the Aftermath of Currency Crises: the Case of Asia', *IMF Working Paper*, WP/98/170, Washington DC. (1999).

Goldfajn, Ilan and Poonam Gupta, 'Does Monetary Policy Stabilize the Exchange Rate Following a Currency Crisis?', *IMF Working Paper*, WP/99/42 (1999).

Goldfajn, Ilan and Rodrigo O. Valdes, *Balance of Payments Crises and Capital Flows: the Role of Liquidity* (mimeo, MIT, 1995).

Goldstein, Morris and Philip Turner, 'Banking Crises in Emerging Economies: Origins and Policy Options', *BIS Economic Papers*, 46 (October 1996).

Goldman Sachs, *Asian Banks NPLs: How High, How Structural? Tying NPL Estimates to the Real Sector* (Goldman Sachs Investment Research, mimeo, 1998).

Gramlish Edward, *Inflation Targeting* (Charlotte, NC: The Federal Reserve Board Economic Club, 2000).

Green, Duncan, 'The Indonesian Economic Crisis', CAFOD, London (March 1998).

Greider, William, *One World, Ready or Not: the Manic Logic of Global Capitalism* (New York: Touchstone, Simon & Schuster, 1997).

Griffith-Jones, Stephany, 'Regulatory Challenges for Source Countries of Surges in Capital Flows', a paper presented for a FONDAD workshop, 1998.

Goodhart, Charles, *Monetary Theory and Practice: the U.K. Experience* (London: Macmillan, 1984).

Goodhart, Charles, 'The Operational Role of the Bank of England', *Economic Review*, London (1985).

Goodhart, Charles, *The Evolution of Central Banks: a Natural Development?* (London: London School Of Economics and Political Science, 1985).

Goodhart, Charles, 'Why do Banks Need a Central Bank?', *Oxford Economic Papers*, 39 (March 1987).

Goodhart, Charles, *The Evolution of Central Banks* (Cambridge, MA: MIT Press, 1988).

Goodhart, Charles, *Money, Information and Uncertainty*, 2nd edn, (London: Macmillan, 1989).

Goodhart, Charles, 'Central Bank Independence', The AC Goode Address to CEDA, November 1993a.

Goodhart, Charles, 'Price Stability and Financial Fragility', paper presented at Bank of Japan Conference, Tokyo, on Financial Stability in a Changing Environment, 1993b.

Goodhart, Charles, 'Game Theory for Central Bankers, A Report to the Governor of the Bank of England', 1993c.

Goodhart, Charles, 'What Should the Central Bank Do? What Should Be Their Macroeconomic Objectives and Operations?', *policy forum of the Economic Journal*, 104 (November 1994).

Goodhart, Charles, C. Capie, F. and Schnadt, N., 'The Development of Central Banking', paper presented at the Bank of England's Tercentenary Celebration, London, June 1994.

Goodhart, Charles, and Schoenmaker, D., 'Institutional Separation Between Supervisory and Monetary Agencies' (LSE Financial Markets Group, April 1993).

Gordon, Robert, 'Understanding Inflation in the 1980s', *Brookings Papers on Economic Activity*, 1 (1985) 263–99.

Gordon, Robert, 'Why Stopping Inflation may be Costly: Evidence from Fourteen Historical Episodes', in R.E. Hall (ed.), *Inflation: Causes and Effects* (Chicago, IL: University of Chicago Press, 1982), pp. 11–40.

Gould, David M. and Steven B. Kamin, 'The Impact of Monetary Policy on Exchange Rates During Financial Crisis', paper presented at the 1999 Pacific Basin Conference, San Francisco, September.

Gould, Stephen Jay, *The Panda's Thumb: More Reflections in Natural History* (New York: Norton, 1980).

The Government of Japan, Ministry of Foreign Affairs, *Waga Kuni No Seifu Kaihatsu Enjo* (Tokyo, 1990).

Grabel, Ilene, 'Marketing the Third World: the Contradictions of Portfolio Investment in the Global Economy', *World Development*, 24 (11) (November 1996) 1761–76.

Grossman, Sanford and Oliver Hart, 'The Costs and Benefits of Ownership: a Theory of Vertical and Lateral Integration', *Journal of Political Economy*, 94 (1986) 691–719.

Griffith-Jones, Stephany (1998) 'The East Asian Financial Crisis: its Causes, Consequences, Policy and Research Implications', *IDS Discussion Paper Draft*, Sussex.

Guttmann, Robert, *How Credit-Money Shapes the Economy: the United States in a Global System* (New York: M.E. Sharpe, 1994).

Haldane, Andrew (ed.), *Targeting Inflation* (London: Bank of England, 1995).

Hamada, Koichi, 'A Comparison of Currency Crises Between Asia and Latin America', a paper presented at the 12th Congress of the International Economic Association in Buenos Aires, August 1999.

Hallward-Driemeier, Mary, Dominique Dwor-Frecaut, and Francis Colaco, *Asian Corporate Recovery: a Firm-Level Analysis* (mimeo, 1999).

Hamilton, Gary (ed.), *Business Networks and Economic Development in East and Southeast Asia* (Hong Kong: Centre of Asian Studies, University of Hong Kong, 1991).

Hart, Oliver and John Moore, 'Incomplete Contracts and Renegotiation', *Econometrica*, 56 (1988) 755–86.

Hart, Oliver and John Moore, 'Foundations of Incomplete Contracts', *NBER Working Papers*, 6726 (1998).

Haussmann, Ricardo and Michael Gavin, *Macroeconomic Volatility in Latin America: Causes, Consequences, Policies to Assure Stability* (Inter-American Development Bank, mimeo, July 1995).

Haussmann, Ricardo, Ugo Panizza, and Ernesto Stein, *Why Do Countries Float the Way They Float?* (mimeo, Stanford Graduate School of Business, 1999).

Hayek, Frederich, *Monetary Nationalism and International Stability* (New York: Augustus M. Kelley, 1971, 1973 reprints).

Hayek, Frederich, *Denationalization of Money* (London: Institute of Economic Affairs, 1976).

Hayek, Frederich, *Denationalization of Money: The Arguments Refined; An Analysis of the Theory and Practice of Concurrent Currencies* (London: Institute of Economic Affairs, 1978).

Hayek, Frederich, 'Market Standards for Money', *Economic Affairs*, 6(4) (1986) 8–10.

Hayes, Samuel and Frank Vogel, *Islamic Law and Finance: Religion, Risk and Return* (Cambridge: Kluwer Law International, 1998).

Heilbroner, Robert, and William Milberg, *The Making of Economic Society* (Upper Saddle River, NJ: Prentice Hall International, 1998).

Helleiner, G.K., 'Capital Accounts Regime and Developing Countries', in UNCTAD, *International Monetary and Financial Issues for the 1990s*, VIII (Geneva: UNCTAD, 1997).

Heller, Peter S., 'A Model of Public Fiscal Behavior in Developing Countries: Aid, Investment and Taxation', *American Economic Review*, 65 (1975) 429–45.

Henry, Peter Blair, *Stock Market Liberalization, Economic Reform, and Emerging Market Equity Prices* (mimeo, Stanford Graduate School of Business, 1999a).

Henry, Peter Blair, *Do Stock Market Liberalizations Cause Investment Booms?* (mimeo, Stanford Graduate School of Business, 1999b).

Herrera, Luis Oscar and Rodrigo Valdes-Prieto, *Encaje y Autonomia Monetaria en Chile* (mimeo, Central Bank of Chile, 1997).

Hikino, Takashi, 'Managerial Control, Capital Markets, and the Wealth of Nations', in Alfred D. Chandler, Franco Amatori and Takashi Hikino (eds), *Big Business and the Wealth of Nations* (Cambridge: Cambridge University Press, 1997).

Holt, C.C., 'Linear Decision Rules for Economic Stabilization and Growth', *Quarterly Journal of Economics*, 56 (1962) 20–45.

Hoshi, Takeo, 'Benefits and Costs of the Japanese System of Corporate Governance', *Global Economic Review*, 26(3) (1997) 77–95.

Hoshi, Takeo, Anil Kasyap and David Scharfstein, 'Corporate Structure, Liquidity and Investment: Evidence from Japanese Industrial Groups', *Quarterly Journal of Economics*, 106 (1991) 33–66.

Howitt, Peter, 'Zero Inflation as a Long Run Target for Monetary Policy', in R. Lipsey (ed.), *Zero Inflation: the Goal of Price Stability* (Toronto: E.D. Howe Institute, 1990).

International Bank for Reconstruction and Development (World Bank), 'Bangladesh: Recent Economic Developments and Medium Term Prospects', *The World Development Report* 1 (March 1986); *The World Development Report* (1986, 1987).

International Monetary Fund, *IMF-Supported Programs in Indonesia, Korea and Thailand: a Preliminary Assessment* (Washington, DC, January 1999).

International Monetary Fund, *Involving the Private Sector in Forestalling and Resolving Financial Crises* (Policy Development and Review Department, 1999).

International Monetary Fund, *Experience with Basle Core Principle Assessments* (prepared by the Monetary and Exchange Affairs Department, 12 April 2000).

Islam, Shafiqul (ed.), *Yen for Development* (New York: Council on Foreign Relations Press, 1991).

Ito, Takatoshi, 'Ajia Tsuka Kiki to IMF (The Asian Currency Crisis and the IMF)', *Keizai Kenkyu* 50(1) (January 1999) 68–94.

Ito, Takatoshi and Richard Portes, 'Crisis Management, European Economic Perspective', *CEPR EEP*, 17 (1999).

Iwai, Katsuhito, 'Persons, Things and Corporations: the Corporate Personality Controversy and Comparative Corporate Governance', *The American Journal of Comparative Law*, XLVII(4) (Fall 1999) 583–632.

Jensen, Michael, 'Takeovers: Their Causes and Consequences', *Journal of Economic Perspectives*, 2 (1988) 21–48.

Jensen, Michael, 'The Modern Industrial Revolution, Exit, and the Failure of Internal Control Systems', *Journal of Finance*, 48 (1993) 831–80.

Jensen, M. and Meckling, W.H. 'Theory of the Firm: Managerial Behavior, Agency Costs and Ownership Structure', *Journal of Financial Economics*, 3 (1976) 305–60.

Jeong, Kap-Young and Jongryn Mo, 'The Political Economy of Corporate Governance Reform in Korea', *Global Economic Review*, 26(3) (1997) 59–75.

Johnson, C., *MITI and the Japanese Miracle* (Stanford, CA: Stanford University Press).

Johnston, Barry R. and Inci Otker-Robe, 'A Modernized Approach to Managing the Risks in Cross-Border Capital Movements', *IMF Policy Discussion Paper*, PDP/99/6 (1999).

Johnston, Barry R., Salim M. Darbar, and Claudia Echeverria, 'Sequencing Capital Account Liberalization – Lessons from the Experiences in Chile, Indonesia, Korea, and Thailand', *IMF Working Paper*, WP/97/157 (Washington, DC, 1997).

Jomo, K.S. et al., *Southeast Asia's Misunderstood Miracle: Industrial Policy and Economic Development in Thailand, Malaysia and Indonesia* (Boulder, CO: Westview Press, 1997).

Kaminsky, Graciela L. and Sergio Schmukler, *The Relationship between Interest Rates and Exchange Rates in Six Asian Countries* (mimeo, Federal Reserve Board and World Bank, 1998).

Kaminsky, Graciela L. and Carmen M. Reinhart, 'The Twin Cases: the Causes of Banking and Balance-of-Payments Problems', *American Economic Review*, 89(3) (1999a) 473–500.

Kaminsky, Graciela L. and Carmen M. Reinhart, 'On Crises, Contagion, and Confusion', *Journal of International Economics* (1999b).

Kaminsky, Graciela L. and Carmen M. Reinhart, *Bank Lending and Contagion: Evidence from the Asian Crisis* (mimeo, 1999c).

Kanda, Hideki, 'Legal and Regulatory Reforms for Effective Corporate Governance', paper presented at the Workshop on Reforming Corporate Governance in Asia, the Asian Development Bank Institute, 15–19 May 2000, Tokyo.

Kane, Edward J., 'Capital Movements, Banking Insolvency, and Silent Runs in the Asian Financial Crisis', *NBER Working Paper*, 7514 (2000).

Kashyap, Anil K. and Jeremy C. Stein, 'What do a Million Observations on Banks Say About the Transmission of Monetary Policy?', *American Economic Review*, 90(3) (June 2000) 407–28.

Kaufman, Henry 'Preventing the Next Global Financial Crisis', *Washington Post* (28 January 1998), A17.

Kesley, Jane, *Economic Fundamentalism* (London: Pluto Press, 1995).

Keynes, John Maynard, *The General Theory of Employment, Interest, and Money* (London: Macmillan, 1936, 1973 edition).

Keynes, J.M., *The Collected Writings of John Maynard Keynes*, 29 vols, ed. D.E. Moggridge for the Royal Economic Society (London: Macmillan, 1971–1979).

Keynes, John Maynard, ed. E. Johnson, *The Collected Writings Volume XV: Activities 1906–1914 India and Cambridge* (London: Macmillan, 1973).

Khan, H.A., 'Technology, Energy and Balance of Payments: a Macroeconomic Framework for Planning with Application to South Korea', unpublished dissertation, Cornell University, 1983.

Khan, Haider A., 'Econometrics', in W. Outhwaite and T. Bottomore (eds), *Encyclopaedia of Twentieth Century Social Thought* (Oxford: Basil Blackwell, 1993).

Khan, Haider Ali, 'Does Bilateral Foreign Aid Affect Fiscal Behavior of a Recipient?', *Journal of Asian Economies* (March 1994).

Khan, Haider Ali, 'Does the Policy-Maker Make a Difference?' paper presented at AEA/ASSA meetings, Washington, DC, January 1995.

Khan, Haider Ali, 'Does Japan's Aid Work?' unpublished paper, University of Denver.

Khan, Haider Ali, 'Does Japanese Bilateral Aid Work? Foreign Aid and Fiscal Behavior in a Bounded Rationality Model', *Regional Development Studies*, 3 (Winter, 1996/97) 283–97.

Khan, Haider Ali, *Technology, Energy and Development: the South Korean Transition* (Cheltenham: Edward Elgar, 1997a).

Khan, Haider Ali, *African Debt and Sustainable Development* (New York: Phelps-Stokes Foundation, 1997b).

Khan, Haider Ali, *Technology, Development and Democracy: Limits of National Innovation Systems in the Age of Postmodernism* (Cheltenham: Edward Elgar, 1998).

Khan, Haider Ali, *Global Markets and Financial Crisis: Asia's Mangled Miracle* (Basingstoke: Macmillan and St. Martin's Press, forthcoming a).

Khan, Haider Ali, *Innovation and Growth in East Asia: The Future of Miracles* (London: Macmillan, forthcoming b).

Khan, Haider Ali, 'Corporate Governance of Family Businesses in Asia: What's Right and What's Wrong?' *ADBI paper* 3, Tokyo (1999a).

Khan, Haider Ali, 'Corporate Governance in Asia: Which Road to Take?', paper presented at 2nd high level symposium in ADBI, Tokyo, 1999b.

Khan, Haider Ali, 'A Note on Path Dependence', unpublished manuscript, 2001.

Khan, Haider Ali, 'Can Banks Learn to Be Rational?', Discussion Paper no. 2002-CF-151, Graduate School of Economics, University of Tokyo, 2002a.

Khan, Haider Ali, 'Corporate Governance: the Limits of the Principal–Agent Model', Working Paper, GSIS, University of Denver, 2002b.

Khan, Haider Ali, 'The Extended Panda's Thumb and a New Global Financial Architecture: an Evolutionary Theory of the Role of the IMF and Regional Financial Architectures', Working paper GSIS, University of Denver, 2002c.

Khan, Haider Ali, 'Does Aid Work? Japanese Foreign Aid, Development Expenditures and Taxation in Malaysia: Some Results from a Bounded Rationanlity Model of Fiscal Behavior', *Journal of the Centre for International Studies*, Aichi Gakuin University, 4, (2002d) 1–19.

Khan, Haider Ali, 'What Can the African Countries Learn from the Macroeconomics of Foreign aid in Southeast Asia?', in E. Aryeetey, J. Court, M. Nissanke and B. Weder (eds), *Asia and Africa in the Global Economy* (Tokyo: UNU Press, 2002e).

Khan, Haider Ali and Ari Basuseno, 'Analyzing Financial Liberalization in a CGE Model: the Possibility of Crises', Working Paper, GSIS, University of Denver.

Khan, Haider Ali and Elichi Hoshino, 'Impact of Foreign Aid on the Fiscal Behavior of LDC Governments', *World Development*, 20 (1992) 1481–8.

Khan, Haider A. and Victor Lippit, 'The Surplus Approach and the Environment', *Review of Radical Political Economics* (1993a).

Khan, Haider A. and Victor Lippit, '*Sustainability and Surplus*' manuscript, University of California, Riverside and University of Denver, 1993b.

Khan, Haider A. and Toru Yanagihara, 'Asian Development Before and After the Crisis: Some Stylized Facts and Paradigmatic Features with an Agenda for Future Research', manuscript, ADBI, February 1999.

Khanna, Tarun and Palepu Krishna, *Corporate Scope and (Severe) Market Imperfections: an Empirical Analysis of Diversified Business Groups in an Emerging Economy* (Boston, MA: Graduate School of Business Administration, Harvard University, March 1996).

Khanna, Tarun and Krishna Palepu, 'Emerging Market Business Groups, Foreign Investors, and Corporate Governance', *NBER Working Paper*, 6955 (1999).

Kim, Hyun E., 'Was Credit Channel a Key Monetary Transmission Mechanism Following the Recent Financial Crisis in the Republic of Korea?', *Policy Research Working Paper*, 3003 (Washington DC: World Bank, 1999).

Kim, Kenneth A. and S. Ghon Rhee, 'Shareholder Oversight and the Regulatory Environment', working paper, 1999.

Kim, Yun-Hwan, 'Policy Agenda for Bond Market Development in Asia', paper presented at the Round Table on Capital Market Reforms in Asia, the Organization of Economic Co-operation and Development and Asian Development Bank Institute, 11–12 April, 2000, Tokyo.

Kindelberger, Charles, *A Financial History of Western Europe* (Oxford: Oxford University Press, 1993).

Klein, B., 'Vertical Integration as Organizational Ownership: the Fisher Body–General Motors Relationship Revisited', *Journal of Law, Economics and Organization*, 4(1) (1988) 199–213.

Klein, B., R. Crawford and A. Alchian, 'Vertical Integration, Appropriable Rents and the Competitive Contracting Process', *Journal of Law and Economics*, 21 (1978) 297–326.

Klein, Michael W. and Giovanni Olivei, 'Capital Account Liberalization, Financial Depth, and Economic Growth', *NBER Working Paper*, 7384 (1999).

Kletzer, Kenneth and Ashoka Mody, *Will Self-protection Policies Safeguard Emerging Markets from Crises?* (mimeo, 2000).

Klir, G.J. and B. Yuan, *Fuzzy Sets and Fuzzy Logic* (Upper Saddle River, NJ: Prentice-Hall, 1995).

Knight, Malcolm, 'Developing Countries and the Globalization of Financial Markets', *IMF Working Paper* WP/98/105 (July 1998).

Kodres, Laura and Mathew Pritsker, *A Rational Expectations Model of Financial Contagion* (mimeo, IMF and Board of Governors of the Federal Reserve System, 1999).

Koike, Kenji, 'The Ayala Group during the Aquino Period: Diversification along with a Changing Ownership and Management Structure', *Developing Economies*, 31 (1993) 442–63.

Kosko, B., *Neural Networks and Fuzzy Systems: a Dynamical Systems Approach to Machine Intelligence* (Englewood Cliffs, NJ: Prentice Hall, 1992).

Kraay, Aart (1998) *Do High Interest Rates Defend Currencies During Speculative Attacks?* (mimeo, World Bank, 1998).

Krueger, Anne O., 'Conflicting Demands on the International Monetary Fund', *American Economic Review*, 90(2) (May 2000) 38–42.

Krugman, Paul, 'A Model of Balance-of-Payments Crises', *Journal of Money, Credit, and Banking*, 11 (1979) 311–25.

Krugman, Paul, *Pop Internationalism* (Cambridge, MA: MIT Press, 1996).

Krugman, Paul, 'Currency Crises', Paper prepared for MBER conference, October, 1997.

Krugman, Paul, *Analytical Afterthoughts on the Asian Crisis* (mimeo, MIT, 1999a).

Krugman, Paul, Keynote Speech, at the International Conference on Exchange Rate Regimes in Emerging Markets Economies, 17–18 December, ABDI, 1999b.

Kuroda, Haruhoko and Masahiro Kawai, 'Strengthing Regional Financial Cooperation in East Asia', revised paper presented in the Seminar on Regional Economic and Financial Cooperation, April 2002.

Kwon, Jae Yeol, 'Strong Insiders, Weak Outsiders: a Critical Look at the Korean System of Corporate Governance', *Global Economic Review*, 26(3) (1997) 97–111.

Kydland, Finn and Edward Prescott, 'Rules Rather Than Discretion: the Inconsistency of Optimal Plans', *Journal of Political Economy*, 85, 473–92.

Laban, Raul and Felipe B. Larrain, 'The Chilean Experience with Capital Mobility', in Barry P. Bosworth, Rudiger Dornbusch, and Raul Laban (eds), *The Chilean Economy: Policy Lessons and Challenges* (Washington, DC: The Brookings Institution, 1994).

Lacher, R., P. Coats, S. Sharma, and L. Fant, 'A Neural Network for Classifying the Financial Health of a Firm', *European Journal of Operational Research*, 85(1) (1995) 53–65.

Lamberte, Mario B., 'A Second Look at Credit Crunch: the Philippine Case', *PIDS Discussion Paper Series*, 99-23 (1999).

Lane, Timothy, A. Gosh, J. Hamman, S. Phillips, M. Schulze-Ghattas, and Tsidi Tsikata, *IMF-Supported Programs in Indonesia, Korea and Thailand: a Preliminary Assessment* (Washington, DC: IMF, 1999).

La Porta, Rafael, Florencio Lopez-de-Silanes, Andrei Shleifer and Robert W. Vishny, 'Trust in Large Organizations', *NBER Working Paper* 5864 (1996).

La Porta, Rafael, Florencio Lopez-de-Silanes, Andrei Shleifer and Robert W. Vishny, 'Legal Determinants of External Finance', *Journal of Finance*, 52 (1997) 1131–1150.

La Porta, Rafael, Florencio Lopez-de-Silanes, Andrei Shleifer and Robert W. Vishny, 'Law and Finance', *Journal of Political Economy* 106(6) (1998) 1113–1155.

La Porta, Rafael, Florencio Lopez-de-Silanes, Andrei Shleifer, and Robert Vishny, *Investor Protection and Corporate Governance* (mimeo, 2000).

Lastra, R., 'Central Banking & Banking Regulation', Financial Markets Group, London School of Economics and Political Science, London, 1996.

Laubach, Thomas, *Three Essays on Monetary Policy* (Princeton, NJ: Princeton University Press, 1997).

Laurens, Bernard and Jaime Cardoso, 'Managing Capital Flows: Lessons from the Experience of Chile', *IMF Working Paper*, WP/98/168 (1998).

Lehmann, Jean-Pierre, *Comparative Perspective of Corporate Governance: Europe and East Asia*, (1997), pp. 3–36.

Lenard, M.J., P. Alam, and G.R. Madey, 'The Application of Neural Networks and a Qualitative Response Model to the Auditor's Going Concern Uncertainty Decision', *Decision Science*, 26 (1995) 209–27.

Leszczynski, K., P. Penczek, and W. Grochulskki, 'Sugeno's Fuzzy Measure and Fuzzy Clustering', *Fuzzy Sets and Systems*, 15 (1985) 147–58.

Levine, Ross, 'Foreign Bank, Financial Development, and Economic Growth', in Claude E. Barfield (ed.), *International Monetary Markets: Harmonization versus Competition* (Washington: The American Enterprise Institute Press, 1996).

Levy, J., E. Mallach, and P. Duchessi, 'A Fuzzy Logic Evaluation System for Commercial Loan Analysis', *OMEGA International Journal of Management Science*, 19(6) (1991) 651–69.

Lim, Linda, 'Singapore's Success: the Myth of the Free Market Economy', *Asian Survey*, 23(6) (1983) 752–64.

Lim, Linda, 'Evolution of Southeast Asian Business Systems', *Journal of Asian Business*, 12(1) (1996).

Lim, Linda and Peter Gosling, *The Chinese in Southeast Asia vol. 1, Ethnicity and Economic Activity, vol.2, Identity, Culture and Politics* (Singapore: Maruzen Asia, 1983).

Lindgren, Carl, G. Garcia, and M. Saal, *Bank Soundness and Macroeconomic Policy* (IMF, 1996).

Lin, C.-T. and Lee, C.G., *Neural Fuzzy Systems: a Neuro-Fuzzy Synergism to Intelligent Systems* (New York: Prentice Hall, 1996).

Lipsey, Richard, *Zero Inflation: the Goal of Price Stability* (Toronto: E.D. Howe Institute, 1990).

Lipton, M. and John Toye, *Does Aid Work in India? A Country Study of the Impact of Official Development Assistance* (London: Routledge, 1990).

Litan, Robert, *What Should Banks Do?* (Washington, DC: Brookings Institution, 1987).

Litan, Robert and Richard Herring, 'Statement of the Shadow Financial Regulatory Committee on International Monetary Fund Assistance and International Crises', Statement No. 145, Shadow Financial Regulatory Committee, May 1998.

Little, Jane, R. Cooper, W. Corden, and S. Rajapatirana, *Boom, Crisis, and Adjustment: the Macroeconomic Experience of Developing Countries* (Oxford: Oxford University Press for the World Bank, 1993).

Lloyd, Michelle, *The New Zealand Approach to Central Bank Autonomy* (Reserve Bank Bulletin, 1992).

Long, Simon, 'The Limits to Golf: Regional Implications of the Southeast Asian Currency Depreciations of 1997', paper presented at the ISIS/CSIS Conference on 'Political Change and Regional Security in Southeast Asia', Bali, 7–10 December 1997.

Lucas, Robert, 'The Bank of Canada and Zero Inflation: a New Cross of Gold?', *Canadian Public Policy*, 25 (1989) 84–93.

Macmillan, Rory, 'Toward a Sovereign Debt Work-out System', *Northwestern Journal of International Law and Business*, 16(1) (1995) 57–106.

Mag, Ignacio, 'Central Bank Independence: a Critical View from a Developing Country Perspective', *World Development*, 23(10) (1995) 1639–1652.

Maizels, Alfred and Machiko K. Nissanke, 'Motivations for Aid to Developing Countries', *World Development*, 12 (1984) 879–900.

Mankiw, Gregory, *Macro-Economics* (New York: Worth Publishers, 2000).

Marais, M.L., J.M. Patell, and M.A. Wolfson, 'The Experimental Design of Classification Models: an Application of Recursive Partitioning and Bootstrapping to Commercial Bank Loan Classifications', *Journal of Accounting Research*, 22 (1984) 87–114.

Marfan, Manuel and Barry P. Bosworth, 'Saving, Investment, and Economic Growth', in Barry P. Bosworth, Rudiger Dornbusch, and Raul Laban (eds), *The Chilean Economy: Policy Lessons and Challenges*, (Washington, D.C: The Brookings Institution, 1994).

Masciandaro, Donato and Guido Tabellini, 'Monetary Regimes and Fiscal Deficits: a Comparative Analysis', in H.-S. Cheng (ed.), *Monetary Policy in Pacific Basin Countries* (Boston: Kluwer Academic Publishers, 1988), pp. 125–52.

Massad, Carlos, 'The Liberalization of the Capital Account: Chile in the 1990s', in *Should the IMF Pursue Capital Account Convertibility?: Essays in International Finance*, 207 (1998).

Masson, P., E. Jadresic and P. Mauro, 'Exchange Rate Regimes of Developing Countries: Global Context and Individual Choices', paper presented at the International Conference on Exchange Rate Regimes in Emerging Market Economies, Tokyo, Japan, 17–18 December 1999.

Mayer, M., *The Bankers* (New York: Truman Talley Books, 1997).

Mayer, M., *The Feds* (New York: Free Press, 2001).

McKinnon, Ronald I., *Money and Capital in Economic Development* (Washington, DC: The Brookings Institution, 1973).

McKinnon, Ronald I. and Huw Pill (1996) 'Credible Liberalization and International Capital Flows: the Overborrowing Syndrome', in Takatoshi Ito and Anne O. Krueger (eds), *Financial Deregulation and Integration in East Asia* (Chicago: Chicago University Press, 1996), pp. 7–42.

McKinnon, Ronald I., 'The East Asia Dollar Standard, Life After Death?', presented at the World Bank Economic Development Institute Workshop on Rethinking the East Asian Miracle, San Francisco, 16–17, February 1999.

McKinnon, Ronald I., and Kenichi Ohno, *Dollar and Yen: Resolving Economic Conflict between the United States and Japan* (Cambridge, MA: MIT Press, 1997).

Meese, R. and K. Rogoff, 'Empirical Exchange Rate Models of the Seventies: Do They Fit Out of Sample?', *Journal of International Economics*, 14 (1983) 3–24.

Meyer, Laurence, *The Strategy of Monetary Policy* (The Federal Reserve Board. Middlebury College, 1998).

Michie, J. and J. Grieve Smith (eds), *Managing the Global Economy* (Oxford: Oxford University Press, 1995).

Michie, J. and J. Grieve Smith (1999) *Global Instability: the Political Economy of World Economic Governance* (London: Routledge, 1999).

Milgrom, P., 'Employment Contracts, Influence Activities, and the Efficient Organization Design', *Journal of Political Economy*, 42 (1988) 42–61.

Min, Hong G., 'Dynamic Capital Mobility, Capital Market Risk and Exchange Rate Misalignment: Evidence from Seven Asian Countries', *World Bank Policy Research Working Paper*, 2025 (1998).

Minsky, H., *Can it Happen Again?* (Armonk, NY: M.E. Sharpe, 1982).

Minsky, H., *Global Consequences of Financial Deregulation* (Washington, DC: International Law Institute, 1986).

Minsky, H., *Stabilizing an Unstable Economy* (New Haven: Yale University Press, 1986).

Minsky, H., *John Maynard Keynes* (New York: Columbia University Press, 1975).

Mishkin, Frederic S., 'Understanding Financial Crises: a Developing Country Perspective', in Michael Bruno and Boris Pleskovic (eds), *Annual World Bank Conference on Development Economics* (Washington, DC: World Bank 1996), pp. 29–62.

Mishkin F., 'What Should Central Bank Do?', *Federal Reserve Bank of St. Louis*, 82(6) (November/December 2000).

Miwa Yoshiro and J. Mark Ramseyer, 'Banks and Economic Growth: Implications from Japanese History', University of Tokyo, CIRJE discussion paper no. F-87, 2000.

Monetary Authority of Singapore (MAS), 'Notices to Banks', MAS 757, November 26, 1999.

Monetary Authority of Singapore (MAS), 'Exchange Rate Policy in East Asia After the Fall: How Much Have Things Changed?,' *Occasional paper*, 19, Economics Department (February 2000.)

Montes, Manuel F., 'Diagnoses of the Asian Crisis: Implications for Currency Arrangements', presented at the IDE-JETRO International Symposium on the Asian Economic Crisis, Tokyo (November 1998).

Montes, Manuel F. and J. Lim, 'Macroeconomic Volatility, Investment Anemia and Environmental Struggles in the Philippines', *World Development*, 24(2) (1996).

Morris, Christopher, Presentation at the APF Brainstorming Workshop on How to Prevent Another Crisis, Asian Development Bank Institute, 10–11 March, 2000.

Mosley, P., J. Hudson and Sara Horrell, 'Aid, the Public Sector and the Market in Less Developed Countries', *Economic Journal*, 97 (1987) 616–41.

Nadal-De Simone, Francisco and Piritta Sorsa, 'A Review of Capital Account Restrictions in Chile in the 1990s', *IMF Working Paper*, WP/99/52 (1999).

Naris, Chaiyasoot, 'Industrializiation, Financial Reform and Monetary Policy', in Medhi Korngkraw (ed.), *Thailand's Industrialization and Its Consequences* (London: Macmillan, 1995).

Nasution, Anwar, 'An Evaluation of the Banking Sector Reforms in Indonesia, 1983–1993', *The Asia Pacific Development Journal*, 1(1) (Bangkok: UN-ESCAP, 1994).

Nasution, Anwar, 'Banking Sector Reforms in Indonesia, 1983–93', in Ross H. McLeod (ed.), *Indonesia Assessment 1994: Finance as a Key Sector in Indonesia's Development* (Singapore: Research School of Pacific and Asian Studies, Australian National University and Institute of Southeast Asian Studies, 1995), pp. 130–57.

Nasution, Anwar, 'The Banking System and Monetary Aggregates Following Financial Sector Reforms: Lessons from Indonesia', United Nations University/World Institute for Development Economics Research (UNU/WIDER), Helsinki, Finland, *Research for Action*, 27, 1996.

Nasution, Anwar, 'Lessons from the Recent Financial Crisis in Indonesia', paper presented at the AT10 Researcher's Meeting of the Tokyo Club Foundation for Global Studies, Tokyo, February 1998.

Nasica, E., *Finance, Investment and Economic Fluctuations* (Northampton, MA: Edward Elgar, 2000).

National Development Information Office (Indonesia), *Indonesia Source Book, 1990/91* (Jakarta: NDIO 1991).

Nauck, D. and R. Kruse 'Neuro-Fuzzy Systems Research and Applications outside of Japan', *Fuzzy-Neural Networks, Soft Computing Series* (Tokyo: Asakura Publ., 1996), pp. 108–34.

Nussbaum, Martha, *Women and Human Development: the Capabilities Approach* (Cambridge: Cambridge University Press, 2000).

Nussbaum, Martha and Amartya Sen, *The Quality of Life* (Oxford: Clarendon Press, 1993).

Obstfeld, Maurice, 'Destabilizing Effects of Exchange Rate Escape Clauses', *NBER Working Paper*, 2603 (1991).

Obstfeld, Maurice, 'The Logic of Currency Crises', *NBER Working Paper*, 4640 (1994).

Obstfeld, Maurice, 'The Logic of Currency Crises', *Cahiers Economiques et Monetaires*, Bank of France 43 (1994) 189–213.

Obstfeld, Maurice, 'Models of Currency Crises with Self-Fulfilling Features', *NBER Working Paper*, 5285 (1995).

Obstfeld, Maurice, 'Destabilizing Effects of Exchange-Rate Escape Clauses', *Journal of International Economics*, 43(1/2) (1997) 61–77.

Obstfeld, Maurice, 'The Global Capital Market: Benefactor or Menace?', *Journal of Economic Perspectives*, 12(4) (Autumn 1998) 9–30.

Obstfeld, Maurice and Kenneth Rogoff, *Foundations of International Macroeconomics* (Cambridge, MA: MIT Press, 1996).

OECD, *Economic Survey: Australia*, various issues.

OECD, *Economic Survey: Canada*, various issues

OECD, *Economic Survey: New Zealand*, various issues.

OECD, *World Economic Outlook*, various issues.

Ohno, Kenichi, 'Exchange Rate Management in Developing Asia: Reassessment of the Pre-crisis Soft Dollar Zone', *ADBI Working Paper* I (January 1999).

Ohno, Kenichi, Kazuko Shirono, and Elif Sisli, *Can High Interest Rates Stop Regional Currency Falls?*, Working Paper, Asian Development Bank Institute (ADBI), No. 6, December 1999.

Okazaki, Tetsuji, 'The Role of Holding Companies in Pre-war Japanese Economic Development', *Social Science Japan Journal*, 4(2) (2001) 243–68.

Omori, Takuma, 'Suffolk Banking System against the Crisis of 1837–39 – the Spontaneous Development of "Lender of Last Resort" by a Commercial Bank–

University of Tokyo, Graduate School of Economics Discussion Paper 2002-CJ-79 (June 2002).

Pack, Howard and Janet Rothenberg Pack, 'Is Foreign Aid Fungible?: the Case of Indonesia', *Economic Journal*, 100 (1990) 188–94.

Pack, Howard and Janet Rothenberg Pack, 'Foreign Aid and the Question of Fungibility', *Review of Economics and Statistics*, (1993) 258–65.

Pakorn, Vichyanond, *Thailand's Financial System: Structure and Liberalization* (Bangkok: Thailand Development Research Institute, 1994).

Perkins, Dwight Heald and Wing Thye Woo, *Malaysia in Turmoil: Growth Prospects and Future Competitiveness* (mimeo, December 1998).

Perry, Guillermo and Danny M. Lepziger (eds), *Chile: Recent Policy Lessons and Emerging Challenges* (Washington, DC: WBI Development Studies, World Bank, 1999).

Person, Torsten and Guido Tabellini, *Carnegie-Rochester Series on Public Policy, Designing Institutions for Monetary Stability'*, 39 (1993) 53–84.

Peterson, Wallace, *Silent Depression* (New York: W.W. Norton, 1994).

Pindyck, R. and A. Solimano, 'Economic Instability and Aggregate Investment', *NBER Macroeconomics Annual*, 8 (1993) 259–303.

Pindyck, R.S. and D.L. Rubinfeld, *Econometric Models and Economic Forecasts*, 4th edn (New York: McGraw-Hill, 1998).

Polanyi, Karl, *The Great Transformation* (New York: Rinehart & Co., 1944).

Pollard, P., 'Central Bank Independence and Economic Performance', *Federal Reserve Bank of St Louis Review* (1993) 21–36.

Pomerleano, Michael, 'The East Asian Crisis and Corporate Finances: the Untold Micro Story', *Policy Research Working Paper*, World Bank, 1998.

Posen, Adam, *Central Bank and the Political Economy of Disinflation* (Cambridge, MA: Harvard University Press, 1997).

President's Working Group on Financial Markets, 'Hedge Funds, Leverage, and the Lessons of Long-Term Capital Management-Report of the President's Working Group on Financial Markets', April 1999.

Quinlan, J.R., 'Comparing Connectionist and Symbolic Learning Methods', in G. Hanson, G. Drastal and R. Rivest (eds), *Computational Learning Theory and Natural Learning Systems: Constraints and Prospects* (Cambridge, MA: MIT Press, 1993).

Radelet, Steven and Jeffrey D. Sachs, 'The East Asian Financial Crisis: Diagnosis, Remedies, Prospects', *Brookings Papers on Economic Activity*, 1 (1998) 1–90.

Radelet, Steven and Jeffrey D. Sachs, *What Have We Learned So Far From the Asian Financial Crisis?* (mimeo, January 1999).

Raghavan, C., 'BIS Banks Kept Shoveling Funds to Asia, Despite Warnings', *Third World Economics* (16–31 January 1998).

Rajan, Raghuram, 'Insiders and Outsiders: the Choice Between Relationship and Arm's-Length Debt', *Journal of Finance*, 47 (1992) 1367–1400.

Rajan, Raghuram and Luigi Zingales, 'The Tyranny of the Inefficient: an Inquiry into the Adverse Consequences of Power Struggles', *NBER Working Paper*, 5396 (1996).

Rajan, Raghuram and Luigi Zingales, 'Which Capitalism? Lessons from the East Asian Crisis', *Journal of Applied Corporate Finance* (1998).

Rajan, Ramkishen S., 'Examining the Case for an Asian Monetary Fund', *Policy Discussion Paper*, No. 0002 (Adelaide: Center for International Economic Studies, University of Adelaide, 2000).

Ramey, G. and V. Ramey, 'Cross-Country Evidence on the Link between Volatility and Growth', *American Economic Review* (1995) 1138–51.

Reinhart, Carmen M. and Steven Dunaway, 'Dealing with Capital Inflows: Are There Any Lessons?', manuscript, University of Maryland, June 1996.

Reisen, Helmut, 'Sustainable and Excessive Current Account Deficits', United Nations University/World Institute for Development Economics Research (UNU/WIDER) Working Paper No. 151, Helsinki, May 1997.

Rescher, N., *Many-Valued Logic* (New York: McGraw-Hill, 1969).

Reserve Bank of Australia, *Bulletin*, various issues.

Rhee, S. Ghon, 'Regionalized Bond Markets: Are the Region's Markets Ready?', paper presented at the Asia Development Forum entitled 'East Asia: From Crisis to Opportunity', Singapore, 5–8 June 2000.

Richter, Jurgen (ed.), *Economic Growth, Institutional Failure and the Aftermath of the Crisis* (London: Macmillan Press Ltd – now Palgrave Macmillan, 2000).

Rodrik, Dani, *Has Globalization Gone too Far?* (Washington DC: Institute for International Economics, 1997).

Rodrik, Dani, 'The Global Fix: a Plan to Save the World Economy', *New Republic*, (November 1998a).

Rodrik, Dani, 'Symposium on Globalization in Perspective: an Introduction', *Journal of Economic Perspectives* (Fall 1998b).

Rodrik, Dani, 'Who Needs Capital-Account Convertibility?', in *Should the IMF Pursue Capital Account Convertibility, Essays in International Finance*, 207 (Princeton, NJ: Princeton University Press 1998c).

Rodrik, Dani and Andres Velasco, *Financial Market Trends* (Paris: OECD, 1999).

Rogoff, Kenneth, 'The Optimal Degree of Commitment to an Intermediate Target', *Quarterly Journal of Economics*, 100(4) (1985) 1169–89.

Rogoff, Kenneth, *Perspectives on Exchange Rate Volatility* (mimeo, 1998a).

Rogoff, Kenneth, 'International Institutions for Reducing Global Financial Instability', *NBER Working Paper*, 7265 (1998b).

Roll, Eric et al., *Independent and Accountable: a New Mandate for the Bank of England* (London: Center for Economic Policy Research, October 1993).

Romaniuk, D.G. and L.O. Hall, 'Decision Making on Creditworthiness, Using a fuzzy Connectionist Model', *Fuzzy Sets and Systems*, 48(9) (1992) 15–22.

Romer, David, *Advanced Macroeconomics* (New York: McGraw Hill, 2001).

Root, Hilton L., *Small Countries, Big Lessons: Governance and the Rise of East Asia* (Hong Kong: Oxford University Press, 1996).

Rose, Andrew K., *Limiting Currency Crises and Contagion: Is There a Case for an Asian Monetary Fund?* (mimeo, 1998).

Sachs, Jeffrey D., 'Alternative Approaches to Financial Crises in Emerging Markets', in Miles Kahler (ed.), *Capital Flows and Financial Crises* (Ithaca: Cornell University Press, 1998), pp. 247–62.

Sachs, Jeffrey D., 'International Lender of Last Resort: What Are the Alternatives?', in Jane S. Little and Giovanni P. Olivei (eds), *Rethinking the International Monetary System* (Conference Proceedings, Federal Reserve Bank of Boston, 1999).

Sachs, Jeffrey D., A. Tornell. and A. Velasco, 'Financial Crises in Emerging Markets: the Lessons From 1995', *Brookings Papers on Economic Activity*, 1 (1996).

Sachs, Jeffrey D, and Wing Thye Woo, 'Understanding the Asian Financial Crisis', in Wing Thye Woo, Jeffrey D. Sachs, and Klaus Schwab (eds), *The Asian Financial Crisis: Lessons for a Resilient Asia* (Cambridge, MA: MIT Press, 2000).

Sachs, Jeffrey D., and Wing Thye Woo, *The Asian Financial Crisis: What Happened, and What is to be Done* (mimeo, 1999).

Sangsubhan, Kanit, *Capital Account Crisis: Some Findings in the Case of Thailand* (mimeo, 1999).

Sargent, Thomas, 'The Ends of Four Big Inflations', in R.E. Hall (ed.), *Inflation: Causes and Effects* (Chicago, IL: University of Chicago Press, 1982), pp. 41–98.

Sargent, T.J., 'A Classical Macroeconomic Model for the United States', *Journal of Political Economy*, 84 (1976) 207–38.

Sargent, T.J., *Bounded Rationality in Macroeconomics* (Oxford: Clarendon Press, 1993).

Sato, Yuri, 'The Salim Group in Indonesia: the Development Behavior of the Largest Conglomerate in Southeast Asia', *Developing Economies*, 31 (1993) 408–41.

Sawyer, Malcolm and Philip Arestis, *The Political Economy of Central Banking* (Cheltenham: Edward Elgar, 1998).

Sayer, Richard, *The Bank of England 1891–1944* (Cambridge: Cambridge University Press).

Scharfstein, David S., 'The Dark Side of Internal Capital Markets II: Evidence from Diversified Conglomerates', *NBER Working Paper* 6352 (1998).

Scharfstein, David S. and Jeremy C. Stein, 'The Dark Side of Internal Capital Markets: Divisional Rent-Seeking and Inefficient Investment', *NBER Working Paper* 5969 (1997).

Selody, Jack, '1976. The Goal of Price Stability: a Review of the Issues', *Bank of Canada Technical Report*, 54, 1990.

Sen, Amartya, *Development as Freedom* (New York: A. Knopf, 1999, 2000).

Sen, Amartya, *Commodities and Capabilities* (New York: Elsevier Science Pub. Co., 1985).

Sen, Amartya, *Inequality Reexamined* (New York: Russell Sage Foundation, 1992).

Sengupta, G.K., 'Optimal Stabilization Policy with a Quadratic Criterion Function', *Review of Economic Studies* 36 (1970) 127–46.

Serven, Luis, *Macroeconomic Uncertainty and Private Investment in LDCs: an Empirical Investigation* (mimeo, World Bank, 1998).

Serven, Luis and A. Solimano (1993) 'Debt Crisis, Adjustment Policies and Capital Formation in Developing Countries: Where Do We Stand?', *World Development*, 21 (1993) 127–40.

Setboonsargn, Suthad, presentation at the APF Brainstorming Workshop on How to Prevent Another Crisis, Asian Development Bank Institute, 10–11 March 2000.

Sharda, R., and R.L. Wilson, 'Neural Network Experiments in Business-Failure Forecasting: Predictive Performance Measurement Issues', *International Journal of Computational Intelligence and Organizations*, 1(2) (1996) 107–17.

Sharma, S., *Applied Multivariate Techniques* (New York: John Wiley & Sons, Inc., 1996).

SHAZAM User's Reference Manual Version 7.0 (New York: McGraw Hill, 1993).

Shiller, Robert, 'Conversation, Information, and Herd Behavior', *American Economic Review Papers and Proceedings*, 85 (1995) 181–5.

Shleifer, Andrei and Robert W. Vishny, 'Management Entrenchment: the Case of Manager-Specific Investments', *Journal of Financial Economics*, 25 (1989) 123–40.

Shleifer, Andrei and Robert W. Vishny, 'A Survey of Corporate Governance', *Journal of Finance*, L11 (1997) 737–83.

Shirai, Sayuri, *Kensho IMF Keizai Seisaku–Higashi Asia Kiki o Koete (Examining IMF's Economic Policies: Beyond the East Asian Crisis)* (Tokyo: Toyo Keizai Shimposha, 1999).

Singh, Ajit, 'Financial Liberalisation and Globalisation: Implications for Industrial and Industrialising Economies', in K.S. Jomo and Nagaraj Shyamala (eds), *Globalisations and Development: Heterodox Perspectives* (Basingstok: Palgrave – now Palgrave Macmillan, 2001).

Simon, Herbert A., *Models of Bounded Rationality* (Cambridge, MA: MIT Press, 1982).

Smith, Vera, *The Rational of Central Banking and the Free Banking Alternative* (Indianapolis: Liberty Press, 1936, 1990 edition).

Soto, Claudio, 'Controles a los Movimientos de Capitales: Evaluacion Empirica del Caso Chileno' (Banco Central de Chile, 1997).

Srinivasan, V. and Y.H. Kim, 'Credit Granting: a Comparative Analysis of Classification Procedures', *Journal of Finance*, 42(3) (1987) 665–83.

Stiglitz, Joseph E., 'The Role of the State in Financial Markets', *Proceedings of the World Bank Conference on Development Economics 1993* (Washington DC: World Bank, 1994).

Stiglitz, Joseph E., 'Knowledge for Development: Economic Science, Economic Policy, and Economic Advice, the Role of the State in Financial Markets', paper presented at the Annual World Bank Conference on Development Economics, Washington DC, 20–1, April 1998.

Stiglitz, Joseph E., 'Bleak Growth Prospects for the Developing World', *International Herald Tribune*, 6 (10–11, April 1999a).

Stiglitz, Joseph E., 'Lessons from East Asia', presented at the Sixth Symposium of the Institute for International Monetary Affairs, Tokyo (February 1999b).

Stiglitz, Joseph E. and Andrew Weiss, 'Credit Rationing in Markets with Imperfect Information', *American Economic Review*, 71(3) (1981) 393–410

Suehiro, Akira, 'Family Business Reassessed: Corporate Structure and Late-Starting Industrialization in Thailand', *The Developing Economies*, 31(4) (1993) 378–407.

Suehiro, Akira, 'Modern Family Business and Corporate Capability in Thailand', *Japanese Yearbook on Business History*, no. 14 (1997) 31–57.

Sugeno, M., Y. Nishiwaki, H. Kawai and Y. Harima, 'Fuzzy Measure Analysis of Public Attitude Towards the Use of Nuclear Energy', *Fuzzy Sets and Systems*, 20 (1986) 259–89.

Summers, Lawrence H., 'International Financial Crises: Causes, Prevention, and Cures', *American Economic Review*, 90(2) (2000).

Summers, Lawrence H. and Victoria Summers, 'When Financial Markets Work Too Well: a Cautious Case for Securities Transactions Tax', *Journal of Financial Services Research* (December 1989) 261–86.

Tahani, H., and Keller, J.M. 'Information Fusion in Computer Vision using Fuzzy Integral', *IEEE Transaction of System, Man and Cybernetics*, 20(3) (1990) 733–41.

Takagi, Shinji, 'Developing a Viable Corporate Bond Market under a Bank-dominated System: Analytical Issues and Policy Implications', paper presented at the Round Table on Capital Market Reforms in Asia, the Asian Development Bank Institute, Tokyo, 11–12 April 2000.

Tam, K.Y., and Kiang, M.Y., 'Managerial Applications of Neural Networks: the Case of Bank Failure Predictions', *Management Science*, 38(7) (1992) 926–47.

Taniura, Takao, 'Management in Taiwan: the Case of the Formosa Plastics Group', *East Asian Cultural Studies*, 28 (1989) 21–46.

Taniura, Takao, 'The Lucky Goldstar Group in the Republic of Korea', *Developing Economies*, 31 (1993) 465–84.

Thornton, Henry, *An Enquiry into the Nature and Effects of the Paper Credit of Great Britain 1802* (London: Frank Cass and Company, 1962 edition).

Tobin, James, and Gustav Ranis, 'The IMF's Misplaced Priorities: Flawed Funds', *The New Republic*, available online at the following address: http://www.thenewrepublic.com/archive/0398/030998/tobin030998.html (1998).

Tong, R.M. and P.P. Bonissone, 'Linguistic Solutions to Fuzzy Decision Problems', in H.-J. Zimmermann, L.A. Zadeh and B.R. Gaines (eds), *Fuzzy Sets and Decision Analysis* (Amsterdam: North-Holland, 1984).

Toniolo, Gianni (ed.), *Central Banks' Independence in Historical Perspective* (Berlin: Walter de Gruyter, 1988).

UNCTAD, *Least Developed Countries Report* (Geneva and New York: UNCTAD, 2002).

Valdes-Prieto, Salvador and Marcelo Soto, 'New Selective Controls in Chile: Are They Effective?', *Working Paper Catholic University of Chile* (1996).

Viner, Jacob, 'Problems of Monetary Control', *Essays in International Finance*, Princeton University 45 (1964).

Wade, Robert, 'The Asian Debt-and-development Crisis of 1997–?: Causes and Consequences', *World Development*, 26(8) (1998a) 1535–53.

Wade, Robert, 'From "Miracle" to "cronyism": Explaining the Great Asian Slump', *Cambridge Journal of Economics*, 22(6) (November 1998b) 693–706.

Waiquamdee, Atchana, Soravis Krairiksh, and Wasana Phongsanarakul, 'Corporates' Views of the Constraints to Recovery', paper presented at the Conference on Asian Corporate Recovery, Bangkok, (March–April 1999).

Wang, Yunjong, *The Asian Financial Crisis and Its Aftermath: Do We Need a Regional Financial Arrangement?* (mimeo, 1999).

Webb, David, 'Some Institutional Issues in Corporate Governance and Finance', paper presented at The Asian Development Bank, Manila, 1998.

Werner, Richard A., 'Bank Restructuring and Macroeconomic Stability', note presented at the Eighth Seminar on International Finance, Asian Development Bank, Tokyo (November 1998).

West, R.C., 'A Factor-Analysis Approach to Bank Condition', *Journal of Banking and Finance*, 9 (1985) 253–66.

Williamson, John, 'Capital Mobility Contagion, and Crises', paper presented at a conference on 'What Financial System for the Year 2000?', Portugal, 4 December 1999.

Williamson, John, 'Development of the Financial System in Post-Crisis Asia', *Asian Development Bank Institute Working Paper*, 8 (2000).

Williamson, Oliver E., *The Economic Institutions of Capitalism* (New York: Free Press, 1985).

Williamson, Oliver E., 'The Institutions and Governance of Economic Development and Reform', in *Proceedings of the World Bank Annual Conference on Development Economics 1994* (Washington, DC: World Bank, 1995).

Wilson, R.L., and R. Sharda 'Bankruptcy Prediction Using Neural Networks', *Decision Support Systems*, 11 (1994) 545–57.

Wong, Sui-lun, 'The Chinese Family Firm: a Model', *British Journal of Sociology*, 36(1) (1985) 58–72.

Wooley, John T., *Monetary Politics: the Federal Reserve and the Politics of Monetary Policy* (Cambridge: Cambridge University Press, 1984).

Working Group of G-22, 'Report of the Working Group on International Financial Crises', October 1998.

World Bank, *The East Asian Miracle: Economic Growth and Public Policy* (Washington, DC: The World Bank, 1993).

World Bank, *Private Capital Flows to Developing Countries: the Road to Financial Integration* (New York: Oxford University Press, 1997).

World Bank, *East Asia: the Road to Recovery* (Washington, DC: The World Bank, 1998).

Yang, B., L.X. Li, H. Ji, and J. Xu, 'An Early Warning System for Loan Risk Assessment Using Artificial Neural Networks', *Knowledge-Based Systems*, 14 (2001) 303–6.

Yang, Z.R., 'Probabilistic Neural Networks in Bankruptcy Prediction', *Journal of Business Research*, 44 (1999) 67–74.

Yergin, Daniel and Joseph Stanislaw, *The Battle Between Government and the Marketplace That is Remaking the Modern World* (New York: Simon & Schuster, 1998).

Yoshitomi, Masaru, *Nihon Keizai no Shinjitsu: Tsusetsu o Koete (The Reality of the Japanese Economy: Beyond Common Views)* (Tokyo: Toyo Keizai Shimposha, 1998).

Yoshitomi, Masaru and Kenichi Ohno, 'Capital Account Crisis and Credit Contraction: the New Nature of Crisis Requires New Policy Responses', paper presented at ADB Annual Meeting, 29 April 1999, Manila (ADB Institute Working Paper Series, No. 2, May 1999).

Yoshitomi, Masaru and Sayuri Shirai, *How to Prevent Another Capital Account Crisis: a Critical Reference Review* (mimeo, Asian Development Bank Institute, 2000).

Young, John, *European Currency and Finance*, US Commission of Gold and Silver Enquiry (Washington,: DC Government Printing Office, 1925).

Zavgren, C.V., 'Assessing the Vulnerability to Failure of American Industrial Firms: a Logistic Analysis', *Journal of Business Finance and Accounting*, 12 (1985) 19–45.

Zhuang, Juzhong, *Corporate Governance in Asia: Some Conceptual Issues* (Manila: Asian Development Bank, 1999).

Zimmermann, H.J., *Fuzzy Sets, Decision Making, and Expert Systems* (Boston: Kluwer Academic Publishers, 1987).

Zimmermann, H.J., *Fuzzy Set Theory and its Applications* (Dordrecht: Kluwer, 1991).

Zimmermann, H.J. and U. Thole, 'On the Suitability of Minimum and Product Operators for the Intersection of Fuzzy Sets', *Fuzzy Sets and Systems*, 2 (1978) 173–86.

Zimmermann, H.J. and P. Zysno, 'Decision and Evaluation by Hierarchical Aggregation of Information', *Fuzzy Sets and Systems*, 10 (1983) 243–60.

Zingales, Luigi, 'Corporate Governance', *NBER Working Paper* (1997).

Index